Risk and Insurance Analysis
Techniques

Risk and Insurance Analysis Techniques

Edited by

Michael W. Elliott, MBA, CPCU, AIAF

1st Edition • 1st Printing

The Institutes
720 Providence Road, Suite 100
Malvern, Pennsylvania 19355-3433

1st Edition • 1st Printing • September 2016

Library of Congress Control Number: 2016952272

ISBN: 978-0-89463-906-7

Foreword

The Institutes are the trusted leader in delivering proven knowledge solutions that drive powerful business results for the risk management and property-casualty insurance industry. For more than 100 years, The Institutes have been meeting the industry's changing professional development needs with customer-driven products and services.

In conjunction with industry experts and members of the academic community, our Knowledge Resources Department develops our course and program content, including Institutes study materials. Practical and technical knowledge gained from Institutes courses enhances qualifications, improves performance, and contributes to professional growth—all of which drive results.

The Institutes' proven knowledge helps individuals and organizations achieve powerful results with a variety of flexible, customer-focused options:

Recognized Credentials—The Institutes offer an unmatched range of widely recognized and industry-respected specialty credentials. The Institutes' Chartered Property Casualty Underwriter (CPCU®) professional designation is designed to provide a broad understanding of the property-casualty insurance industry. Depending on professional needs, CPCU students may select either a commercial insurance focus or a personal risk management and insurance focus and may choose from a variety of electives.

In addition, The Institutes offer certificate or designation programs in a variety of disciplines, including these:

- Claims
- Commercial underwriting
- Fidelity and surety bonding
- General insurance
- Insurance accounting and finance
- Insurance information technology
- Insurance production and agency management
- Insurance regulation and compliance
- Management
- Marine insurance
- Personal insurance
- Premium auditing
- Quality insurance services
- Reinsurance
- Risk management
- Surplus lines

Ethics—Ethical behavior is crucial to preserving not only the trust on which insurance transactions are based, but also the public's trust in our industry as a whole. All Institutes designations now have an ethics requirement, which is delivered online and free of charge. The ethics requirement content is designed specifically for insurance practitioners and uses insurance-based case studies to outline an ethical framework. More information is available in the Programs section of our website, TheInstitutes.org.

Flexible Online Learning—The Institutes have an unmatched variety of technical insurance content covering topics from accounting to under-writing, which we now deliver through hundreds of online courses. These cost-effective self-study courses are a convenient way to fill gaps in technical knowledge in a matter of hours without ever leaving the office.

Continuing Education—A majority of The Institutes' courses are filed for CE credit in most states. We also deliver quality, affordable, online CE courses quickly and conveniently through CEU. Visit CEU.com to learn more. CEU is powered by The Institutes.

College Credits—Most Institutes courses carry college credit recommendations from the American Council on Education. A variety of courses also qualify for credits toward certain associate, bachelor's, and master's degrees at several prestigious colleges and universities. More information is available in the Student Services section of our website, TheInstitutes.org.

Custom Applications—The Institutes collaborate with corporate customers to use our trusted course content and flexible delivery options in developing customized solutions that help them achieve their unique organizational goals.

Insightful Analysis—Our Insurance Research Council (IRC) division conducts public policy research on important contemporary issues in property-casualty insurance and risk management. Visit www.insurance-research.org to learn more or purchase its most recent studies.

The Institutes look forward to serving the risk management and property-casualty insurance industry for another 100 years. We welcome comments from our students and course leaders; your feedback helps us continue to improve the quality of our study materials.

Peter L. Miller, CPCU
President and CEO
The Institutes

Preface

Risk and Insurance Analysis Techniques is the assigned textbook for the AIDA 182 course in The Institutes' Associate in Insurance Data Analytics (AIDA) designation program. This course provides an overview of conventional analytical techniques and their application to risk management and property-casualty insurance. It also introduces some emerging analytical techniques using big data.

The course starts with an explanation of fundamental risk classifications and measures. Probability distributions and risk modeling are covered in detail. The course then explains how analytical concepts are applied to loss exposures, ratemaking, risk control, and operational processes.

Assignment 1 examines various ways that risk can be classified and measured, including its likelihood of occurring, time horizon, and correlation with other risks. Linear regression analysis is introduced with examples showing how it can be used to project losses.

Assignments 2 and 3 explain probability distributions and various methods for modeling risks. Included are various risk distribution measures, including central tendency and dispersion, as well as decision trees and influence diagrams. Catastrophe models are explained in detail.

Assignments 4 through 8 apply additional risk analysis techniques to risk management and property-casualty insurance:

*   Assignment 4 covers loss exposures, including methods for analyzing them.
*   Assignment 5 explains loss reserves, including methods for establishing case and bulk reserves.
*   Assignment 6 explores ratemaking and the ratemaking process. It also describes the ratemaking factors that vary by type of insurance.
*   Assignment 7 discusses risk control techniques and root cause analysis. Included are analytical examples employing failure mode and effects analysis (FMEA) and fault-tree analysis.
*   Assignment 8 covers performance and process management. It introduces key risk indicators and business process management.

Over the next several years, risk and insurance analysis techniques will continue to change, given the advent of big data and increasingly powerful data storage and processing capabilities. This will increase the operating efficiency of insurance companies and their customer organizations.

For more information about The Institutes' programs, please call our Customer Success Department at (800) 644-2101, email us at CustomerSuccess@TheInstitutes.org, or visit our website at TheInstitutes.org.

Michael W. Elliott

Contributor

The Institutes acknowledge with deep appreciation the contributions made to the content of this text by the following person:

Judith M. Vaughan, CPCU, AIC

Contents

1

Classifying and Analyzing Risk

Educational Objectives

After learning the content of this assignment, you should be able to:

▷ Explain how the following classifications of risk apply and how they help in risk management:

- Pure and speculative risk

- Subjective and objective risk

- Diversifiable and nondiversifiable risk

- Quadrants of risk (hazard, operational, financial, and strategic)

▷ Explain how basic risk measures apply to the management of risk.

▷ Describe the importance of correlation and covariance when analyzing an organization's risks.

▷ Explain how regression analysis can be used to forecast gains or losses.

Classifying and Analyzing Risk

1

RISK CLASSIFICATIONS

To successfully apply analysis techniques, risk management and insurance professionals should understand the risks their organizations face. All types of predictive analyses should begin with a clear definition of the business purpose. The risk may involve a threat to the organization or, in some cases, both a threat and an opportunity.

Classifying the various types of risk can help an organization understand and manage its risks. The categories should align with an organization's objectives and risk management goals.

Classification can help with assessing risks, because many risks in the same classification have similar attributes. It also can help with managing risk, because many risks in the same classification can be managed with similar techniques. Finally, classification helps with the administrative function of risk management by helping to ensure that risks in the same classification are less likely to be overlooked.

These classifications of risk are some of the most commonly used:

- Pure and speculative risk
- Subjective and objective risk
- Diversifiable and nondiversifiable risk
- Quadrants of risk (hazard, operational, financial, and strategic)

These classifications are not mutually exclusive and can be applied to any given risk.

Pure and Speculative Risk

A **pure risk** is a chance of loss or no loss, but no chance of gain. For example, the owner of a commercial building faces the risk associated with a possible fire loss. The building will either burn or not burn. If the building burns, the owner suffers a financial loss. If the building does not burn, the owner's financial condition is unchanged. Neither of the possible outcomes would produce a gain. Because there is no opportunity for financial gain, pure risks are always undesirable. See the exhibit "Classifications of Risk."

In comparison, **speculative risk** involves a chance of gain. As a result, it can be desirable, as evidenced by the fact that every business venture involves

Pure risk
A chance of loss or no loss, but no chance of gain.

Speculative risk
A chance of loss, no loss, or gain.

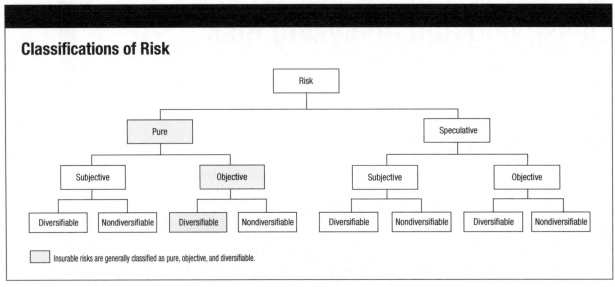

Classifications of Risk

[DA02396]

speculative risks. For example, an investor who purchases an apartment building to rent to tenants expects to profit from this investment, so it is a desirable speculative risk. However, the venture could be unprofitable if rental price controls limit the amount of rent that can be charged.

Certain businesses involve speculative risks, such as these:

- Price risk—Uncertainty over the size of cash flows resulting from possible changes in the cost of raw materials and other inputs (such as lumber, gas, or electricity), as well as cost-related changes in the market for completed products and other outputs.

- Credit risk—Although a credit risk is particularly significant for banks and other financial institutions, it can be relevant to any organization with accounts receivable.

Financial investments, such as the purchase of stock shares, involve a distinct set of speculative risks. See the exhibit "Speculative Risks in Investments."

Insurance deals primarily with risks of loss, not risks of gain; that is, with pure risks rather than speculative risks. However, the distinction between these two classifications of risk is not always precise—many risks have both pure and speculative aspects.

Distinguishing between pure and speculative risks is important because those risks must often be managed differently. For example, although a commercial building owner faces a pure risk from causes of loss such as fire, he or she also faces the speculative risk that the market value of the building will increase or decrease during any one year. Similarly, although an investor who purchases an apartment building to rent to tenants faces speculative risk because rental income may produce a profit or loss, the investor also faces a pure risk from causes of loss such as fire.

Credit risk

The risk that customers or other creditors will fail to make promised payments as they come due.

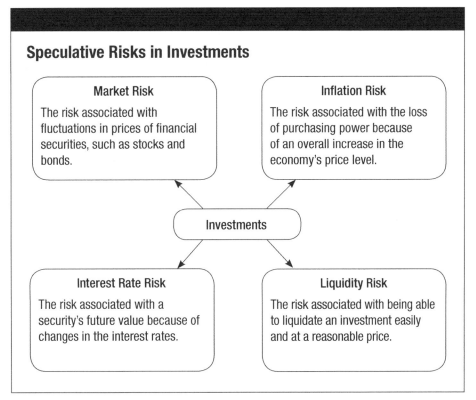

Speculative Risks in Investments

Market Risk
The risk associated with fluctuations in prices of financial securities, such as stocks and bonds.

Inflation Risk
The risk associated with the loss of purchasing power because of an overall increase in the economy's price level.

Investments

Interest Rate Risk
The risk associated with a security's future value because of changes in the interest rates.

Liquidity Risk
The risk associated with being able to liquidate an investment easily and at a reasonable price.

[DA02398]

To properly manage these investments, the commercial building owner and the apartment owner must consider both the speculative and the pure risks. For example, they may choose to manage the pure risk by buying insurance or taking other measures to address property loss exposures. The speculative risk might be managed by obtaining a favorable mortgage and maintaining the property to enhance its resale value.

Subjective and Objective Risk

When individuals and organizations must make a decision that involves risk, they usually base it on the individual's or organization's assessment of the risk. The assessment can be based on opinions, which are subjective, or facts, which are objective.

Because it is based on opinion rather than fact, **subjective risk** may be quite different from the actual underlying risk that is present. In fact, subjective risk can exist even where **objective risk** does not. The closer an individual's or organization's subjective interpretation of risk is to the objective risk, the more effective its risk management plan will likely be.

Subjective risk
The perceived amount of risk based on an individual's or organization's opinion.

Objective risk
The measurable variation in uncertain outcomes based on facts and data.

The reasons that subjective and objective risk can differ substantially include these:

- Familiarity and control—For example, although many people consider air travel (over which they have no control) to carry a high degree of risk, they are much more likely to suffer a serious injury when driving their cars, where the perception of control is much greater.

- Consequences over likelihood—People often have two views of low-likelihood, high-consequence events. The first misconception is the "It can't happen to me" view, which assigns a probability of zero to low-likelihood events such as natural disasters, murder, fires, accidents, and so on. The second misconception is overstating the probability of a low-likelihood event, which is common for people who have personally been exposed to the event previously. If the effect of a particular event can be severe, such as the potentially destructive effects of a hurricane or earthquake, the perception of the likelihood of deaths resulting from such an event is heightened. This perception may be enhanced by the increased media coverage given to high-severity events.

- Risk awareness—Organizations differ in terms of their level of risk awareness and, therefore, perceive risks differently. An organization that is not aware of its risks would perceive the likelihood of something happening as very low.

Both risk management and insurance depend on the ability to objectively identify and analyze risks. However, subjectivity is also necessary because facts are often not available to objectively assess risk.

Diversifiable and Nondiversifiable Risk

Diversifiable risk is not highly correlated and can be managed through diversification, or spread, of risk. An example of a diversifiable risk is a fire, which is likely to affect only one or a small number of businesses. For instance, an insurer can diversify the risks associated with fire insurance by insuring many buildings in several different locations. Similarly, business investors often diversify their holdings, as opposed to investing in only one business, hoping those that succeed will more than offset those that fail.

Examples of **nondiversifiable risks** include inflation, unemployment, and natural disasters such as hurricanes. Nondiversifiable risks are correlated—that is, their gains or losses tend to occur simultaneously rather than randomly. For example, under certain monetary conditions, interest rates increase for all firms at the same time. If an insurer were to insure firms against interest rate increases, it would not be able to diversify its portfolio of interest rate risks by underwriting a large number of insureds, because all of them would suffer losses at the same time.

Systemic risks are generally nondiversifiable. For example, if excess leverage by financial institutions causes systemic risk resulting in an event that disrupts

Diversifiable risk

A risk that affects only some individuals, businesses, or small groups.

Nondiversifiable risk

A risk that affects a large segment of society at the same time.

Systemic risk

The potential for a major disruption in the function of an entire market or financial system.

the financial system, this risk will have an effect on the entire economy and, therefore, on all organizations. Because of the global interconnections in finance and industry, many risks that were once viewed as nonsystemic (affecting only one organization) are now viewed as systemic. For instance, many economists view the failure of Lehman Brothers in early 2008 as a trigger event: highlighting the systemic risk in the banking sector that resulted in the financial crisis.

Quadrants of Risk: Hazard, Operational, Financial, and Strategic

Although no consensus exists about how an organization should categorize its risks, one approach involves dividing them into risk quadrants:

- Hazard risks arise from property, liability, or personnel loss exposures and are generally the subject of insurance.
- Operational risks fall outside the hazard risk category and arise from people or a failure in processes, systems, or controls, including those involving information technology.
- Financial risks arise from the effect of market forces on financial assets or liabilities and include **market risk**, credit risk, **liquidity risk**, and price risk.
- Strategic risks arise from trends in the economy and society, including changes in the economic, political, and competitive environments, as well as from demographic shifts.

Hazard and operational risks are classified as pure risks, and financial and strategic risks are classified as speculative risks.

The focus of the risk quadrants is different from the risk classifications previously discussed. Whereas the classifications of risk focus on some aspect of the risk itself, the four quadrants of risk focus on the risk source and who traditionally manages it. For example, the chief financial officer traditionally manages financial risk, and the risk manager traditionally manages hazard risk. Just as a particular risk can fall into more than one classification, a risk can also fall into multiple risk quadrants. For example, embezzlement of funds by an employee can be considered both a hazard risk, because it is an insurable pure risk, and an operational risk, because it involves a failure of controls. See the exhibit "Risk Quadrants."

Organizations define types of risk differently. Some organizations consider legal risks as operational risk, and some may characterize certain hazard risks as operational risk. Financial institutions generally use the categories of market, credit, and operational risk (defined as all other risk, including hazard risk). Each organization should select categories that align with its objectives and processes.

Market risk

Uncertainty about an investment's future value because of potential changes in the market for that type of investment.

Liquidity risk

The risk that an asset cannot be sold on short notice without incurring a loss.

Risk Quadrants

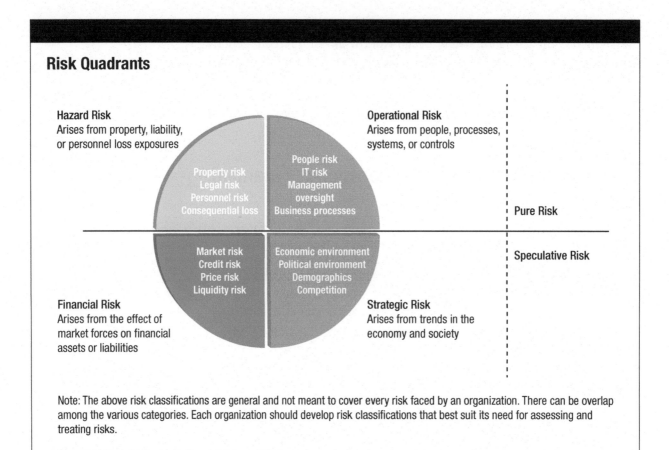

Hazard Risk
Arises from property, liability, or personnel loss exposures

Property risk
Legal risk
Personnel risk
Consequential loss

Operational Risk
Arises from people, processes, systems, or controls

People risk
IT risk
Management oversight
Business processes

Pure Risk

Market risk
Credit risk
Price risk
Liquidity risk

Economic environment
Political environment
Demographics
Competition

Speculative Risk

Financial Risk
Arises from the effect of market forces on financial assets or liabilities

Strategic Risk
Arises from trends in the economy and society

Note: The above risk classifications are general and not meant to cover every risk faced by an organization. There can be overlap among the various categories. Each organization should develop risk classifications that best suit its need for assessing and treating risks.

[DA08677]

Apply Your Knowledge

The New Company manufactures electronic consumer products. The company's manufacturing plant is highly automated and located in the United States. However, it purchases components from three companies in Asia. The majority of its sales are in the U.S., but European sales represent a growing percentage.

Describe the types of risk New Company would have in each of the four risk quadrants.

Feedback: In the hazard risk quadrant, New Company would have property damage risks to its plant and equipment resulting from fire, storms, or other events. It would also have risk of injury to its employees and liability risks associated with its products.

In the operational risk quadrant, New Company would have risks from employee turnover or the inability to find skilled employees. It would also have business process risk related to how it manages its supply chain and information technology risk related to its automated manufacturing process.

In the financial risk quadrant, New Company would have exchange rate risk related to its European sales. It would also have price risk for raw materials and supplies.

Strategic risks include competition, economic factors that could affect consumer demand, and the political risk arising from countries in which the company's component suppliers are located.

BASIC RISK MEASURES

The physicist Lord Kelvin said, "To measure is to know" and "If you cannot measure it, you cannot improve it." Risk management requires measures of risk in order to both know the nature of risks and manage them to help an organization meet its objectives.

Although it is not possible to measure all the risks that could potentially affect an organization's ability to meet its objectives, quantifying those risks that can be measured should form the basis of risk assessment. Additionally, ongoing measurement provides benchmarks to monitor and evaluate the success of an organization's risk management program.

These are the basic measures that apply to risk management:

- Exposure
- Volatility
- Likelihood
- Consequences
- Time horizon
- Correlation

Exposure provides a measure of the maximum potential damage associated with an occurrence. Generally, the risk increases as the exposure increases, assuming the risk is nondiversifiable. For example, if a bank underwrites mortgages to subprime borrowers, the credit risk increases as the amount of subprime mortgages increases because the exposure to default increases. An insurer that writes homeowners policies in coastal areas increases its exposure to windstorms as its coastal book of business increases. In these examples, the exposure can be quantified based on the amount of mortgages or policy coverage issued. Other exposures, such as the risk of a data breach or reputational risk, are not as easily quantified. However, even if an exposure cannot be readily quantified, there should be an attempt to qualitatively measure its effect on the organization to effectively manage the risk. For example, the effect of reputational risk could be measured in terms of its potential influence on an organization's stock price, customer loyalty, and employee turnover.

Exposure
Any condition that presents a possibility of gain or loss, whether or not an actual loss occurs.

Volatility
Frequent fluctuations, such as in the price of an asset.

Law of large numbers
A mathematical principle stating that as the number of similar but independent exposure units increases, the relative accuracy of predictions about future outcomes (losses) also increases.

Volatility provides a basic measure that can be applied to risk. Generally, risk increases as volatility increases. Volatility can often be quantified. For example, VIX, the Chicago Board Options Exchange Market Volatility Index, provides a measure of stock market volatility. The volatility of energy prices, for example, is a major risk for many organizations. Utility companies, airlines, trucking companies, and other types of organizations that are highly dependent on fuel use strategies such as hedging to manage the risk associated with volatility in the price of oil. However, organizations that may be only indirectly affected by energy price volatility, such as retailers whose customers have less disposable income when gas prices rise, may also want to assess and manage this risk through inventory and pricing adjustments.

The likelihood of an occurrence is a key measure in risk management. The ability to determine the probability of an event mathematically is the foundation of insurance and risk management.[1] The term "likelihood" is used rather than "probability" because probability analysis relies on the **law of large numbers**. Although insurers and some other organizations can use the law of large numbers to accurately determine the probability of various risks, most organizations need to determine the likelihood of an occurrence without the benefit of a probability analysis of large numbers.

For example, a bank can probably determine and quantify the likelihood of default on a loan based on credit scores and other factors in the bank's extensive data. However, it would be more difficult for the bank to determine the likelihood of a cyber attack in which customer data are taken, resulting in liability. It would be even more difficult for the bank to predict the likelihood of a terrorist attack that could be catastrophic. Similarly, it is easier to determine the likelihood that certain risks undertaken to improve an organization's performance will have a positive outcome than it is for others. If a bank decides to issue credit to borrowers with slightly lower credit scores than its current borrowers, the bank probably has sufficient data to determine the likelihood of a positive outcome. However, if the bank decides to expand into a new and unfamiliar region, it may be more difficult to predict the likelihood of a successful outcome.

The relationship between likelihood and consequences is critical for risk management in assessing risk and deciding whether and how to manage it. Therefore, organizations must determine to the extent possible the likelihood of an event and then determine the potential consequences if the event occurs.

Consequences are the measure of the degree to which an occurrence could positively or negatively affect an organization. The greater the consequences, the greater the risk. In assessing the level of risk, the risk management professional must understand to the extent possible both the likelihood and the consequences. If there is a low likelihood of an occurrence with minor consequences, it may not be necessary for an organization to actively manage the risk. For example, a bank may decide that the likelihood of employees taking office supplies for personal use is low, and the consequences if this occurs are minor. Therefore, the bank may decide not to manage this risk.

Risks with high likelihood and minor consequences should usually be managed through an organization's routine business procedures. For example, there is a significant likelihood that a customer will be a few days late in making a loan payment. The consequences of payments that are a few days late are relatively minor. However, the bank should manage this risk through normal business procedures such as late charges or sending reminder notices if the payment is not received by the due date.

Risks with potentially major consequences should be managed even if the likelihood of their occurrence is low. For example, the risk of a fire at a bank, although unlikely, must be managed. Risks with significant likelihood and major consequences require significant, continuous risk management. For example, an international bank faces exchange rate risk that is likely and that could result in considerable losses. The bank may use hedging strategies and other techniques to modify this type of risk.

The **time horizon** of an exposure is another basic measure that is applied in risk management. A risk's time horizon can be measured in various ways. The time horizon associated with an investment risk, such as a stock or bond, can be determined by specified bond duration or by how quickly a stock can be traded. Longer time horizons are generally riskier than shorter ones. For example, a thirty-year mortgage is usually riskier for a bank than a fifteen-year mortgage. A business strategy that involves purchase of real estate and building new structures is not as easily reversed as one that involves only a new advertising campaign and is therefore riskier.

Time horizon
Estimated duration.

Although an organization may have little or no control over the time horizon of a risk, the organization should evaluate and manage this risk just as it would manage other risks over which it has no control, such as weather-related risks. For example, diversification in financial investments can help manage the risks associated with the time horizon of those investments. An insurance company that matches the durations of its assets (investments) and liabilities (loss reserves) neutralizes the risks associated with time horizon. When real estate prices are highly volatile, an organization may defer an expansion strategy that involves a long time horizon, such as purchasing or building new facilities.

Correlation is a measure that should be applied to the management of an organization's overall risk portfolio. If two or more risks are similar, they are usually highly correlated. The greater the correlation, the greater the risk. For example, if a bank makes mortgage loans primarily to the employees of a local manufacturer and business loans primarily to that same manufacturer, the bank's loan risks are highly correlated. The failure of the manufacturing business would likely be catastrophic for the bank's entire loan book of business. If a manufacturer contracts with three major suppliers in the same earthquake-prone region in Asia, the manufacturer's supply-chain risks are highly

Correlation
A relationship between variables.

correlated. Diversification is a risk management strategy that can reduce the risk of correlation.[2]

Risk management professionals should evaluate all of these measures and their overall effect on an organization's risk portfolio. Highly correlated risks with a high likelihood, major consequences, high volatility, and significant exposure over a long time horizon should be a key focus of risk management. The global financial crisis that started in 2007 resulted in part from the failure to recognize or address this type of risk. Subprime mortgages represented highly correlated risk to the same types of risky borrowers, large exposure with major consequences, high volatility due to fluctuations in their market value (and in the market value of the underlying real estate collateral), and a long time horizon because of their duration. Therefore, it is essential that organizations apply these basic measures when assessing their risk.

Apply Your Knowledge

An insurer decides to achieve growth in its auto insurance line by offering a discount to its homeowners insurance customers who also purchase auto insurance. Which of the following risk measures is or are likely to increase as a result of this business decision? Select all that apply.

a. Exposure

b. Volatility

c. Time horizon

d. Correlation

Feedback: a. and d. The insurer increases its exposure to its existing customer base by offering discounted auto insurance to its homeowners customers. The insurer also increases its risk correlation because it insures the same customers for both the homeowners and auto lines. Presumably, the insurer can manage its risk volatility through diversification, and its time horizon for risk is largely limited by the length of the auto and homeowners policy terms.

CORRELATION AND COVARIANCE

Correlation and covariance provide a common statistical language for describing the relationships among various sources of risk. The interaction among risk sources can have a significant impact on risk management decision making.

Risk professionals should understand these concepts with regard to correlation and covariance:

- The definition, similarities, and differences between correlation and covariance
- The uses of correlation and covariance to evaluate risk
- The relationship between correlation and causality
- The relationships shown of correlation or causality of risk sources reported in the form of a matrix

Correlation and Covariance Defined

Correlation and **covariance** are key statistical metrics that are useful for selecting sources of risk for a portfolio. Both convey the direction of and strength of the association between two variables—that is, the extent to which the values of two variables change together. Correlation is a scaled version of covariance and is expressed as a number from –1 to +1, which is called the correlation coefficient. While both metrics can show whether the two variables are positively related (move in the same direction) or negatively related (move in opposite directions), correlation gives the degree to which this is indicated.

Covariance
The relative association between variables to move in tandem or independently of each other.

Uses of Correlation and Covariance

Risk professionals use correlation and covariance measurements for several purposes:

- Identifying and quantifying relationships among various sources of risk
- Communicating throughout the organization the degree of uncertainty in a risk portfolio
- Prioritizing investments in loss control
- Optimizing financing for multiple sources of risk
- Evaluating risk management program effectiveness

Correlation and covariance can also be used to evaluate competitive risk. For example, assume surveys reveal a strong covariance between only two out of ten features in a new product's design and consumers' preferences. Using this information, the product is then redesigned to emphasize the features most important to consumers, improving its competitive position.

If two variables' values tend to move together, then their covariance (and correlation coefficient) is positive. For example, the covariance of the price of gasoline and the cost of operating a fleet of vehicles is usually positive. Conversely, if two variables' values tend to move in opposite directions, their covariance (and correlation coefficient) is negative. For example, the demand for hot chocolate will likely have a negative covariance with the demand for popsicles. Variables that are independent, or uncorrelated, will have a covariance (and correlation coefficient) of zero. See the exhibit "Correlation Coefficient Values."

Correlation Coefficient Values

Correlation coefficient values range from perfectly negative (-1) to perfectly positive (+1):

−1 Perfectly negative correlation	If one variable's value goes up, the other variable's value goes down in a direct proportion. For example, if the demand for heating oil is perfectly negatively correlated with temperature, every time the temperature goes up, the demand for heating oil goes down by the same magnitude.
Between −1 and 0 Negative correlation	If one variable's value goes up, the other variable's value goes down, but less than with perfectly negative correlation. If the demand for heating oil is negatively correlated with temperature, every time the temperature goes up, the demand for heating oil goes down, but less than it would if there were perfectly negative correlation.
0 No correlation	There is no relationship between the variables. Variables with no correlation are independent. For example, the revenues of a restaurant in California and the likelihood of a tornado touching down in Kansas are not correlated. Because there is no relationship between the two, the restaurant sales and probability of a tornado in Kansas are independent variables.
Between 0 and +1 Positive correlation	If one variable goes up, the other goes up, but less than with perfectly positive correlation. For example, the probability of a fire at a warehouse increases if the warehouse next door is on fire. The probabilities of fire at the two warehouses are positively correlated, but less than they would be if there were perfectly positive correlation.
+1 Perfectly positive correlation	If one variable's value goes up, the other variable's value goes up in a direct proportion. For example, if an organization holds an investment portfolio that exactly mimics the S&P 500 index and the value of the S&P 500 index goes up by 2 percentage points, the value of the organization's investment portfolio also goes up by 2 percentage points.

[DA03925]

Monte Carlo simulation

A computerized statistical model that simulates the effects of various types of uncertainty.

The **Monte Carlo simulation** is a mathematically based computer technique used to solve complex problems in a numerical format for finance, manufacturing, science, engineering, and many other business applications. This technique provides a probability distribution of outcomes that can occur after applying a range of random conditions (or variables) to simulate an event or series of events hundreds or even thousands of times. The resulting probability distribution can be used to forecast and better understand the correlations among the variables.

A risk manager could employ the Monte Carlo simulation technique to attribute values to potential investment options under consideration. The unknowns applied could be sources of uncertainty such as a range of interest rates, inflation rates, currency exchange rates, or even possible environmental or technological influences. If the conclusion after many iterations (the random pairing of variables) is that the options are negatively correlated or not correlated, the spread of results is reduced; if they are positively correlated, the spread of results is increased. This method can therefore be used to simulate outcomes when combining selected financial instruments into a coordinated portfolio. The result can reveal that a risky asset with its high yield can be included with a company's portfolio if balanced with and negatively correlated with a different asset, creating a diversified portfolio.

Correlation and Causality

Correlation does not measure **causality**. Causality defines and measures cause and effect—how one variable influences another. Correlation is a statistical relationship between the movements of two variables and is not a measure or implication of causality.

Causality

The relationship between two events, where the second is brought about by the first.

For example, there is a strong positive correlation between an increase in the demand for popsicles and an increase in the demand for window air conditioners (as one increases, the other increases as well). However, an increased demand for popsicles does not cause an increase in demand for window air conditioners. This would be an incorrect conclusion, although both demand patterns are tied to an underlying condition of warm weather. Common underlying factors are frequent reasons for positive or negative correlations between two variables but do not indicate causality between the variables.

As with any statistical measure, care must be used in interpreting the results of correlation analysis. Correlation results may be skewed by abnormal observations, inaccuracy of data, or an insufficient number of observations. A risk professional should not rely solely on correlation analysis.

Correlation Matrices

When a risk professional considers how a source of risk interacts with other risk sources, correlation or covariance is typically reported in the form of a matrix, which shows the correlation or covariance for pairs of risk sources. A correlation matrix always has a value of +1 along the diagonal, meaning that a risk source is always perfectly positively correlated with itself. See the exhibit "Correlation Matrix for the Return on Various Financial Investments."

Sources of risk that have a low positive correlation, no correlation, or a negative correlation with other risk sources in a portfolio are generally good risk sources to add to the portfolio (all factors that could influence the correlations

Correlation Matrix for the Return on Various Financial Investments

	Symbol	FYY	TYY	$/Y	SIL	OIL
U.S. Treasury Bill 5-Year Yield	FYY	1	0.907	−0.517	−0.344	−0.236
U.S. Treasury Bill 10-Year Yield	TYY	0.907	1	−0.495	−0.286	−0.231
$/ Yen	$/Y	−0.517	−0.495	1	0.409	0.273
Silver	SIL	−0.344	−0.286	0.409	1	0.39
Oil	OIL	−0.236	−0.231	0.273	0.39	1

[DA03926]

being equal) and tend to improve the organization's risk-return position. This is because the portfolio will benefit from increased risk diversification, with the exposure to risk from individual risk sources reduced. Risk sources that have a high positive correlation with others in the portfolio, all else being equal, often will not improve the organization's risk-return position because there is little or no risk diversification and the additional expected return may not be high enough to justify the greater risk to the portfolio.

TREND ANALYSIS

Risk management uses trend analysis to forecast losses or gains. Such forecasts help an organization's management make cost-effective risk management decisions.

Trend analysis

An analysis that identifies patterns in past data and then projects these patterns into the future.

Regression analysis

A statistical technique that is used to estimate relationships between variables.

Organizations use **trend analysis** to identify predictable patterns of change in dynamic environments and, from those patterns, develop forecasts. **Regression analysis**, a type of statistical trend analysis, can increase the accuracy of forecasting by examining variables that affect trends. For example, changes in hazard loss frequency or severity might coincide with changes in some other variable, such as production, in such a way that loss frequency or severity can be forecast more accurately. Trend analysis and regression analysis can also be used to detect and forecast patterns of gains.

Organizations must develop sound forecasts of their property, liability, personnel, and net income losses, as well as any gains associated with risk exposures. To develop these forecasts, risk management professionals examine data on past losses and gains and subject these data to probability analysis and/or trend analysis to project the expected value of future losses and gains. Resulting projections help management determine the costs and benefits of each alternative and choose the one(s) with the greatest benefits over costs.

Trend analysis is commonly used to adjust forecasted future dollar amounts of losses or gains using an anticipated inflation rate. For example, projected inflationary trends would increase the cost of future physical damage losses; therefore, inflation must be considered in an estimate of the property losses an organization will finance through retention if it adopts a particular deductible.

Regression Analysis

Regression analysis assumes that the variable being forecast varies predictably with another variable. The variable being forecast is the dependent variable. The variable that determines the value of the variable being forecast is the independent variable. **Linear regression analysis** deals with a constant rate of change. For example, if the independent variable is time measured in years, then a linear regression analysis assumes that the change in the dependent variable is the same from year to year. In this case, the regression line is straight (or linear), not curved. See the exhibit "Diagram of Linear Time Series Analysis Trend Line."

Linear regression analysis
A form of regression analysis that assumes that the change in the dependent variable is constant for each unit of change in the independent variable.

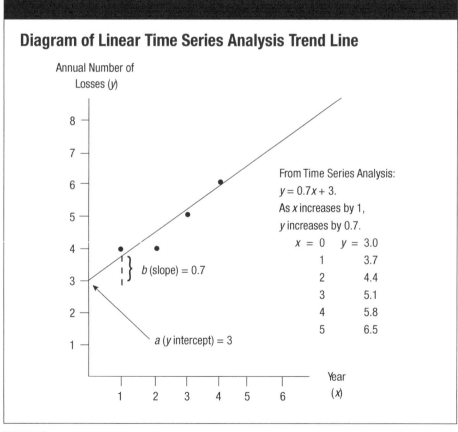

Diagram of Linear Time Series Analysis Trend Line

Annual Number of Losses (y)

From Time Series Analysis:
$y = 0.7x + 3$.
As x increases by 1,
y increases by 0.7.

$x =$	$y =$
0	3.0
1	3.7
2	4.4
3	5.1
4	5.8
5	6.5

b (slope) = 0.7

a (y intercept) = 3

Year (x)

[DA02077]

The exhibit plots annual machinery losses on a graph. The dependent variable (annual number of losses) is charted on the vertical (y) axis; the independent variable (years) is charted on the horizontal (x) axis. The data points show that 4, 4, 5, and 6 losses occurred, respectively, in Year 1 through Year 4. The goal of regression analysis is to find the equation for the line that best fits these four data points and to project this line to forecast the number of future losses.

A logical first step in calculating a linear regression line is to plot the data points and sketch an approximate line. Such a sketch helps to intuitively estimate the two determinants of any linear regression line. The first determinant is the point at which the line crosses the vertical y axis, labeled "a" in the diagram (y-intercept) or the value of y when x equals zero. The second determinant is the slope of the line, the amount by which y increases or decreases with a one-unit increase in x. The length of the dashed line labeled "b" signifies the slope. A line slanting upward from left to right has positive slope; a line slanting downward has negative slope. Therefore, the y-intercept and the slope determine a line.

This is the equation of a line:

$$y = bx + a,$$

Where

y is the dependent variable

x is the independent variable

a is the y-intercept

b is the slope of the line

In the machinery example, y is the number of machinery losses, and x is the number of years beyond year zero. Given the values for x and y, the values of a and b that provide the best fit for the data can be determined. This calculation is typically accomplished with computer software or a calculator.

Two aspects of interpreting linear regression lines need to be recognized. First, a linear regression line might not be accurate when it gets very far away from the actual data values used. For example, it may be suitable to use this linear trend line to forecast losses in Year 5 or Year 6, but it probably would not be accurate for forecasting losses in Year 25 or Year 26.

Second, for any past year, the dependent variable's value calculated by the linear regression line is not likely to exactly equal the historical value for that past year. Any regression line represents the "best fit" of a straight or smoothly curved line to actual historical data for all past years. For any given year, the projected trend value will probably differ from the actual outcome, both in the past and in the future. The size of this difference between actual and projected values will also vary. For example, in the preceding exhibit, the historical outcome for Year 2 is farther from the projected regression line than is the outcome for Year 1.

In the machinery loss example, the dependent variable (the annual number of losses) varies only with the passage of time (the independent variable). An alternative possibility is to assume that the annual number of machinery losses is affected by a variable such as the volume of items processed or the number of hours in operation. Therefore, one of these other variables (such as volume of output) could be substituted for time as the independent variable that projects the number of future machinery losses. Indeed, any reasonable causative variable that can be measured and projected with more accuracy than accidental losses can be an independent variable.

Regression Analysis Example

Assume a risk management professional wants to use a firm's annual output (in 100,000-ton units) to project the annual number of machinery losses. The professional compiles data that show the number of machinery losses sustained and the tons of output (in hundreds of thousands) in each year from Year 1 to Year 4. See the exhibit "Relationship of Losses to Exposure (Tons of Output)."

Relationship of Losses to Exposure (Tons of Output)

Year	Annual Number of Losses	Tons of Output (× 100,000)
1	4	35
2	4	60
3	5	72
4	6	95
	19	262

This information can be used to project trends that relate the number of machinery losses to time and to annual tons of rubber output.

[DA02079]

With this information, regression analysis can be used to project trends that relate the number of machinery losses to tons of output. The risk manager graphs the annual tons of output horizontally on the *x* axis as the independent variable and graphs the annual number of machinery losses vertically on the *y* axis as the dependent variable. See the exhibit "Diagram of Linear Regression Line."

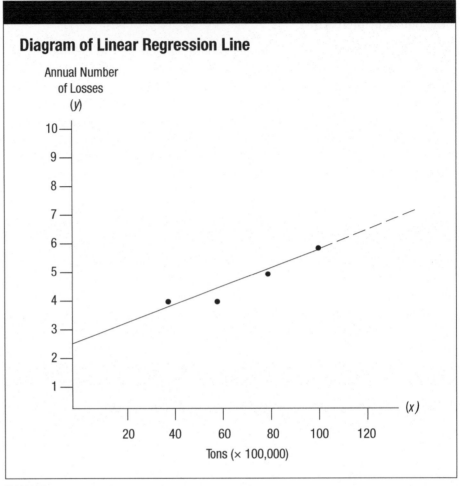

Diagram of Linear Regression Line

[DA02080]

The four data points in the graph correspond to the pairs of numbers of losses and tons of output shown in the preceding exhibit, and the solid portion of the linear regression line approximates the trend of the historical data. The dashed extension of the regression line projects annual numbers of machinery losses for levels of output (in units of 100,000) beyond the range of these particular historical data. Developing such a diagram and approximating a regression line can help in visualizing this relationship.

A computer program or calculator can be used to determine the values of *a* and *b* for the actual linear regression line. In this example, the indicated value for *a* is 2.46 machinery losses, and the value for *b* is 0.035. If the number of losses is linearly related to output for all possible levels of output, the 2.46 value for *a* means that, even if annual output were zero, it would still sustain 2.46 (actually 2 or 3) machinery losses each year. The indicated value for *b* is 0.035, implying that, with each 100,000-ton increase in output, 0.035 additional machinery losses can be expected. Also, one more machinery loss can be expected with approximately each additional 2,900,000 tons of output (calculated as 100,000 tons × [1 ÷ 0.035]).

Although arithmetically correct, these values may not be valid for very low or very high volumes of output, as the regression extends the line too far beyond the bounds of past experience.

To forecast losses from these regression results, assume the organization expects to produce 10 million (or 100 hundred thousand) tons of products next year. The expected number of machinery losses for next year can then be calculated:

$$y = bx + a$$

$$= 2.46 + (0.035 \times 100)$$

$$= 2.46 + 3.50$$

$$= 5.96 \text{ losses}$$

Because fractional numbers of machine losses are impossible, a reasonable forecast would be for six machinery losses in a year when production is expected to be 10 million tons.

A risk management professional can apply more than one linear regression line by incorporating several independent variables simultaneously. An example is a series of equations that would forecast the total dollar amount of losses in a future year based on combined effects of forecast freight volumes, weather conditions, price levels, and perhaps other independent variables more easily forecast than the losses themselves.

In some cases, a risk manager may need to apply a curvilinear regression line. This technique is used to measure a relationship between the independent and dependent variables that changes at an accelerating or decelerating rate rather than at a constant rate.

Forecasts should be accepted only if the underlying assumptions are valid. Therefore, knowing these assumptions and recognizing the potential limitations in these forecasting techniques are important.

Trend analyses can be powerful tools for forecasting future losses and gains, but they must be used with care. Results must be interpreted with reason and not with automatic acceptance just because they are mathematically based. Furthermore, perhaps more for risk management than for some other uses of these forecasting techniques, the seeming scarcity of loss data, when compared with the apparent wealth of data in other management specialties, makes forecasts of accidental losses more difficult.

Apply Your Knowledge

Green Mountain Trucking (GMT) has a regular schedule of maintenance and service for each of its trucks. GMT's risk manager wants to know, for each truck, how each 10,000 miles of travel beyond 60,000 affects the cost of repairs.

The risk manager begins by creating a simple linear regression analysis. Identify the variables the risk manager will use for the *x* axis and the *y* axis.

Feedback: The risk manager designates as *x* (the independent variable) the trucks' odometer readings (in 10,000 mile increments), and as *y* (the dependent variable) the total road-trip repair costs.

The risk manager uses a calculator to determine the regression's value of *a* and *b* and has found a linear relation between truck mileage beyond 60,000 and road-trip repair costs. For purposes of this linear regression, describe what *b* represents.

Feedback: For purposes of this linear regression, *b* implies that, with each additional 10,000 miles a truck travels beyond 60,000 miles, repair costs would increase by *b*'s value.

SUMMARY

Classifying the various types of risk can help organizations manage risk. Some of the most commonly used classifications are pure and speculative risk, subjective and objective risk, and diversifiable and nondiversifiable risk. An organization's risks can also be categorized into quadrants as hazard risk, operational risk, financial risk, and strategic risk.

Effective risk management should quantify risks and the results of risk management efforts to the extent possible. The basic measures that are applied to risk management include exposure, volatility, likelihood, consequences, time horizon, and correlation.

Correlation and covariance show the relationship between two variables and the extent to which they change together. This relationship is used to measure how two risk sources interact, which can help direct a company's investments, plan new projects for its future, or gain a competitive edge in product development. The Monte Carlo simulation is a tool utilized to mathematically produce outcomes after applying random variables to a scenario in order to gain additional insight into a risk source or situation affected by many different conditions. Correlation or covariance can be reported in a matrix, showing the correlation or covariance for pairs of risk sources.

Trend analysis seeks predictable patterns of change in a dynamic, changing environment. Organizations use trend analysis to develop forecasts based on patterns of change. Regression analysis can increase the accuracy of an organization's forecasts by using statistical analysis to examine related variables that affect trends.

ASSIGNMENT NOTES

1. Peter L. Bernstein, Against the Gods: The Remarkable Story of Risk (New York: John Wiley & Sons, Inc., 1998), p. 3.

2. James Lam, Enterprise Risk Management: From Incentives to Controls (Hoboken, N.J.: John Wiley & Sons, Inc., 2003), p. 26.

Direct Your Learning ▶▶

Probability Distributions for Analyzing Risk

Educational Objectives

After learning the content of this assignment, you should be able to:

▷ Describe the nature of probability with respect to theoretical and empirical probability and the law of large numbers.

▷ Explain how the information provided in a simple probability distribution can be used in making basic risk management decisions.

▷ Describe the various measures of central tendency and how they can be used in analyzing the probabilities associated with risk.

▷ Describe the measures of dispersion and how they can be used in analyzing the probabilities associated with risk.

▷ Describe the characteristics of normal distributions and how they can be used to analyze loss exposures and project future losses more accurately.

▶▶

Probability Distributions for Analyzing Risk

2

NATURE OF PROBABILITY

The probability of an event is the relative frequency with which the event can be expected to occur in the long run in a stable environment. Determining the probability that a certain event will occur can be an important part of exposure analysis in the risk management process.

Many risk analysis techniques involve the determination of probability (the likelihood that an event will occur) and probability distributions (a presentation—table, chart, or graph—of probability estimates of a particular set of circumstances and of the probability of each possible outcome). The importance of probability in insurance cannot be overstated. Without the ability to determine the probability of losses, insurers would not be able to successfully underwrite insurance. Risk management and insurance professionals should have an understanding of the nature of probability and its role in risk management and insurance.

Concepts affecting the basic nature of probability include theoretical probability, empirical probability, and the law of large numbers.

Theoretical Probability and Empirical Probability

Any probability can be expressed as a fraction, percentage, or decimal. For example, the probability of a head on a coin toss can be expressed as 1/2, 50 percent, or .50. The probability of an event that is totally impossible is 0 and the probability of an absolutely certain event is 1.0. Therefore, the probabilities of all events that are neither totally impossible nor absolutely certain are greater than 0 but less than 1.0.

Probabilities can be developed either from theoretical considerations or from historical data. **Theoretical probability** is probability that is based on theoretical principles rather than on actual experience. Probabilities associated with events such as coin tosses or dice throws can be developed from theoretical considerations and are unchanging. For example, from a description of a fair coin or die, a person who has never seen either a coin or a die can calculate the probability of flipping a head or rolling a four.

Empirical probability is probability that is based on actual experience. For example, the probability that a sixty-two-year-old male will die in a particular year cannot be theoretically determined, but must be estimated by studying the loss experience of a sample of men aged sixty-two. The empirical

Theoretical probability
Probability that is based on theoretical principles rather than on actual experience.

Empirical probability (a posteriori probability)
A probability measure that is based on actual experience through historical data or from the observation of facts.

probabilities deduced solely from historical data may change as new data are discovered or as the environment that produces those events changes.

Empirical probabilities are only estimates whose accuracy depends on the size and representative nature of the samples being studied. In contrast, theoretical probabilities are constant as long as the physical conditions that generate them remain unchanged.

Although it may be preferable to use theoretical probabilities because of their unchanging nature, they are not applicable or available in most of the situations that insurance and risk management professionals are likely to analyze, such as automobile accidents or workers compensation claims. As a result, empirical probabilities must be used.

Law of Large Numbers

Probability analysis

A technique for forecasting events, such as accidental and business losses, on the assumption that they are governed by an unchanging probability distribution.

Probability analysis is particularly effective for projecting losses in organizations that have (1) a substantial volume of data on past losses and (2) fairly stable operations so that (except for price level changes) patterns of past losses presumably will continue in the future. In organizations with this type of unchanging environment, past losses can be viewed as a sample of all possible losses that the organization might suffer.

The larger the number of past losses an organization has experienced, the larger the sample of losses that can be used in the analysis. Consequently, the forecasts of future losses are more reliable (consistent over time) because the forecast is based on a larger sample of the environment that produced the losses. This is an application of the law of large numbers.

As an example, suppose an urn holds four marbles. One of the marbles is red and three are black. Assume that the number of red or black marbles is not known. The task is to estimate the theoretical probability of choosing a red marble on one draw (sample) from the urn by repeatedly sampling the marbles and replacing each in the urn after the sampling.

After twenty samples a red marble has been chosen eight times, which yields an empirical frequency of 40 percent (8/20). However, this estimate is inaccurate because the theoretical probability is 25 percent (1/4), given that only one of the four marbles is red.

According to the law of large numbers, the relative inaccuracy between the empirical frequency (40 percent in this case) and the theoretical probability (25 percent) will decline, on average, as the sample size increases. That is, as the number of samples increases from 20 to 200 or 2,000, the empirical frequency of choosing a red marble gets closer and closer to 25 percent.

The law of large numbers has some limitations. It can be used to more accurately forecast future events only when the events being forecast meet all three of these criteria:

- The events have occurred in the past under substantially identical conditions and have resulted from unchanging, basic causal forces.
- The events can be expected to occur in the future under the same, unchanging conditions.
- The events have been, and will continue to be, both independent of one another and sufficiently numerous.

USING PROBABILITY DISTRIBUTIONS

Once empirical probabilities are determined, probability distributions can be constructed. The information provided by probability distributions can be instrumental in analyzing loss exposures and making risk management decisions.

A properly constructed **probability distribution** always contains outcomes that are both mutually exclusive and collectively exhaustive. There are two forms of probability distributions: discrete and continuous. Discrete probability distributions have a finite number of possible outcomes and are typically used as frequency distributions. Continuous probability distributions have an infinite number of possible outcomes and are typically used as severity distributions.

Probability distribution

A presentation (table, chart, or graph) of probability estimates of a particular set of circumstances and of the probability of each possible outcome.

Outcomes of a Properly Constructed Probability Distribution

Both theoretical probabilities (such as those involving tossing coins or rolling dice) and empirical probabilities (such as those involving the number or size of losses) have outcomes that are mutually exclusive and collectively exhaustive. For example, on a particular flip of a coin, only one outcome is possible: heads or tails. Therefore, these outcomes are mutually exclusive.

Similarly, these two outcomes are the only possible outcomes and, therefore, are collectively exhaustive. A properly constructed probability distribution always contains outcomes that are both mutually exclusive and collectively exhaustive. For example, the exhibit shows the hypothetical probability distribution of the number of hurricanes making landfall in Florida during any given hurricane season. Each outcome (hurricane) is mutually exclusive and the sum of the outcomes is 1.0, so they are collectively exhaustive. See the exhibit "Number of Hurricanes Making Landfall in Florida During One Hurricane Season."

Number of Hurricanes Making Landfall in Florida During One Hurricane Season

Number of Hurricanes Making Landfall	Probability
0	.300
1	.350
2	.200
3	.147
4	.002
5+	.001
Total Probability	**1.000**

[DA02572]

The second exhibit shows the distribution as a pie chart. See the exhibit "Probability of Hurricanes Making Landfall in Florida During One Hurricane Season."

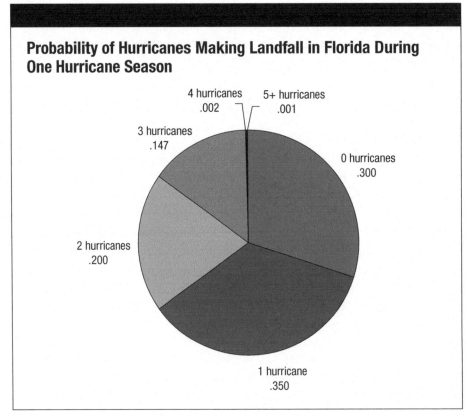

Probability of Hurricanes Making Landfall in Florida During One Hurricane Season

[DA02573]

Theoretical Probability Distributions

Consider the probability distribution of the total number of points on one throw of two dice, one red and one green. There are thirty-six equally likely outcomes (green 1, red 1; green 1, red 2; ... green 6, red 6). The exhibit shows three alternate presentations of this probability distribution—a table, a chart and a graph.

- All possible outcomes are accounted for (they are collectively exhaustive), and the occurrence of any possible outcome (such as green 1, red 1) excludes any other outcome.

- Eleven point values are possible (ranging from a total of two points to a total of twelve points), and the probability of each of these eleven possible point values is proportional to the number of times each point value appears in the table of outcomes.

- As the chart in the exhibit indicates, the probability of a total of two points is 1/36 because only one of the thirty-six possible outcomes (green 1, red 1) produces a total of two points.

- Similarly, 1/36 is the probability of a total of twelve points. The most likely total point value, seven points, has a probability of 6/36, represented in the table of outcomes by the diagonal southwest-northeast row of sevens. When the outcomes are presented as a graph, the height of the vertical line above each outcome indicates the probability of that outcome.

Although insurance and risk management professionals work with theoretical distributions on occasion, relatively few of the loss exposures they analyze involve theoretical probabilities. Therefore, most of the work they do involves empirical probability distributions. See the exhibit "Probability Distribution of Total Points on One Roll of Two Dice."

Empirical Probability Distributions

Empirical probability distributions (estimated from historical data) are constructed in the same way as theoretical probability distributions. The exhibit shows a hypothetical empirical probability distribution for auto physical damage losses. See the exhibit "Estimated Probability Distribution of Auto Physical Damage Losses."

Because the first requirement of a probability distribution is that it provide a mutually exclusive, collectively exhaustive list of outcomes, loss categories (bins) must be designed so that all losses can be included. One method is to divide the bins into equal sizes, similar to the exhibit, with each bin size being a standard size (in this case, $5,000).

The second requirement of a probability distribution is that it define the set of probabilities associated with each of the possible outcomes. The exhibit shows empirical probabilities for each size category in Column 3.

Probability Distribution of Total Points on One Roll of Two Dice

A. Table of Outcomes

		Red Die					
		1	2	3	4	5	6
Green Die	1	2	3	4	5	6	7
	2	3	4	5	6	7	8
	3	4	5	6	7	8	9
	4	5	6	7	8	9	10
	5	6	7	8	9	10	11
	6	7	8	9	10	11	12

B. Chart Format

Total Points Both Dice	Probability				
2	1/36	or	.028	or	2.8%
3	2/36	or	.056	or	5.6
4	3/36	or	.083	or	8.3
5	4/36	or	.111	or	11.1
6	5/36	or	.139	or	13.9
7	6/36	or	.167	or	16.7
8	5/36	or	.139	or	13.9
9	4/36	or	.111	or	11.1
10	3/36	or	.083	or	8.3
11	2/36	or	.056	or	5.6
12	1/36	or	.028	or	2.8
Total	36/36	or	1.000	or	100.0%

Note: Total may not sum to 1 or 100% because of rounding.

C. Graph Format

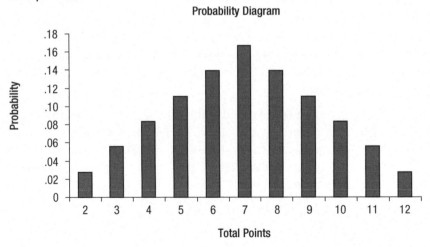

[DA02574]

Estimated Probability Distribution of Auto Physical Damage Losses

	(1)	(2)	(3)	(4)	(5)
	Size Category of Losses (bins)	Number of Losses	Percentage of Number of Losses	Dollar Amount of Losses	Percentage of Dollar Amount
	$0–$5,000	7	36.84%	$18,007	10.64%
	$5,001–$10,000	7	36.84	51,448	30.39
	$10,001–$15,000	2	10.53	27,298	16.13
	$15,001–$20,000	1	5.26	15,589	9.21
	$20,001–$25,000	1	5.26	21,425	12.66
	$25,001+	1	5.26	35,508	20.98
	Total	19	100.00%	$169,275	100.00%

Mean dollar amount = $8,909

[DA02575]

To determine the empirical probabilities in Column 3, the number of losses for each category (Column 2) is divided by the total number of losses. The sum of the resulting empirical probabilities is 100 percent (that is, the outcomes are collectively exhaustive) and any given loss falls into only one category (the outcomes are mutually exclusive). Therefore, the empirical probability distribution for losses is described by Columns 1 and 3 and satisfies all the requirements of a probability distribution.

The empirical probability distribution for auto physical damage losses presented in the exhibit differs in two ways from the theoretical probability distributions of the dice rolls shown in the "Probability Distribution of Total Points on One Roll of Two Dice" exhibit:

- First, the outcomes shown in Column 1 of the auto physical damage exhibit (size categories of losses) are arbitrarily defined boundaries, whereas the outcomes of a roll of dice are specific and observable.
- Second, whereas the maximum possible dice total is twelve, the largest size of auto physical damage losses ($25,000+) has no evident upper limit.

Discrete and Continuous Probability Distributions

Probability distributions come in two forms: discrete probability distributions and continuous probability distributions. Discrete probability distributions have a finite number of possible outcomes, whereas continuous probability distributions have an infinite number of possible outcomes.

Discrete probability distributions are usually displayed in a table that lists all possible outcomes and the probability of each outcome. These distributions are typically used to analyze how often something will occur; that is, they are shown as frequency distributions. The number of hurricanes making landfall in Florida (shown in the "Number of Hurricanes Making Landfall in Florida During One Hurricane Season" exhibit) is an example of a frequency distribution.

Discrete probability distributions have a countable number of outcomes. For example, it is impossible to have 2.5 outcomes. In contrast, continuous probability distributions have an infinite number of possible outcome values and are generally represented in one of two ways: either as a graph or by dividing the distribution into a countable number of bins (shown in the "Estimated Probability Distribution of Auto Physical Damage Losses" exhibit).

The "Continuous Probability Distributions" exhibit illustrates two representations of continuous probability distributions. The possible outcomes are presented on the horizontal axes, and the likelihood of those outcomes is shown in the vertical axes. The height of the line or curve above the outcomes indicates the likelihood of that outcome. The outcomes in a continuous probability distribution are called probability density functions. Continuous probability distributions are typically used for severity distributions—they depict the value of the loss rather than the number of outcomes.

Figure (a) in the "Continuous Probability Distributions" exhibit, which has a flat line above the interval $0 to $1,000, illustrates that all of the outcomes between $0 and $1,000 are equally likely. Figure (b), which has a curve that starts at $0 and increases until it reaches a peak at $500 and then declines to $0 again at $1,000, illustrates that the very low (close to $0) and very high (close to $1,000) outcomes are unlikely and that the outcomes around $500 are much more likely. See the exhibit "Continuous Probability Distributions."

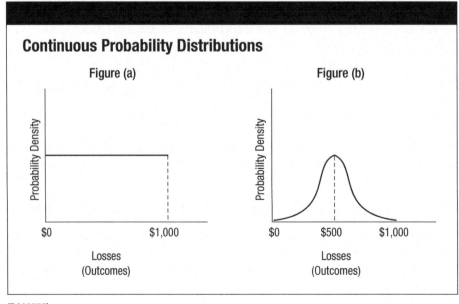

Continuous Probability Distributions

Figure (a)

Figure (b)

[DA02576]

The other way of presenting a continuous probability distribution is to divide the distribution into a countable number of bins. The "Estimated Probability Distribution of Auto Physical Damage Losses" exhibit displays auto physical damage losses in a continuous probability distribution that has been divided into six bins described by various ranges of losses. Although the auto physical damage distribution is a continuous probability distribution, the dividing of the losses into bins makes the continuous distribution resemble a discrete probability distribution with several outcomes.

In continuous probability distributions used as severity distributions, the value lost can take any value between $0 and some upper limit (such as $1,000,000). By definition, continuous probability distributions have an infinite number of possible outcomes (otherwise they are discrete distributions). Therefore, the probability of any given outcome is zero, as there are an uncountable number of other outcomes.

As a result, an insurance or risk management professional has to divide the continuous distribution into a finite number of bins. When divided into bins, a probability of an outcome falling within a certain range can be calculated.

For example, in a discrete frequency distribution, the probability of a high-rise office building not having a fire (zero fires) may be .50, of having one fire—.35, and of having two fires—.15. If a fire occurs, the damage may be anywhere between $0 and $1,000,000,000, which is a continuous severity distribution.

It is almost impossible for an insurance or risk management professional to assign a probability to the likelihood of having a loss amount of $35,456.32. However, if the severity distribution is divided into a finite number of bins, $0–$1,000,000, $1,000,001–$2,000,000, and so on, it is possible to assign a probability to each bin.

For example, the probability of the damage being between $0 and $1,000,000 is .25, and the probability of the damage being between $1,000,001 and $2,000,000 is .30. By dividing a continuous distribution into bins, the insurance or risk management professional simplifies the analysis necessary to develop a forecast of future losses using frequency and severity distributions.

USING CENTRAL TENDENCY

In analyzing a probability distribution, the measures of central tendency represent the best guess as to what the outcome will be. For example, if a manager asked an underwriter what the expected losses from fire would be on a store that the underwriter had insured, the underwriter's best guess would be one of the measures of central tendency of the frequency distribution multiplied by one of the measures of central tendency of the severity distribution. So, if the expected number of fires was two, and each fire had an expected severity of $5,000, the underwriter would expect $10,000 in losses.

Central tendency
The single outcome that is the most representative of all possible outcomes included within a probability distribution.

After determining empirical probabilities and constructing probability distributions, the insurance or risk management professional can use **central tendency** to compare the characteristics of those probability distributions. Many probability distributions cluster around a particular value, which may or may not be in the exact center of the distribution's range of values. The three most widely accepted measures of central tendency are the expected value or mean, the median, and the mode.

Expected Value

Expected value
The weighted average of all of the possible outcomes of a probability distribution.

The **expected value** is the weighted average of all of the possible outcomes of a theoretical probability distribution. The weights are the probabilities of the outcomes. The outcomes of a probability distribution are symbolized as $x1$, $x2$, $x3$, ... xn (xn represents the last outcome in the series), having respective probabilities of $p1$, $p2$, $p3$, ... pn. The distribution's expected value is the sum of ($p1 \times x1$) + ($p2 \times x2$) + ($p3 \times x3$) + ... ($pn \times xn$). See the exhibit "Calculating the Expected Value of a Probability Distribution—The Two Dice Example."

Calculating the Expected Value of a Probability Distribution— The Two Dice Example

(1) Total Points— Both Dice (x)	(2) Probability (p)	(3) $p \times x$	(4) Cumulative Probability (sum of p's)
2	1/36	2/36	1/36
3	2/36	6/36	3/36
4	3/36	12/36	6/36
5	4/36	20/36	10/36
6	5/36	30/36	15/36
7	6/36	42/36	21/36
8	5/36	40/36	26/36
9	4/36	36/36	30/36
10	3/36	30/36	33/36
11	2/36	22/36	35/36
12	1/36	12/36	36/36, or 100%
Total	36/36 = 1	252/36 = 7.0	

Expected Value = 252/36 = 7.0
Median = 7 (There is an equal number of outcomes (15) above and below 7.)
Mode = 7 (The most frequent outcome.)

[DA02577]

In the example of a probability distribution of total points on one roll of a pair of dice, the distribution's expected value of 7.0 is shown in the exhibit as the sum of the values in Column 3.

The procedure for calculating the expected value applies to all theoretical discrete probability distributions, regardless of their shape or dispersion. For continuous distributions, the expected value is also a weighted average of the possible outcomes. However, calculating the expected value for a continuous distribution is much more complex and therefore is not discussed here.

Mean

Probabilities are needed to calculate a theoretical distribution's expected value. However, when considering an empirical distribution constructed from historical data, the measure of central tendency is not called the expected value, it is called the **mean**. In other words, the mean is the numeric average. Just as the expected value is calculated by weighting each possible outcome by its probability, the mean is calculated by weighting each observed outcome by the relative frequency with which it occurs.

Mean
The sum of the values in a data set divided by the number of values.

For example, if the observed outcome values are 2, 3, 4, 4, 5, 5, 5, 6, 6, and 8, then the mean equals 4.8, which is the sum of the values, 48, divided by the number of values, 10. The mean is only a good estimate of the expected outcome if the underlying conditions determining those outcomes remain constant over time.

Unlike the expected value, which is derived from theory, the mean is derived from experience. If the conditions that generated that experience have changed, the mean that was calculated may no longer be an accurate estimate of central tendency. Nonetheless, an insurance or a risk management professional will often use the mean as the single best guess as to forecasting future events.

For example, the best guess as to the number of workers compensation claims that an organization will suffer in the next year is often the mean of the frequency distribution of workers compensation claims from previous years.

Median and Cumulative Probabilities

Another measure of central tendency is the **median**. In order to determine a data set's median, its values must be arranged by size, from highest to lowest or lowest to highest. In the array of nineteen auto physical damage losses in the exhibit, the median loss has an adjusted value of $6,782. This tenth loss is the median because nine losses are greater than $6,782 and nine losses are less than $6,782. See the exhibit "Array of Historical and Adjusted Auto Physical Damage Losses."

Median
The value at the midpoint of a sequential data set with an odd number of values, or the mean of the two middle values of a sequential data set with an even number of values.

A probability distribution's median has a cumulative probability of 50 percent. For example, seven is the median of the probability distribution of points in

Array of Historical and Adjusted Auto Physical Damage Losses

(1) Date	(2) Historical Loss Amount	(3) Adjusted Loss Amount*	(4) Rank
09/29/X3	$ 155	$ 200	19
04/21/X3	1,008	1,300	18
03/18/X4	1,271	1,500	17
12/04/X3	1,783	2,300	16
07/27/X5	3,774	4,000	15
06/14/X6	4,224	4,224	14
04/22/X6	4,483	4,483	13
02/08/X5**	5,189	5,500	12
05/03/X3	4,651	5,999	11
01/02/X6**	6,782	6,782	10
07/12/X4	6,271	7,402	9
05/17/X5**	7,834	8,303	8
08/15/X4	7,119	8,403	7
06/10/X6	9,059	9,059	6
12/19/X5	12,830	13,599	5
08/04/X5	12,925	13,699	4
11/01/X4	13,208	15,589	3
01/09/X6	21,425	21,425	2
10/23/X6	35,508	35,508	1

*   Adjusted amount column is the historical loss amount adjusted to current year dollars using a price index.

** Loss for which adjustment of historical amount to current year dollars changes ranking in array.

[DA02578]

rolling two dice because seven is the only number of points for which the probability of higher outcomes (15/36) is equal to the probability of lower outcomes (15/36). That is, there are fifteen equally probable ways of obtaining an outcome higher than seven and fifteen equally probable ways of obtaining an outcome lower than seven.

The median can also be determined by summing the probabilities of outcomes equal to or less than a given number of points in rolling two dice, as in the "Calculating the Expected Value of a Probability Distribution—The Two Dice Example" exhibit. The cumulative 50 percent probability (18/36) is reached in the seven-points category (actually, in the middle of the seven-point class of results). Therefore, seven is the median of this distribution.

The cumulative probabilities in Column 4 of the exhibit indicate the probability of a die roll yielding a certain number of points or less. For example, the cumulative probability of rolling a three or less is 3/36 (or the sum of 1/36 for rolling a two and 2/36 for rolling a three). Similarly, the cumulative probability of rolling a ten or less is 33/36, calculated by summing the individual Column 2 probabilities of outcomes of ten points or less.

With probability distributions of losses, calculating probabilities of losses equal to or less than a given number of losses or dollar amounts of losses, individually and cumulatively, can be helpful in selecting retention levels. Similarly, calculating individual and cumulative probabilities of losses equal to or greater than a given number of losses or dollar amounts can help in selecting upper limits of insurance coverage.

The "Cumulative Probabilities" exhibit shows how to derive a cumulative probability distribution of loss sizes from the individual probabilities of loss size in the exhibit. See the exhibit "Cumulative Probabilities That Auto Physical Damage Losses Will Not Exceed Specified Amounts."

Column 3 of the "Cumulative Probabilities" exhibit indicates that, on the basis of the available data, 36.84 percent of all losses are less than or equal to $5,000 and that another 36.84 percent are greater than $5,000 but less than or equal to $10,000. Therefore, the probability of a loss being $10,000 or less is calculated as the sum of these two probabilities, or 73.68 percent, as shown in Column 4 of the "Cumulative Probabilities" exhibit. Similarly, as shown in Column 7 of the same exhibit, individual losses of $10,000 or less can be expected to account for 41.03 percent of the total dollar amount of all losses.

Understanding the cumulative probability distribution will enable an insurance or risk management professional to evaluate the effect of various deductibles and policy limits on insured loss exposures. For example, if an insurance policy has a $5,000 deductible, the insurance or risk management professional would know that 36.84 percent of losses covered by that policy would be below the deductible level and therefore would not be paid by the insurer.

The summed probabilities in Column 4 of the "Cumulative Probabilities" exhibit indicate that the median individual loss is between $5,001 and $10,000, the category in which the 50 percent cumulative probability is reached. This result is consistent with the $6,782 median loss found by examining the "Array of Historical and Adjusted Auto Physical Damage Losses" exhibit.

Mode

In addition to mean and median, a further measure of central tendency is the **mode**. For a continuous distribution, the mode is the value of the

Mode
The most frequently occurring value in a distribution.

Cumulative Probabilities That Auto Physical Damage Losses Will Not Exceed Specified Amounts

(1) Loss Size Category	(2) Number of Losses	(3) Percentage of Number of Losses	(4) Cumulative Percentage of Number of Losses Not Exceeding Category	(5) Dollar Amount of Losses	(6) Percentage of Dollar Amount	(7) Cumulative Percentage of Dollar Amount of Losses Not Exceeding Category
$0–$5,000	7	36.84%	36.84%	$18,007	10.64%	10.64%
$5,001–$10,000	7	36.84	73.68	51,448	30.39	41.03
$10,001–$15,000	2	10.53	84.21	27,298	16.13	57.16
$15,001–$20,000	1	5.26	89.47	15,589	9.21	66.37
$20,001–$25,000	1	5.26	94.74	21,425	12.66	79.02
$25,001+	1	5.26	100.00	35,508	20.98	100.00
Total		100.00%			100.00%	

[DA02579]

outcome directly beneath the peak of the probability density function. In the distribution of total points of two dice throws, the mode is seven points. In the empirical distribution of auto physical damage losses shown in the "Cumulative Probabilities" exhibit, the mode is the $0–$5,000 range or the $5,001–$10,000 range, because those ranges have the highest frequency of losses (seven).

Knowing the mode of a distribution allows insurance and risk management professionals to focus on the outcomes that are the most common. For example, knowing that the most common auto physical damage losses are in the $0–$10,000 range may influence the risk financing decisions regarding deductible levels for potential insurance coverages.

The relationships among the mean (average), median, and mode for any data set are illustrated by the distribution's shape. The shape of a particular relative frequency or severity probability distribution can be seen by graphing a curve of the data as shown in the "Typical Shapes" exhibit and can be either symmetrical or asymmetrical. See the exhibit "Typical Shapes of Symmetrical and Skewed Distributions Showing Relative Locations of Mean, Median, and Mode."

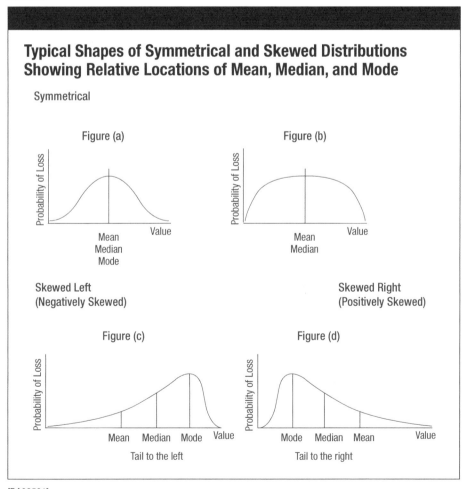

Typical Shapes of Symmetrical and Skewed Distributions Showing Relative Locations of Mean, Median, and Mode

Symmetrical

Figure (a)

Figure (b)

Skewed Left (Negatively Skewed)

Skewed Right (Positively Skewed)

Figure (c)

Figure (d)

[DA02581]

In a symmetrical distribution, one side of the curve is a mirror image of the other. The distribution in Figure (a) of the exhibit is the standard (normal) distribution commonly called a bell-shaped curve, but the distributions in both Figure (a) and Figure (b) are symmetrical. In a symmetrical distribution, the mean and median have the same value. In a standard bell-shaped distribution, the mode also has the same value as that of the mean and the median.

If a distribution is asymmetrical, it is skewed. Skewed distributions are shown in both Figure (c) and Figure (d) of the exhibit. Many loss distributions are skewed because the probability of small losses is large whereas the probability of large losses is small. Asymmetrical distributions are common for severity distributions where most losses are small losses but there is a small probability of a large loss occurring. If the distribution is skewed, the mean and median values will differ and the median value of the distribution is often a better guess than the mean as to what is most likely to occur.

For example, if the distribution of workers compensation claims was skewed by two years in which an organization experienced an unusually high level of claims, the mean would be higher than the median. In that situation, the median is more likely a better estimate of next year's claims than the mean. See the exhibit "Practice Exercise."

Practice Exercise

Based on the mean of the total workers compensation losses for each year, the risk manager of an airline company expects the total amount of such losses next year to be $2 million. The chief financial officer has assured the risk manager that the company can afford to retain half of that amount ($1 million) in an effort to reduce the insurance premium. Using the values provided in the chart, what is the highest aggregate annual deductible the risk manager should consider?

Loss Size Category	Dollar Amount of Losses	Percentage of Total Dollar Amount of Losses
$0 – $10,000	$500,000	25%
$10,001 – $20,000	$300,000	15%
$20,001 – $50,000	$300,000	15%
$50,001 – $100,000	$400,000	20%
$100,001 +	$500,000	25%
Total	$2,000,000	100%

Answer

By adding the percentages of total dollar amounts to obtain cumulative percentages (shown in the new column, far right), the risk manager can see that 50 percent, or $1 million, will likely be retained by the company if it chooses a deductible of slightly less than $50,000. The risk manager may want to resize the loss size categories to derive a more accurate number.

Loss Size Category	Dollar Amount of Losses	Percentage of Total Dollar Amount of Losses	Cumulative Percentage of Dollar Amount of Losses Not Exceeding Category
$0 – $10,000	$500,000	25%	25%
$10,001 – $20,000	$300,000	15%	40%
$20,001 – $50,000	$300,000	15%	55%
$50,001 – $100,000	$400,000	20%	75%
$100,001 +	$500,000	25%	100%
Total	$2,000,000	100%	

[DA05840]

USING DISPERSION

When analyzing probability distributions, insurance and risk management professionals use measures of dispersion to assess the credibility of the measures of central tendency used in analyzing loss exposures.

Dispersion

The variation among values in a distribution.

Measures of central tendency for a distribution of outcomes include the expected value (or mean), which can provide useful information for comparing characteristics of distributions. However, another important characteristic of a distribution is its **dispersion**. Dispersion describes the extent to which the distribution is spread out rather than concentrated around the expected value. The less dispersion around the distribution's expected value, the greater the likelihood that actual results will fall within a given range of that expected value.

Therefore, less dispersion means less uncertainty about the expected outcomes. Insurance professionals may be able to use measures of dispersion around estimated losses to determine whether to offer insurance coverage to a possible insured. Dispersion also affects the shape of a distribution. The more dispersed a distribution (larger standard deviation), the flatter the distribution. A less dispersed distribution forms a more peaked distribution. Two symmetrical distributions with the same mean but with different standard deviations are shown in the "Dispersion" exhibit. See the exhibit "Dispersion."

Dispersion

Smaller Standard Deviation

Mean

Larger Standard Deviation

[DA02582]

For example, if an underwriter is choosing between two accounts, both with the same expected loss, but one account has more variation in possible losses then the other, the underwriter will likely choose to insure the account with less variation (lower dispersion). In general, the less dispersion around the central tendency, the less risk is involved in the loss exposure.

There are two widely used statistical measures of dispersion:

- Standard deviation
- Coefficient of variation

Standard Deviation

The **standard deviation** is the average of the differences (deviations) between the values in a distribution and the expected value (or mean) of that distribution. The standard deviation therefore indicates how widely dispersed the values in a distribution are.

To calculate the standard deviation of a probability distribution, one must perform these steps:

1. Calculate the distribution's expected value or mean
2. Subtract this expected value from each distribution value to find the differences
3. Square each of the resulting differences
4. Multiply each square by the probability associated with the value
5. Sum the resulting products
6. Find the square root of the sum

The "Calculation of Standard Deviation of the Probability Distribution of Two Dice" exhibit illustrates how to calculate a standard deviation for the distribution of values in rolling two dice. The distribution's expected value or mean is seven. See the exhibit "Calculation of Standard Deviation of the Probability Distribution of Two Dice."

The standard deviation of auto physical damage losses can be estimated using the individual loss amounts shown in Column (1) of the "Calculation of Standard Deviation of Individual Outcomes" exhibit. Calculating a standard deviation using a sample of actual outcomes is done in much the same way as for a probability distribution. To calculate the standard deviation using the actual sample of outcomes, it is not necessary to know the probability of each outcome, just how often each outcome occurred. See the exhibit "Calculation of Standard Deviation of Individual Outcomes."

Standard deviation

A measure of dispersion between the values in a distribution and the expected value (or mean) of that distribution, calculated by taking the square root of the variance.

Calculation of Standard Deviation of the Probability Distribution of Two Dice

(1) Points (x_i)	(2) Probability (p)	(3) Step 1 EV	(4) Step 2 $x_i - EV$	(5) Step 3 $(x_i - EV)^2$	(6) Step 4 $(x_i - EV)^2 \times p$
2	1/36	7	−5	25	25/36
3	2/36	7	−4	16	32/36
4	3/36	7	−3	9	27/36
5	4/36	7	−2	4	16/36
6	5/36	7	−1	1	5/36
7	6/36	7	0	0	0
8	5/36	7	1	1	5/36
9	4/36	7	2	4	16/36
10	3/36	7	3	9	27/36
11	2/36	7	4	16	32/36
12	1/36	7	5	25	25/36
			Step 5	Total	210/36
			Step 6	$\sqrt{(210/36)} =$	2.42*

*Rounded

[DA02583]

The steps for calculating the standard deviation of a set of individual outcomes not involving probabilities are these:

1. Calculate the mean of the outcomes (the sum of the outcomes divided by the number of outcomes).
2. Subtract the mean from each of the outcomes.
3. Square each of the resulting differences.
4. Sum these squares.
5. Divide this sum by the number of outcomes minus one. (This value is called the variance.)
6. Calculate the square root of the variance.

The "Calculation of Standard Deviation of Individual Outcomes" exhibit illustrates how to calculate a standard deviation using actual loss data rather than a theoretical probability distribution. Insurance and risk management professionals use measurements of dispersion of the distributions of potential outcomes to gain a better understanding of the loss exposures being analyzed.

Calculation of Standard Deviation of Individual Outcomes

(1) Adjusted Loss Amount (ALA)	(2) Step 1 Mean Loss (ML)	(3) Step 2 ALA-ML	(4) Step 3 (ALA-ML)^2
$ 200	$8,909	$–8,709	$ 75,846,681
1,300	8,909	–7,609	57,896,881
1,500	8,909	–7,409	54,893,281
2,300	8,909	–6,609	43,678,881
4,000	8,909	–4,909	24,098,281
4,224	8,909	–4,685	21,949,225
4,483	8,909	–4,426	19,589,476
5,500	8,909	–3,409	11,621,281
5,999	8,909	–2,910	8,468,100
6,782	8,909	–2,127	4,524,129
7,402	8,909	–1,507	2,271,049
8,303	8,909	–606	367,236
8,403	8,909	–506	256,036
9,059	8,909	150	22,500
13,599	8,909	4,690	21,996,100
13,699	8,909	4,790	22,944,100
15,589	8,909	6,680	44,622,400
21,425	8,909	12,516	156,650,256
35,508	8,909	26,599	707,506,801

Step 4	Sum	$1,279,202,694
Step 5	Variance [sum ÷ (n – 1)]	71,066,816
Step 6	Standard deviation (sqrt variance)	$8,430

[DA02584]

For example, knowing the expected number of workers compensation claims in a given year is important, but it is only one element of the information that can be gleaned from a distribution. The standard deviation can be calculated to provide a measure of how sure an insurance or risk management professional can be in his or her estimate of number of workers compensation claims.

Coefficient of Variation

Coefficient of variation

A measure of dispersion calculated by dividing a distribution's standard deviation by its mean.

The **coefficient of variation** is a further measure of the dispersion of a distribution. For example, the coefficient of variation for the distribution of total points in rolling two dice equals 2.4 points (the standard deviation of the distribution) divided by 7.0 points (the mean or expected value), which is 0.34. Similarly the coefficient of variation of the sample of outcomes in the "Calculation of Standard Deviation of Individual Outcomes" exhibit is $8,430 divided by $8,909, or approximately 0.95.

In comparing two distributions, if both distributions have the same mean (or expected value), then the distribution with the larger standard deviation has the greater variability. If the two distributions have different means (or expected values), the coefficient of variation is often used to compare the two distributions to determine which has the greater variability relative to its mean (or expected value).

For insurance and risk management professionals, comparing two distinct distributions with different means and standard deviations is difficult. In the example of an underwriter trying to determine to which account to offer coverage, if the means are the same, all else being equal, the underwriter should choose the account with the lower standard deviation. If the accounts have different means and standard deviations, the underwriter could compare the two accounts using the coefficient of variation and choose the account with the lower coefficient of variation.

Insurance and risk management professionals can use the coefficient of variation to determine whether a particular loss control measure has made losses more or less predictable (that is, whether the distribution is more or less variable).

For example, an insurance or a risk management professional may calculate that an organization's theft losses have a severity distribution with a mean of $3,590 and a standard deviation of $3,432 for a coefficient of variation of 0.96. If the organization installs a new security system, the theft losses may have a severity distribution with a mean of $2,150 and a standard deviation of $2,950 for a coefficient of variation of 1.37.

Although the security system has reduced the mean severity, it has actually made the losses less predictable because the new severity distribution is relatively more variable than the old distribution without the security system.

The coefficient of variation is useful in comparing the variability of distributions that have different shapes, means, or standard deviations. The distribution with the largest coefficient of variation has the greatest relative variability. The higher the variability within a distribution, the more difficult it is to accurately forecast an individual outcome.

USING NORMAL DISTRIBUTIONS

Insurance and risk management professionals use normal probability distributions to predict future losses, which enables them to marshal the resources to control losses that can be prevented or mitigated and to finance those that cannot.

The **normal distribution** is a probability distribution that, when graphed, generates a bell-shaped curve. This particular probability distribution can help to accurately forecast the variability around some central, average, or expected value and has therefore proven useful in accurately forecasting the variability of many physical phenomena.

Normal distribution

A probability distribution that, when graphed, generates a bell-shaped curve.

Characteristics of Normal Distributions

The exhibit illustrates the typical bell-shaped curve of a normal distribution. Note that the normal curve never touches the horizontal line at the base of the diagram. In theory, the normal distribution assigns some probability greater than zero for every outcome, regardless of its distance from the mean. The exhibit also shows the percentage of outcomes that fall within a given number of standard deviations above or below the mean of a distribution. See the exhibit "The Normal Distribution—Percentages of Outcomes Within Specified Standard Deviations of the Mean."

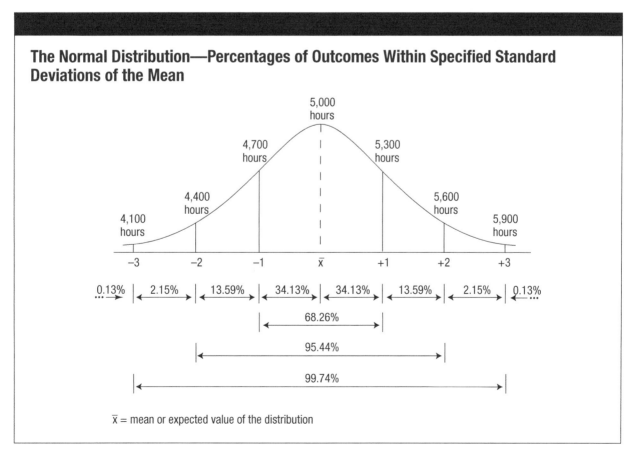

The Normal Distribution—Percentages of Outcomes Within Specified Standard Deviations of the Mean

$\bar{x}$ = mean or expected value of the distribution

For example, for all normal distributions, 34.13 percent of all outcomes are within one standard deviation above the mean and, because every normal distribution is symmetrical, another 34.13 percent of all outcomes fall within one standard deviation below the mean. By addition, 68.26 percent of all outcomes are within one standard deviation above or below the mean. The portion of a normal distribution that is between one and two standard deviations above the mean contains 13.59 percent of all outcomes, as does the portion between one and two standard deviations below the mean. Hence, the area between the mean and two standard deviations above the mean contains 47.72 percent (34.13 percent + 13.59 percent) of the outcomes, and another 47.72 percent are two standard deviations or less below the mean.

Consequently, 95.44 percent of all outcomes are within two standard deviations above or below the mean, and fewer than 5 percent of outcomes are outside two standard deviations above or below the mean. Taking this a step further, 2.15 percent of all outcomes are between two and three standard deviations above the mean, and another 2.15 percent are between two and three standard deviations below the mean. Therefore, 49.87 percent (34.13 percent + 13.59 percent + 2.15 percent) of all outcomes are three standard deviations or less above the mean, and an equal percentage are three standard deviations or less below the mean.

Consequently, the portion of the distribution between three standard deviations above the mean and three standard deviations below it contains 99.74 percent (49.87 percent × 2) of all outcomes. Therefore, only 0.26 percent (100 percent – 99.74 percent) of all outcomes lie beyond three standard deviations from the mean. Half of these outcomes (0.13 percent) are more than three standard deviations below the mean, and the other half (0.13 percent) are more than three standard deviations above the mean.

Practical Application

The relationship between the expected value and the standard deviation of a normal distribution can have useful practical application. For example, suppose that a plant uses 600 electrical elements to heat rubber. The useful life of each element is limited, and an element that is used for too long poses a substantial danger of exploding and starting an electrical fire. An insurance professional underwriting the plant's fire insurance would look for evidence that proper maintenance is performed and the elements are replaced to ensure proper fire safety.

The issue is determining when to replace the elements. Replacing them too soon can be costly, whereas replacing them too late increases the chance of fire. The characteristics of the normal probability distribution provide a way of scheduling maintenance so that the likelihood of an element becoming very dangerous before it is replaced can be kept below a particular margin of safety that is specified by the organization based on its willingness to assume risk.

Assume that the expected safe life of each element conforms to a normal distribution having a mean of 5,000 hours and a standard deviation of 300 hours. Even if the maintenance schedule requires replacing each element after it has been in service only 5,000 hours (the mean, or expected, safe life), a 50 percent chance exists that it will become unsafe before being changed, because 50 percent of the normal distribution is below this 5,000-hour mean.

If each element is changed after having been used only 4,700 hours [one standard deviation below the mean (5,000 – 300)], a 15.87 percent (50 percent – 34.13 percent) chance still exists that an element will become unsafe before being changed. If this probability of high hazard is still too high, changing each element after 4,400 hours [two standard deviations below the mean (5,000 – (2 × 300))] reduces the probability of high hazard to only 2.28 percent, the portion of a normal distribution that is more than two standard deviations below the mean.

A still more cautious practice would be to change elements routinely after only 4,100 hours [three standard deviations below the mean (5,000 – (3 × 300))], so that the probability of an element becoming highly hazardous before replacement would be only 0.13 percent, slightly more than one chance in 1,000.

Using this analysis, management can select an acceptable probability that an element will become unsafe before being replaced and can schedule maintenance accordingly. See the exhibit "Practice Exercise."

Practice Exercise

An insurer is beginning to write policies in a new state. The insurer's claim manager wants to know how many new claim representatives to hire. The insurer's marketing department has provided an estimate of additional premium volume from the new state. Based on that estimate and industry data, the manager has determined the mean number of new claims to be 8,000, with a standard deviation of 2,000 in a normal distribution. If a claim representative can adjust 600 claims per year and the manager wants to be approximately 98 percent certain that she has enough representatives, how many will she need to hire?

Answer

As shown in the exhibit titled "The Normal Distribution—Percentages of Outcomes Within Specified Standard Deviations of the Mean," 2.28 percent of all outcomes (2.15 percent + 0.13 percent) are more than two standard deviations above the mean, and 97.72 percent (100 percent – 2.28 percent) of all outcomes fall under the normal distribution below two standard deviations above the mean. Therefore, by rounding up the 97.72 percent, the claim manager can be approximately 98 percent certain that the actual number of claims will fall at or below two standard deviations above the mean. In the claim manager's distribution, two standard deviations above the mean is 12,000 claims (calculated as 8,000 + 2,000 + 2,000). Because each claim representative can adjust 600 claims per year, the manager will need to hire 12,000/600 or 20 new representatives.

SUMMARY

Concepts affecting the use of probability in risk analysis include theoretical probability, empirical probability, and the law of large numbers. Although it may be preferable to use theoretical probabilities because of their unchanging nature, theoretical probabilities are not applicable or available in most situations that insurance and risk management professionals are likely to analyze. Applying the law of large numbers to probability reveals that a forecast of future losses will be more reliable if the forecast is based on a larger sample of the losses used in the analysis.

A properly constructed probability distribution always contains outcomes that are both mutually exclusive and collectively exhaustive. All probability distributions can be classified as either discrete or continuous.

The central tendency is the single outcome that is the most representative of all possible outcomes included within a probability distribution. The three most widely accepted measures of central tendency are expected value or mean, median, and mode.

Dispersion, which is the variation between values in a distribution, can be used as well as central tendency to compare the characteristics of probability distributions. The less dispersion around a distribution's expected value, the greater the likelihood that actual results will fall within a given range of that expected value. Two widely used statistical measures of dispersion are standard deviation and the coefficient of variation.

The normal distribution is a probability frequency distribution that, when graphed, generates a bell-shaped curve. This particular probability distribution can help to accurately forecast the variability around some central, average, or expected value and has therefore proven useful in accurately forecasting the variability of many physical phenomena.

3

Risk Modeling Techniques

Educational Objectives

After learning the content of this assignment, you should be able to:

▷ Describe the methods and associated limitations of risk modeling.

▷ Compare decision tree analysis and event tree analysis in terms of the methods they use to evaluate event consequences.

▷ Describe the purpose and components of an influence diagram.

▷ Given a scenario, apply influence diagrams and probabilities.

▷ Apply the concepts of value at risk and earnings at risk to financial risk.

▷ Summarize the key components and outputs of a catastrophe model.

Risk Modeling Techniques

METHODS AND LIMITATIONS OF RISK MODELING

Analytical tools that measure uncertainty allow risk management professionals to predict how decisions will influence the variability of an organization's future results.

A wide variety of risk models can be applied to a risk, with many customized to meet an organization's specific needs. When and how each model is used is partially determined by its limitations. No single organization is likely to use all of the modeling methods, which are organized into these three groups:

- Methods based on historical data
- Methods based on expert input
- Methods based on combining historical data and expert input

---

Big Data Analysis Techniques

Big data, which is data that is too large to be gathered and analyzed by traditional methods, and new data analysis techniques, such as text mining and social network analysis, are improving risk modeling. Insurers possess vast quantities of data, much of which has remained unused because of the size or type of data. For example, adjusters' notes or customer service conversations have not previously been used to provide data for analysis. With the new data mining techniques, more data is accessible for analysis. Additionally, larger amounts of data can be analyzed more quickly as a result of increasingly powerful data storage and processing capabilities.

Machine learning, in which computers continually teach themselves to make better decisions based on previous results and new data, provides methods to continually improve risk models. As new data is input to a computerized model, the model learns from the new data and produces more accurate results.

[OV_12091]

Methods Based on Historical Data

Certain techniques for modeling uncertainty are rooted in an analysis of past patterns and historical data. The most popular risk modeling methods that are based on historical data feature these approaches:

- Empirical probability distribution
- Theoretical probability distribution
- Extreme value theory
- Regression analysis

Empirical Probability Distribution

An empirical probability distribution is constructed from values of a random variable. An example of such a variable is the frequency of workers compensation claims for an organization. When constructing the empirical probability distribution, the most direct and simple approach is to assume that the observed values of the random variable fully define the probabilities of various values for the variable in future periods. For example, an organization's annual frequency of workers compensation claims over a given period of time may have ranged from a low of 700 to a high of 1,000. In the simplest case, these historical data are used to predict the probability of various annual frequency amounts for the organization going forward.

A deck of cards can be used to illustrate how empirical (historical) data can be used to construct an empirical probability distribution. For example, a standard deck of fifty-two cards contains thirteen cards of each suit (hearts, diamonds, clubs, and spades). When randomly drawing a card from a newly shuffled deck 100 separate times, these results were observed:

- A heart was drawn eighteen times
- A diamond was drawn twenty-five times
- A club was drawn thirty times
- A spade was drawn twenty-seven times

The probability of drawing a heart was 18 percent; a diamond, 25 percent; a club, 30 percent; and a spade, 27 percent (times drawn/total cards drawn × 100 = probability percentage), which can be displayed on a graph. See the exhibit "Empirical Probability."

Theoretical Probability Distribution

In contrast to empirical probability distributions, theoretical probability distributions are constructed using mathematical or analytical formulas and are then used as a statistical reference or comparison. If an empirical distribution is based on an insufficient number of historical data points, a risk analyst will often insert the historical data into a theoretical probability distribution to improve the forecast.

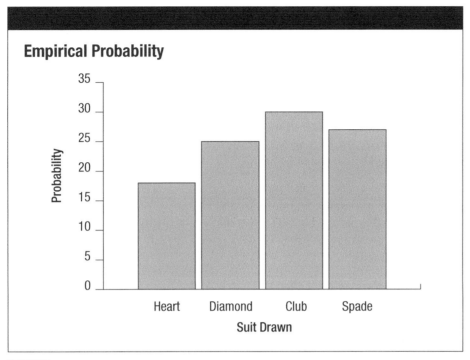

[DA10433]

Continuing with the example of drawing a playing card, the theoretical probability of drawing a card of one particular suit would be 25 percent, as there are thirteen of each suit (13/52 × 100 = 25 percent). With enough trials (well over 100), each suit should be represented by 25 percent of the cards drawn. The theoretical distribution provides mathematically predictable results without having to actually draw the cards to achieve the same purpose.

Theoretical probability distributions are useful in explaining the potential variability of categories of risk. For example, claim frequency is often assumed to follow a certain distribution, either a negative binomial or Poisson distribution. By contrast, claim severity is often assumed to follow a lognormal or a Pareto (or conditional claim or tail) distribution. Probability distribution modeling is complicated, and actuaries are often relied upon to create the models.

Securities and stock prices are often represented by a normal distribution. The majority of results fall within the expected bell-shaped parameters. The tail to the right of the bell continues on indefinitely. The left tail continues on indefinitely into negative numbers. This distribution therefore does include the very low probability (barely above the x and y intersection on the y-axis of probability) but very high severity (the tail greatly extended on the x-axis of severity) of an unexpected catastrophic event.

Extreme Value Theory

Extreme value theory (EVT)

Statistical probability estimations of extreme deviations from the median of probability distributions.

Extreme value theory (EVT) addresses the tail of a probability distribution—the unlikely but possible downside risk that is difficult to forecast accurately. As an analytical and a statistical tool, it aims to analyze probability distributions generated by occurrences, such as natural forces such as erratic weather, 100-year floods, or earthquakes. Recently, EVT stress tests have included finance and banking organizations' significant or extreme exposure to poorly performing collateralized debt obligations (securities such as bonds that are typically backed by pooled mortgages).

The difficulty in analyzing and forecasting rare events is in the lack of data available. EVT attempts to model the tail extremities of a rarely occurring or unknown variable. It can be used to predict the probability of certain events at certain values and is useful in assessing risk from infrequently occurring but high-severity losses.

Regression Analysis

Regression analysis assumes that the variable being forecast varies predictably with another variable. The variable being forecast is the dependent variable, and the variable that determines the value of the variable being forecast is the independent variable. For example, a company wants to use its production output to project the number of annual losses. Its output in hundred thousand tons of output is the independent variable and the number of annual losses is the dependent variable. The output is charted on the *x*-axis of a graph and the number of losses is charted on the *y*-axis. After plotting multiple points on the graph of the number of losses for multiple years, a straight or curved line is drawn from the *y*-axis roughly connecting the points.

The goal of regression analysis is to find an equation for the line that connects the points and to continue this line to forecast future losses. The slope of the line and the point of intersection on the *y*-axis are used in the mathematical formula to determine the relationship between the two variables. Therefore, further points can be plotted for subsequent years by extending the line to predict the number of future losses.

Although a helpful forecasting tool, regression analysis may not be accurate when it is used to forecast values far into the future. Nevertheless, regression models provide risk managers and senior executives with information about the dynamic interactions of specific risk components so that the appropriate threats and opportunities are managed. For example, a production manager who anticipates a reduction in the cost of raw materials could use a regression model to determine an optimal product price.

Methods Based on Expert Input

Other methods of mathematical-uncertainty modeling rely on the input of those with expert knowledge. Risk modeling methods based on expert input feature these approaches:

- Preference among bets
- Judgments of relative likelihood
- The Delphi technique

Preference Among Bets

The preference among bets modeling technique converts expert opinion into probabilities. Probabilities can be determined by presenting an expert with the choosing of sides on a bet of certain events. For example, the expert was asked to choose from these bets:

- Bet—receive x if interest rates rise in the next thirty days, pay y if interest rates do not rise in the next thirty days
- Opposite side of bet—pay x if interest rates rise in the next thirty days, receive y if interest rates do not rise in the next thirty days

The winnings for the wager, x and y, are continually adjusted until the expert is no longer actively taking a position one way or the other. In this example, the expert reached a state of indifference, indicating the values for each side are equal, when the amounts were adjusted to this point:

- Receive $800 if interest rates rise in the next thirty days
- Pay $200 if interest rates do not rise in the next thirty days

Using the formula $P(R) = \$y / (\$x + \$y)$, where $P(R)$ is the probability of interest rates rising in the next thirty days, the estimated subjective probability of this happening is $200/($800 + $200) = 0.20, or 20 percent.

This method is best employed when there is little observable data available, or a particular or functional viewpoint is needed in forecasting, such as specialized **political risk** or legal risk.

Judgments of Relative Likelihood

Judgments of relative likelihood may be a helpful technique in obtaining knowledge or opinions from experts unfamiliar with probability assessments. For example, a model could be constructed to determine which of a collection of investments is most likely to provide the greatest return. One type of relative likelihood model is based on expert input about whether an event is (a) more likely, (b) less likely, or (c) equally likely relative to known probabilities.

A limitation of this method is that input can be influenced by an unintentional bias that causes the expert to characterize less familiar events as less likely and more familiar events as more likely. For example, an expert weather

Political risk

Any action by a government that favors domestic over foreign organizations or poses a threat to foreign organizations.

Judgments of relative likelihood

The representation of probability by means of expert input regarding the likelihood of event outcomes.

forecaster in the midwestern United States might be inclined to assess torna-dos as more likely (given an assumed familiarity with them in that region) and hurricanes as less likely.

Delphi Technique

Delphi technique

A collaborative estimating strategy using expert input to reach consensus by continuously refining individual responses.

The **Delphi technique** attempts to arrive at an uncontested group decision. A facilitator asks the participants to provide answers to questionnaires in several rounds. After each round, the responses are tabulated and revealed to the participants before the next round of questionnaires are answered. The theory is that subsequent answers are influenced by previous replies, and so all the participants move toward consensus with each round. At a predetermined time, either after a certain number of rounds or at a defined level of consen-sus, the process stops.

The Delphi technique is useful when exploring a topic of varying subjective judgments or one encompassing a range of disciplines. The characteristics that work together to create the desired outcome are the anonymity of the experts (which encourages free expression), the control of the shared informa-tion (to encourage feedback and change), and the direction provided by the facilitator (to send out the questionnaires and manage the flow of responses). This technique helps the problem-solving and decision-making processes by encouraging experts to share their opinions and forecasts and continuously converging and synthesizing the answers until a group conclusion is reached. The technique can be more cost-effective than assembling a facilitated workshop of experts, but it may not be as helpful when forecasting concerning a new or unknown entity or when novel ways of approaching a decision are needed.

Methods Based on Combining Historical Data and Expert Input

Several methods use both historical data and expert input. The Monte Carlo simulation and the fuzzy logic method each begin with specific inputs that are used in conjunction with expert simulations to model scenarios and provide results helpful in risk analysis.

Monte Carlo Simulation

A Monte Carlo simulation focuses on specific variables in a project—such as revenues, interest rates, gross margins, and costs. A computer randomly selects values for each variable according to a probability distribution and generates thousands of possible scenarios. The results are assembled into probability distributions representing possible outcomes.

The Monte Carlo simulation is typically used for complex projects or those that involve many areas of uncertainty. It is used when probability can be calculated, and the reliability of the results depends on the number of iterations (individual tries or simulations) that were run.

A spreadsheet can be used for simple simulations. Many companies have developed simulation tools to model more sophisticated projects for engineering, environmental, energy, financial, and many other business applications. Their websites also provide calculators, tutorials, webinars, and templates for a wide variety of applications employing the Monte Carlo simulation.

Fuzzy Logic

Fuzzy logic is often used in modeling complex systems and interactions. Fuzzy logic takes complex, descriptive-language expert inputs and converts them to mathematical equivalents. Inputs (or conditions) such as "too cold, too hot, just right" may produce outputs (or actions) such as "speed up the motor, slow down the motor, do nothing." As opposed to conventional logic or probability based on values of true or false, fuzzy logic probability is based on degrees of what is true or not true.

Fuzzy logic

A type of logic that assigns values to indefinite data fields to facilitate more accurate probability.

Fuzzy logic was developed to address situations that are not entirely absolute or in which interpretations are subjective. The process of inputs, outputs, fuzzy sets, and fuzzy rules is complex, but it is meant to use familiar terms, be flexible, and adapt to imprecise data. Some actual or suggested uses for fuzzy logic are machine use by various controllers, transportation signals based not on predictable timers but on changing traffic patterns, and automation of various industrial processes. See the exhibit "Bayesian Inference."

Apply Your Knowledge

A class was learning about probability and wanted to assess the probability of various dog breeds being a student's favorite. The class conducted a survey listing five favorite dogs—border collie, boxer, Labrador retriever, golden retriever, and beagle. Each student voted for one breed. Explain what method of modeling they would be using, the process itself, and what the results would show.

Feedback: The class would be constructing an empirical probability distribution, based on the observable results of the survey. A class of twenty-five students could have these survey results: eight chose border collie, three chose boxer, three chose Labrador retriever, five chose golden retriever, and six chose beagle. The students would determine the probability of choosing each dog breed by dividing the number of times the breed was chosen by the total number of students and then multiplying the result by 100. For example, the border collie's probability of being a student's favorite dog would be 8/25 × 100 = 32 percent. The other results would be boxer—12 percent, Labrador retriever—12 percent, golden retriever—20 percent, and beagle—24 percent.

After seeing their own results, what class activity and method of modeling could compare the students' results with those from a larger group?

Feedback: To see whether their choices were similar to those of a larger group such as the entire country, the class learned that the number of dog registrations was commonly used as a determination of dog popularity and found a list of over 100 dog breeds and their respective number of registrations. The class discovered only two of their class favorites made the national top five—Labrador retriever and golden retriever. However, they did construct other empirical probability distributions—as these were again based on observable results—of the national five favorites and then the national ten favorites. They did the calculations in the same way as in their class survey results. From this experience, the class learned that the larger the sample, the more accurate and reliable the resulting probability.

Bayesian Inference

Often, claims professionals would like to determine a conditional probability, which is the probability of an outcome, given that another condition exists. An example is the probability that an uninsured motorists claim is fraudulent, given that the only witnesses to the accident are friends of the insured. Representing the former as *B* and the latter as *A*, the conditional probability can be expressed as:

$p(B/A)$

In this example, the conditional probability may be difficult to determine based on available data and the expert input of a claims professional. However, through a method known as Bayes' Rule, the conditional probability can be broken down into three components, each of which may be easier to estimate. These components are shown on the right side of this equation:

$p(B/A) = p(A/B) \times p(B)/p(A)$

$p(A/B)$ is the probability that the only witnesses are friends of the insured, given that there is a fraudulent uninsured motorists claim. $p(B)$ and $p(A)$ are separate probabilities, with $p(B)$ the probability that an uninsured motorists claim is fraudulent and $p(A)$ the probability that, for a claim, the only witnesses are friends of the insured. Assuming these three probabilities can be determined using available data and the expert input of a claims professional, the conditional probability in which we are interested, $p(B/A)$, can be inferred based on the preceding formula for Bayes' Rule. This process is known as Bayesian inference.

Although this is a simple example, it helps to illustrate Bayes' Rule. It is important to understand this rule because it forms the basis for many different types of models used to analyze data.

[OV_12092]

ANALYZING EVENT CONSEQUENCES

The selection of a course of action or the occurrence of an event can generate multiple consequences and/or payoffs. Organizations use decision tree analysis and event tree analysis to predict the likelihood and severity of consequences or payoffs arising from decisions or events.

Decision tree analysis examines the consequences, including costs and gains, of decisions. An organization may use decision tree analysis to compare alternative decisions and select the most effective strategy to achieve a goal.

Event tree analysis examines all possible consequences of an accidental event, their probabilities, and existing measures to prevent or control them. An organization may use this approach to examine the effectiveness of systems, risk treatment, or risk control measures and to identify, recommend, and justify expenditures of money, time, or resources for improvements.

Decision Tree Analysis

A decision tree analyzes the uncertainties of decision outcomes. An organization might use a decision tree in selecting the best course of action from multiple options or to manage risks associated with a project. By analyzing various options and the events that may affect them, decision makers can reduce the uncertainty involved in decision making.

Decision trees can provide both qualitative and quantitative analysis. Qualitatively, they can help generate scenarios, progressions, and consequences that could potentially result from a decision. Quantitatively, they can estimate probabilities and frequencies of various scenarios resulting from a decision.

Constructing a decision tree begins with a statement of the initial decision under consideration, for example, which of two products to develop. From that point, various sequences of events ("pathways") are charted for each alternative; each pathway leads to an outcome. For a quantitative analysis, probabilities are assigned to each event on a pathway, and expected values (costs or gains) of each pathway can be estimated for the outcome. The product of the probabilities of each event in a pathway and the value of its outcome can be compared to determine the pathway that produces the highest expected value. See the exhibit "Example of a Decision Tree Diagram."

Decision tree analysis offers the advantages of visual portrayal of event sequences and outcomes and a means to calculate the best pathway through a problem. However, decision tree diagrams of complicated or many-faceted problems may become so complex that they are ineffective in communicating the rationale for a decision to those not involved in the process. Conversely, a decision tree may oversimplify a problem, reducing the effectiveness of resulting decisions.

Event Tree Analysis

Event trees are similar to decision trees in their portrayal and analysis of various pathways and their outcomes; however, event trees analyze the con-

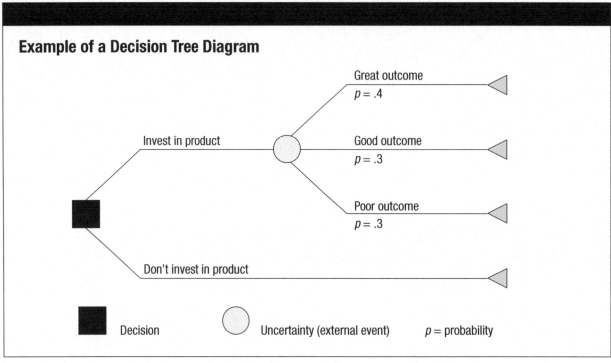

Example of a Decision Tree Diagram

Great outcome
$p = .4$

Good outcome
$p = .3$

Invest in product

Poor outcome
$p = .3$

Don't invest in product

■ Decision   ◯ Uncertainty (external event) p = probability

[DA08712]

sequences of accidental events rather than decisions. An accidental event is defined as the first significant deviation from a normal situation that may lead to unwanted consequences.[1]

Like a decision tree, an event tree can provide both qualitative and quantitative analysis. Qualitatively, it can help generate scenarios, progressions, and consequences that could potentially result from an accidental event. Quantitatively, it can estimate probabilities and frequencies of various scenarios and outcomes and help organizations determine the effectiveness of or need for controls and safeguards. Event trees are often used to determine the need for and to examine the effectiveness of risk treatment methods.

The starting point of an event tree is identification of an accidental event. The various progressions of events that could follow the accidental event are then determined. Progressions may vary because of factors such as other systems, human responses, and even the weather (for example, wind direction during an outdoor fire) or because of the performance or failure of "barriers" to consequences (for example, alarm or detection systems, emergency procedures, or other loss control measures).

This analysis of progressions results in a list of potential consequences of the initial event and identification of any existing barriers for each consequence. From that information, an event tree diagram is constructed. See the exhibit "Example of an Event Tree Analysis."

Example of an Event Tree Analysis

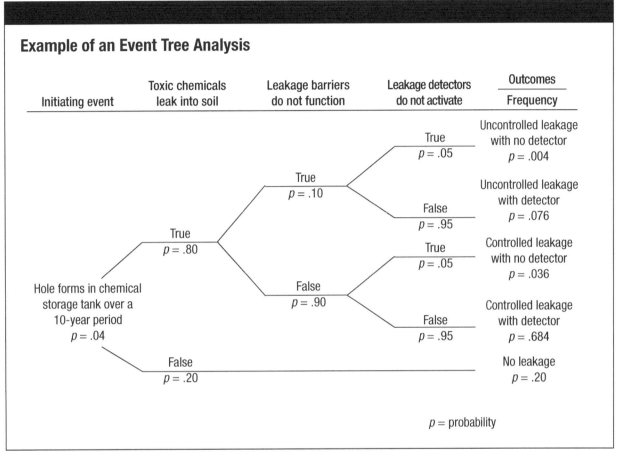

[DA08713]

In an event tree diagram, barriers are listed in the sequence in which they would be activated should the designated event occur. In each pathway, every barrier has the potential to either function or fail; therefore, the pathway splits in two, and an estimated probability—determined by experts or other analysis—is assigned to both potentials.

For each pathway in the diagram, the probability is that all its events will occur. The frequency of the consequence of each pathway is the product of the probabilities in the pathway and the frequency of the initial event. The sum of the probabilities of the outcomes, given that the initial event occurs, should total one.

Like a decision tree, an event tree affords the advantage of visual portrayal of event sequences and outcomes. Specifically, it can illustrate the potential effectiveness of control systems following accidental events and account for timing, other contributing factors, and domino effects. One of the limitations of event tree analysis is that it typically provides only two options—success or failure—and thereby fails to reflect the complexity of some progressions. In addition, some factors that contribute to consequences may be overlooked. See the exhibit "Classification Tree Analysis."

Classification Tree Analysis

Classification tree analysis—often represented visually with a classification tree—is used for data mining, which involves extracting hidden patterns from data. The analysis segments data based on combinations of characteristics that help predict the value of an outcome.

For example, closed workers compensation claims data could be segmented based on characteristics that are predictive of complex claims, with the results used to classify newly reported claims as "complex" or "not complex." The claims classified as complex could then be assigned to more experienced adjusters.

In a data mining context, classification trees are sometimes called decision trees. Decision trees used for data mining describe data, not decisions, although decisions can be made from the data obtained. By contrast, in a decision analysis context, decision trees visually represent decision choices and the uncertainties associated with various outcomes.

[OV_12090]

Comparing Decision Tree Analysis and Event Tree Analysis

Decision tree analysis and event tree analysis share a similar approach, appearance, and process but differ in their purposes, information used, and information produced, among other factors. See the exhibit "Comparison of Decision Tree Analysis and Event Tree Analysis."

INFLUENCE DIAGRAMS

An influence diagram provides a visual graph of a decision, sometimes using mathematical probabilities, to construct a model showing the known and unknown factors related to the decision.

Effective risk management includes evaluating risk during decision making. Organizations may sometimes see the benefits of decisions without considering the risks. An influence diagram provides a method to visualize key organizational decisions, including the probabilities that various events may positively or negatively affect outcomes.

Structure of an Influence Diagram

An influence diagram is a graphical representation of various influences on a decision. The diagram consists of nodes representing events, known information, expected outcome, and uncertainties that could affect the outcome. The interdependencies between nodes are represented by arrows.

The purpose of influence diagrams is to model both known and unknown information, and the value of that information, when making decisions. By

Comparison of Decision Tree Analysis and Event Tree Analysis

	Decision Tree Analysis	Event Tree Analysis
Function	Examines consequences, costs, and gains of decisions Compares alternative decisions	Examines the consequences of accidental events
Use	Aids in the selection of the most effective strategy to achieve a goal	Examines the need for or effectiveness of risk treatment measures Can help in identifying, recommending, and justifying improvements
Features	May analyze both negative and positive consequences (losses and gains)	Typically analyzes negative consequences (risk of loss)
Inputs	Project plan with decision points Information on possible outcomes of decisions or events that might affect them	List of possible events that could lead to loss Information about risk treatments and the probabilities of various barriers failing Understanding of how failure escalates
Process	Definition of problem Construction of pathways to outcome Assignment of probabilities to various events that could affect outcomes Assignment of value to outcome for each pathway	Identification of accidental event Construction of pathways, including barriers, to outcome Assignment of probability of success or failure of each barrier in pathway Determination of frequency of outcomes for each pathway
Outputs	Analysis of risk of each pathway with various options Calculated expected value for each pathway	List of potential problems that could arise, calculated expected values for outcomes and frequencies Recommendations regarding effectiveness of various barriers
Advantages	Presents visual portrayal of problems, sequences, and outcomes Provides a means to calculate the best pathway through a problem Provides both qualitative and quantitative information	Presents visual portrayal of potential sequences of events following accidental event Illustrates the potential effectiveness of control systems following accidental events Provides both qualitative and quantitative information
Disadvantages	May be overly complex and difficult to communicate May be oversimplified, resulting in less accurate information for decision making	May be ineffective unless all potential initiating events are identified Analysis is limited to only two options—success or failure of barriers—possibly overlooking other factors May not address dependencies that arise within a sequence, resulting in inaccurate risk estimations

[DA08714]

presenting the certain and uncertain factors graphically, stakeholders can visualize the relationship of these factors to the potential outcomes of the decision.

An influence diagram can be constructed as a type of Bayesian network, which includes probability tables in addition to a graph. This type of influence diagram includes mathematical probabilities for the uncertainties that could affect the decision's outcome.

Elements of an Influence Diagram

There are three types of nodes in an influence diagram:

- Decision nodes are represented by rectangles.
- Variables are represented by ovals.
- Benefits and costs are represented by diamonds.

The nodes in an influence diagram can include qualitative information as well as data and mathematical probabilities.

As an example, S.M.A.R.T., a United States corporation that manufactures products in the U.S., Mexico, and China, is ready to start production of a new electronic device. S.M.A.R.T is deciding where to manufacture this product. The first rectangle in the influence diagram represents this decision. The second rectangle represents a decision to proceed with a Chinese manufacturer. The diamond represents the costs and benefits from this decision: the lowest product cost and timely receipt of products. S.M.A.R.T. has data from manufacturing its existing products to use in computer modeling for these nodes in the influence diagram.

The oval in the diagram represents the market variables that affect the success of S.M.A.R.T.'s decision. One risk factor is the potential for supply chain interruption. A computerized model could evaluate the probability of a natural or other type of catastrophe, such as war or terrorism, interrupting the supply chain from China to S.M.A.R.T.'s global distribution centers. There are also more subjective variables, such as product quality and customer perceptions of labor practices in China. See the exhibit "Example of an Influence Diagram."

Although the influence diagram focuses on the decision-making process, the variables identified can also be translated into risk management processes. The S.M.A.R.T. influence diagram identified risks of supply chain interruption, product quality, and customer perceptions of Chinese labor practices. If S.M.A.R.T. decides to go forward with manufacturing in China, the organization can also decide to proactively manage these risks.

For example, sufficient supplies of the product could be kept at distribution centers to last through a month of supply chain interruption. Frequent visits to the manufacturing site could address product quality as well as labor conditions, which could help manage risk associated with customer perception. Data from the risk management process could then be incorporated into the probabilities applied to uncertainties illustrated in the influence diagram.

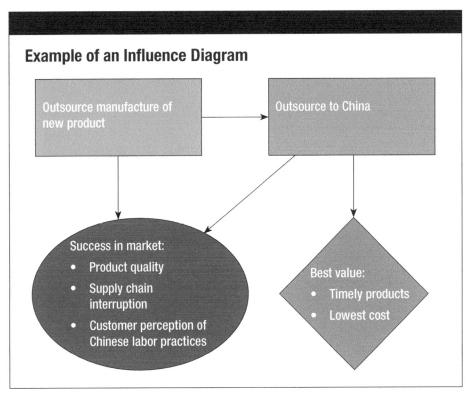

Example of an Influence Diagram

[DA10331]

Comparison With Decision Trees

Decision trees are similar to influence diagrams in their analysis of the uncertainties of decision outcomes. Both provide a general view of variables and potential outcomes, and both can also use mathematical probabilities.

The difference between decision trees and influence diagrams is in their construction. Decision trees have branches that outline each alternative. A branch can also provide the probability for the outcomes it represents. Also, decision trees use somewhat different shapes from influence diagrams to represent alternatives and anticipated outcomes. Similar to influence diagrams, decision trees represent decisions with squares, with the go/no-go alternatives branching out accordingly. Potential outcomes are represented by circles, with different potential outcomes branching out from the circle.

The advantage of a decision tree is the detail it shows for each variable. However, this detail can also be a disadvantage. For complex decisions with many variables, a decision tree can have a large number of branches for each decision component, making it difficult to draw a conclusion.

As shown in the diagram of a decision tree for S.M.A.R.T.'s decision to outsource manufacturing of its new product, multiple branches are required, and they often show a binary decision (go/no go). This is in contrast to the graph of the influence diagram, which presents a holistic view of the decision-making process. See the exhibit "Decision Tree for S.M.A.R.T. New Product Outsourcing."

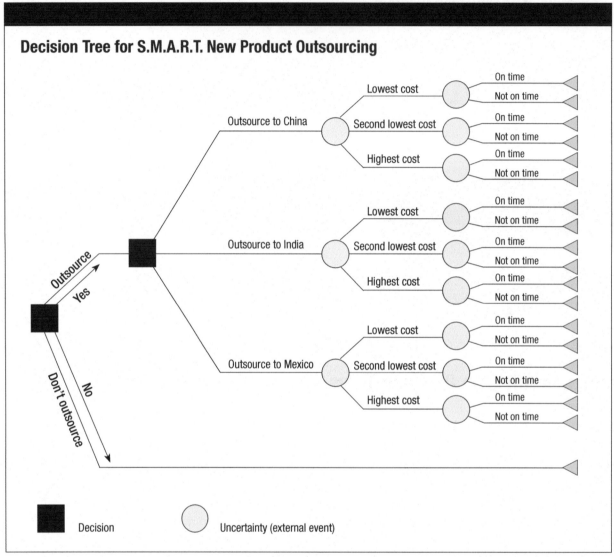

Decision Tree for S.M.A.R.T. New Product Outsourcing

[DA10332]

An influence diagram presents an overview of the decision-making process and can incorporate all of the identified variables and their probabilities. In contrast, the decision tree does not have a method for combining alternatives and outcomes represented by different branches.

Additionally, influence diagrams can be used for ongoing decision making within an organization. In the S.M.A.R.T. example, the organization could decide to evaluate the outsourcing decision on a regular basis, such as quarterly or annually. New data could be entered into the computerized model for each reevaluation. It is more difficult to use a decision tree for an ongoing process because these diagrams are most suitable to a one-time go or no-go type of decision.

APPLYING INFLUENCE DIAGRAMS AND PROBABILITIES

Enterprise risk management (ERM) often involves predicting the probability of future events, including losses, to make strategic decisions and apply appropriate risk management techniques. Uncertainty modeling can improve a risk manager's predictions and recommendations.

Applying an uncertainty model requires several steps. First, a problem or decision is identified, along with the various options to consider. Those options are then analyzed and compared using influence diagrams and probabilities.

Case Facts

GEV Industries is a global conglomerate of various manufacturing businesses. When GEV implemented its ERM program, it installed a **risk dashboard**. One of GEV's **key risk indicators** is its workers compensation costs. Justin, the risk manager, observes increases in these costs over the previous six months. He asks Andrea, the workers compensation manager, to find out what is driving this.

Andrea had already been doing research on the cost increases and identified GEV's Wood Products Division (WPD) as the source. All the other businesses had experienced decreasing workers compensation costs since the organization began a new, comprehensive safety program a year ago. Because WPD had several severe injuries, Andrea started following the results closely to see whether these injuries were anomalies or part of a trend.

After Andrea and Justin review the six-month results, they conclude that the frequency of injuries has increased along with the severity. Because this trend is contrary to the organization's overall results and has persisted for several months, Justin decides that Andrea should visit WPD's plant and analyze what is causing the increases.

WPD's plant uses a variety of machines to manufacture wood products. Some machines saw wood into the various sizes needed. Others assemble and glue the products. Sanders are used in different stages of product assembly. Additionally, there are machines to apply varnish or paint after the products are assembled.

WPD has 200 workers who are assigned to 200 machines on the basis of production needs. Although worker assignments vary, each worker has only one piece of equipment to operate, and each machine is operated by only one worker. Employees are currently expected to operate all of the plant's equipment.

Risk dashboard

A computer interface that reports quantitative data regarding an organization's key risk indicators.

Key risk indicator (KRI)

A tool that an organization uses to measure the uncertainty of meeting an organizational objective.

Case Analysis Tools and Information

Andrea meets with WPD's plant manager, Bill, to review data about the workers' injuries. From their review, they determine this information:

- The accident rate is higher for inexperienced employees.
- The accident rate is higher for complex machines.

To develop a risk management plan to address the injuries, Andrea compiles a table of probabilities relating to the occurrence of accidents over a one-year period at the plant. The exhibit indicates the probabilities resulting from this analysis. See the exhibit "Accident Conditional Probability Table."

Accident Conditional Probability Table

| | Worker Experience | |
Machine Type	Inexperienced	Experienced
Simple	5%	0%
Complex	40%	10%

[DA03739]

The values in the chart represent the percentage of accidents in relation to the workers' levels of experience and the complexity of machines. For example, an inexperienced worker assigned to a simple machine would have a 5 percent chance of having an accident.

To apply these probabilities and determine the overall or average probability that an accident will occur involving a worker, Andrea needs two additional pieces of information:

- The percentage of staff in each of the two categories based on experience
- The percentage of machinery in each of the two levels based on complexity

Bill obtains information from the Human Development Department regarding worker experience and from the plant foreman on machine complexity. He then presents this information to Andrea. See the exhibit "Worker Experience and Machine Complexity Percentages."

After Andrea receives this information, she calculates the probabilities of inexperienced and experienced workers' assignment to simple or complex machines based on random assignment. She multiplies the percentage of employees in each experience category by the percentage of machines in each complexity category to arrive at the probability of an inexperienced or experienced worker's being assigned to a simple or complex machine. See the exhibit "Probability of Worker Assignment to Machine Type."

Worker Experience and Machine Complexity Percentages

Worker Experience	Inexperienced	Experienced
	30%	70%
Machine Complexity	Simple	Complex
	20%	80%

[DA10343]

Probability of Worker Assignment to Machine Type

Machine Type	Worker Experience	
	Inexperienced (30%)	Experienced (70%)
Simple (20%)	30% × 20% = 6% (12 workers)	70% × 20% = 14% (28 workers)
Complex (80%)	80% × 30% = 24% (48 workers)	80% × 70% = 56% (112 workers)

[DA10344]

Andrea then prepares the workers compensation accident probability table. She calculates the probability of an accident occurring with inexperienced and experienced workers operating simple or complex machines by multiplying the accident conditional probability by the worker machine assignment probability. See the exhibit "Random Assignment—Workers Compensation Accident Probability."

The probabilities calculated for each cell are added vertically and horizontally. The sums of probabilities along the bottom row are totaled, as are the sums of the probabilities in the right column. The two totals should be identical. If they are not, a calculation mistake has occurred.

In the table presented here, both totals equal 15.5 percent over a year. This number is the average or overall probability that an accident will occur to a worker based on random assignment of workers to machines. In using data from the accident probability table, Andrea relied on a fundamental hypothesis: worker experience and machine type are independent.

Random Assignment—Workers Compensation Accident Probability

| | Worker Experience | | |
Machine Type	Inexperienced (30%)	Experienced (70%)	Total by Machine Type
Simple (20%)	5% × 6% = 0.3%	0% × 14% = 0%	0.3%
Complex (80%)	40% × 24% = 9.6%	10% × 56% = 5.6%	15.2%
Total by Worker Experience Level	0.3% + 9.6% = 9.9%	0 + 5.6% = 5.6%	15.5%
Total Accident Probability		9.9% + 5.6% = 15.5%	15.5%

[DA03740]

Andrea and Bill conclude that having inexperienced workers operate complex machines is the driver for WPD's high worker injury frequency and severity. Andrea and Bill then discuss these risk management options:

- Assign inexperienced workers to simpler equipment to the extent possible (worker assignment option)
- Provide a training program for inexperienced workers (training program option)

Case Analysis Steps

These are the five steps Andrea applies in choosing a risk management approach for WPD:

1. For each option, evaluate data and draw an influence diagram
2. Determine the probabilities of worker accidents for each option
3. Consider economic and financial issues for each option
4. Compare the options
5. Make a recommendation

Worker Assignment Option

The first option is to assign inexperienced workers to simple machines and experienced workers to complex machines to the extent possible. This would involve assigning forty of the sixty inexperienced workers to the forty simple machines. This option would leave twenty inexperienced workers assigned to complex machines, compared with forty-eight inexperienced workers assigned to complex machines under the current random-assignment approach. See the exhibit "Worker Assignment Option."

Worker Assignment Option

Machine Type	Worker Experience	
	Inexperienced (60)	Experienced (140)
Simple (40)	40 (20%)	0 (0%)
Complex (160)	20 (10%)	140 (70%)

[DA03742]

Worker Assignment Option: Step One—Draw an Influence Diagram

Andrea prepares an influence diagram for the option of reassigning workers to simple or complex machines based on their experience level. The decision to reassign workers is represented by a rectangle. The data for the decision are worker experience and machine type, represented by a diamond. The unknown variable is the accident rate, represented by an oval. The outcome, which results from the data and the unknown variable, is the cost of risk. See the exhibit "Influence Diagram for Worker Assignment Option."

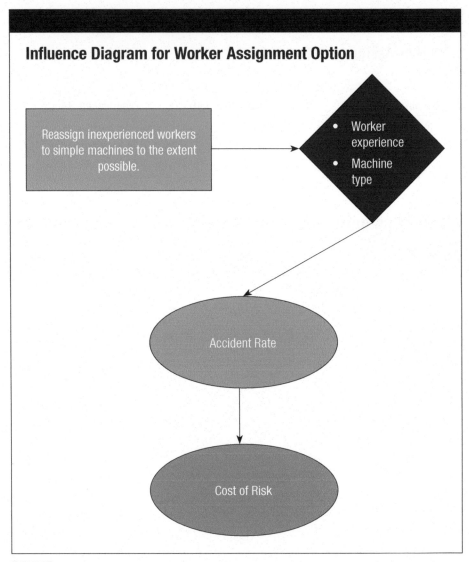

Influence Diagram for Worker Assignment Option

[DA10345]

Worker Assignment Option: Step Two—Determine the Probabilities of Worker Accidents

After developing the influence diagram, Andrea calculates the probabilities for worker accidents using the conditional accident probabilities for each category and the percentage of workers assigned to each type of machine.

Knowledge to Action

Calculate the probability of accidents for the worker assignment option.

Feedback: The worker assignment option results in a total accident probability of 12 percent, compared with the current random assignment probability of 15.5 percent. See the exhibit "Worker Assignment Option—Workers Compensation Accident Probability."

Worker Assignment Option—Workers Compensation Accident Probability

Machine Type	Worker Experience		Total by Machine Type
	Inexperienced (30%)	Experienced (70%)	
Simple (20%)	5% × 20% = 1%	0% × 0% = 0%	1%
Complex (80%)	40% × 10% = 4%	10% × 70% = 7%	11%
Total by Worker Experience Level	1% + 4% = 5%	0% + 7% =7%	12%
Total Accident Probability			12%

[DA10346]

Worker Assignment Option: Step Three—Economic and Financial Considerations

Andrea now needs to determine the cost of risk for this option. The workers compensation and related costs for the past year of the current random assignment of workers to machines is $1.2 million. The worker assignment option would result in a cost reduction:

$$[(15.5\% - 12\%) \div 15.5\%] \times \$1,200,000 = 22.6\% \times \$1,200,000 = \$271,200$$

$$\$1,200,000 - \$271,200 = \$928,800$$

The estimated cost of risk for this option would be $928,800. There are no costs associated with implementing this option.

Training Program Option

Andrea next evaluates the training program option. This option involves hiring a firm to train inexperienced workers on how to safely operate the complex machines. Andrea anticipates that the training program would result in 10 percent of the workforce being inexperienced, compared with the current 30 percent. Because of turnover, Andrea does not anticipate that the workforce would become 100 percent experienced as a result of the training program. Therefore, 20 workers would likely continue to be inexperienced, and 180 workers would be experienced. This compares with 60 inexperienced and 140 experienced workers in the current workforce, resulting in an increase of 40 experienced workers.

Training Program Option: Step One—Draw an Influence Diagram

Andrea now repeats steps one through three for the option of training inexperienced workers.

Knowledge to Action

As with the first option, she begins by preparing an influence diagram.
Draw an influence diagram. See the exhibit "Influence Diagram for Training Program Option."

Influence Diagram for Training Program Option

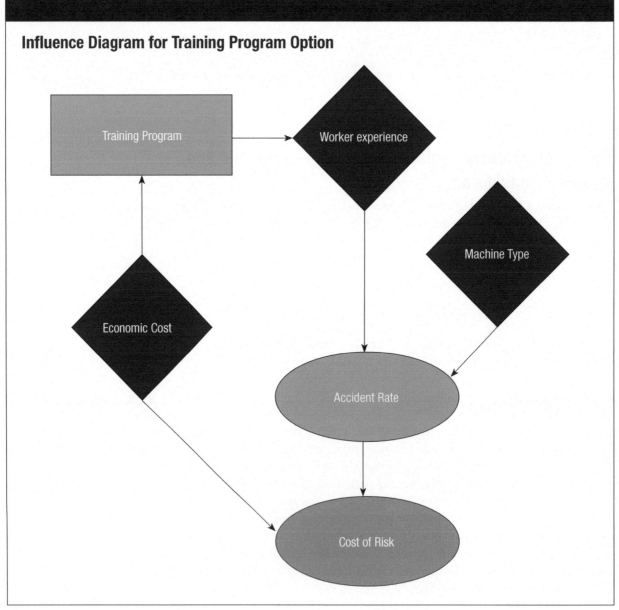

[DA10348]

Feedback: In this diagram, worker experience and machine type are represented in separate diamonds, with an arrow going from the decision rectangle to the worker experience diamond because the training decision affects only worker experience. However, both worker experience and machine type affect the accident rate, which as a variable is presented in an oval. Unlike the first option, there is an economic cost associated with the training program. This cost affects both the cost of risk and the financial viability of the training option.

Training Program Option: Step Two—Determine the Probabilities of Worker Accidents

After developing the influence diagram, Andrea moves to the next step of calculating the probabilities of worker accidents for the training program option. First, she draws a table to outline the expected effect of the program on worker experience levels. See the exhibit "Training Program Effect on Worker Experience."

Training Program Effect on Worker Experience

Inexperienced	Experienced
10% (20 workers)	90% (180 workers)

[DA10349]

Andrea next calculates the probabilities of workers at their post-training experience levels being randomly assigned to simple or complex machines. See the exhibit "Training Program Option—Random Assignment."

Training Program Option—Random Assignment

Machine Type	Worker Experience	
	Inexperienced (10%)	Experienced (90%)
Simple (20%)	10% × 20% = 2%	90% × 20% = 18%
Complex (80%)	10% × 80% = 8%	90% × 80% = 72%

[DA10350]

Knowledge to Action

Calculate the probabilities for the training program option.

Feedback: Andrea then calculates the accident rate probabilities for the training program option by multiplying the conditional accident probabilities by probabilities of an inexperienced or experienced worker's assignment to a simple or complex machine. After training is completed, the probability that 2 percent of inexperienced workers will be assigned to simple machines is multiplied by the 5 percent accident conditional probability for this category, which results in an accident probability of 0.1 percent. Multiplication of the 8 percent probability of inexperienced workers' assignment to complex machines by the 40 percent accident conditional probability for that category results in an accident probability of 3.2 percent. There is a zero accident conditional probability for experienced workers assigned to simple machines. Multiplication of the 72 percent probability of experienced workers assigned to complex machines by the 10 percent accident conditional probability for that category results in an accident probability of 7.2 percent. See the exhibit "Training Program Option—Workers Compensation Accident Probability."

Training Program Option—Workers Compensation Accident Probability

| | Worker Experience | | |
Machine Type	Inexperienced (10%)	Experienced (90%)	Total by Machine Type
Simple (20%)	2 % x 5% = 0.1%	18% x 0% = 0%	0.1%
Complex (80%)	8% x 40% = 3.2%	72% x 10% = 7.2%	10.4%
Total	3.3%	7.2%	10.5%
Total Accident Probability			10.5%

[DA10351]

The total accident rate for the training program option with random machine assignment is 10.5 percent, a reduction of 5 percentage points from the current random-assignment approach without additional training.

Training Program Option: Step Three—Economic and Financial Considerations

Andrea next considers the cost of risk for this option.

Knowledge to Action

Determine the cost of risk for the training program option.

Feedback: First, Andrea looks at the effect of the reduction in accident probability on the cost of risk:

$$[(15.5\% - 10.5\%) \div 15.5\%] \times \$1,200,000 = 32.3\% \times \$1,200,000 = \$387,600$$

$$\$1,200,000 - \$387,600 = \$812,400$$

The cost reduction for this option would be $387,600, resulting in a cost of risk of $812,400. However, the training program costs $100,000. Therefore, the cost reduction would be estimated at $287,600, with a cost of risk of $912,400.

Step Four—Comparison of Options

Andrea next compares the probabilities of accidents for the two proposed options with the current accident probability. See the exhibit "Comparison of Accident Probabilities."

Comparison of Accident Probabilities

	Current	Worker Assignment Option	Training Program Option
Accident Probability	15.5%	12.0%	10.5%

[DA10352]

The table comparing the accident rates indicates that either assigning inexperienced workers to simple machines to the extent possible or implementing the training program would likely result in a better accident rate than randomly assigning workers to machines at current experience levels. The training program is expected to produce a somewhat lower rate than either of the other options, but it involves economic costs that the other options do not.

Andrea decides to consider the effect of combining the options of the training program and the assignment of experienced workers to complex machines whenever possible. In the combined option, the number of experienced workers would increase from the current 140 to 180.

As she did when evaluating each option separately, Andrea begins by developing an influence diagram. She includes a probability table with this diagram showing the accident probabilities obtained by assigning experienced workers to complex machines after the training program. See the exhibit "Influence Diagram for Combined Option, Including Accident Probability Table."

The combined approach would result in fewer inexperienced workers (10 percent), all of whom could be assigned to simple machines. Eighty percent of experienced workers would be assigned to complex machines, with the remaining 10 percent assigned to simple machines. It would also result in a total accident probability of 8.5 percent, which is lower than any of the other options.

Using the costs of $1.2 million, the decrease in accident probability would result in this reduction in the cost of risk:

$$[(15.5\% - 8.5\%) \div 15.5\%] \times \$1,200,000 = 45.2\% \times \$1,200,000 = \$542,400$$

$$\$1,200,000 - \$542,400 = \$657,600$$

The combined approach results in a reduction of $542,400; however, the cost of the training must be factored in. Therefore, the reduction is $442,400, with a cost of risk of $757,600.

Step Five—Make a Recommendation

Andrea outlines the estimated reduction in cost of risk for each option to Justin.

Knowledge to Action

Explain which option Andrea should recommend.

Feedback: The table indicates that either the worker assignment or training program option would reduce the cost of risk. However, combining these two options produces the greatest savings. See the exhibit "Comparison of Cost of Risk."

Andrea recommends the combined approach to Justin. She proposes that reassigning inexperienced workers to simple machines to the extent possible begin immediately. The training program will need to be approved by the GEV vice president responsible for WPD. Andrea's report and recommendations indicate that, in addition to financial savings, GEV's ERM mission includes protection of workers. Therefore, the combined approach will produce a positive qualitative result in addition to the anticipated quantitative savings.

Influence Diagram for Combined Option, Including Accident Probability Table

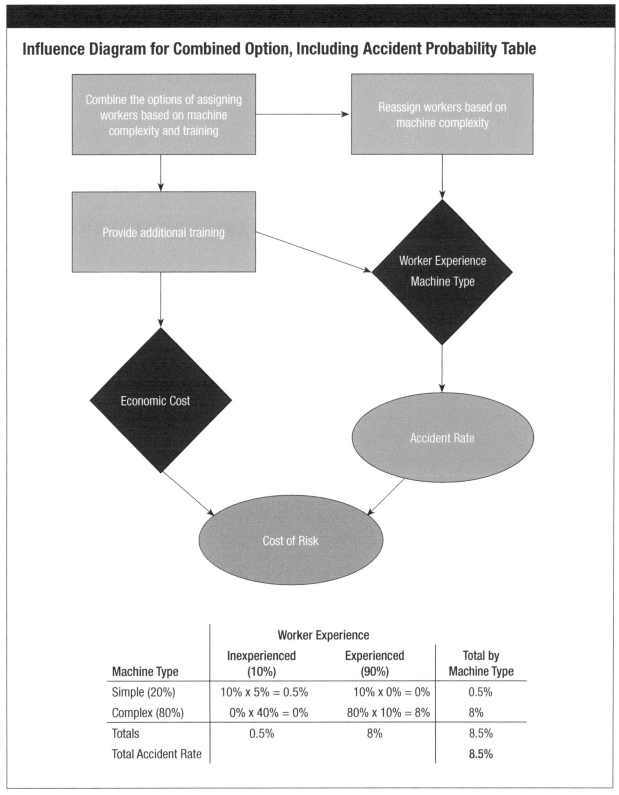

Machine Type	Worker Experience		Total by Machine Type
	Inexperienced (10%)	Experienced (90%)	
Simple (20%)	10% x 5% = 0.5%	10% x 0% = 0%	0.5%
Complex (80%)	0% x 40% = 0%	80% x 10% = 8%	8%
Totals	0.5%	8%	8.5%
Total Accident Rate			8.5%

Comparison of Cost of Risk

	Current	Worker Assignment Option	Training Program Option	Combined Option
Accident Probability	15.5%	12.0%	10.5%	8.5%
Cost of Risk	$1,200,000	$928,800	$912,400	$757,600
Reduction in Cost of Risk	----	$271,200	$287,600	$442,400

[DA10354]

VALUE AT RISK AND EARNINGS AT RISK

To evaluate financial risk, a risk management professional should understand the range of potential financial outcomes.

Risk management professionals can use metrics such as **value at risk (VaR)** or **earnings at risk (EaR)** to determine the probability of various financial outcomes.

VaR is a method of determining the probability of loss on an investment portfolio over a certain, usually short, time horizon. VaR is primarily used by financial institutions that have extensive investments in securities. Similar to VaR, EaR is a financial measure that can be used for nonfinancial organizations.

Value at Risk

VaR measures the probability of a loss in an investment's value exceeding a threshold level. In addition to working within a short time horizon, VaR is typically characterized by low probability. For example, a one-day, 5 percent VaR of $300,000 means there is a 5 percent probability of losing $300,000 or more over the next day.

VaR provides three key benefits as a risk measure:

- The potential loss associated with an investment decision can be quantified.
- Complex positions (typically involving multiple investments) are expressed as a single figure.
- Loss is expressed in easily understood monetary terms.

However, VaR also has a limitation: it does not accurately measure the extent to which a loss may exceed the VaR threshold. This limitation can be addressed with **conditional value at risk (CVaR)**. CVaR provides the same benefits as VaR and also takes into account the extremely large losses that may occur, usually with low probabilities, in the tail of a probability distribution.

Value at risk
A threshold value such that the probability of loss on the portfolio over the given time horizon exceeds this value, assuming normal markets and no trading in the portfolio.

Earnings at risk
The maximum expected loss of earnings within a specific degree of confidence.

Conditional value at risk
A model to determine the likelihood of a loss given that the loss is greater than or equal to the VaR.

CVaR is particularly important in fat-tailed distributions, for which the extremely large losses have higher probabilities than with most other probability distributions. For example, hurricane risk has a fat-tailed distribution. See the exhibit "VaR Distribution."

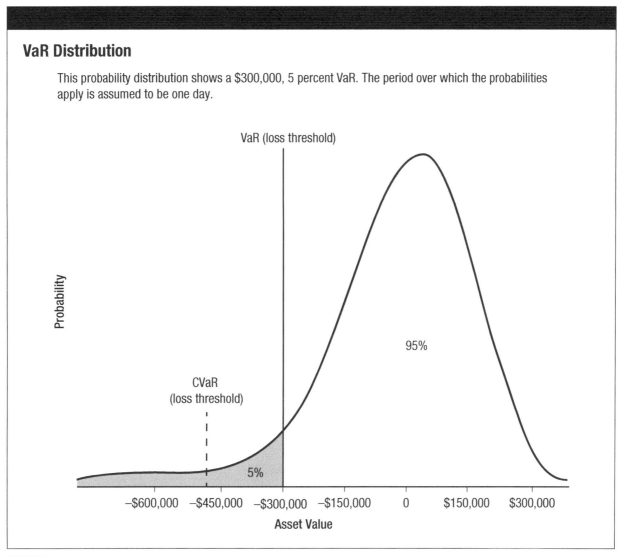

VaR Distribution

This probability distribution shows a $300,000, 5 percent VaR. The period over which the probabilities apply is assumed to be one day.

[DA10431]

Apply Your Knowledge

On a VaR probability distribution curve, a one-day VaR of $20,000 is represented by the area under the curve that is

a. To the right of $20,000.

b. To the left of $20,000.

c. To the right of –$20,000.

d. To the left of –$20,000.

Feedback: d. A one-day VaR of $20,000 is represented by the distribution area under the curve to the left of –$20,000.

Earnings at Risk

Determining EaR entails modeling the influence of factors such as changes in sales; production costs; and the prices of products, commodities, and components used in production. Models are developed using a Monte Carlo simulation, and the results are presented as a probability distribution curve or a histogram of individual probabilities. The EaR threshold represents the lower end of projected earnings within a specific confidence, such as 95 percent. The probability that an organization's earnings will be greater than the EaR threshold is represented by the area under the distribution curve to the right of the EaR threshold. The area under the curve to the left of the EaR threshold represents the probability that earnings will be below the EaR threshold. For example, if earnings at risk are $100,000 with 95 percent confidence, then earnings are projected to be $100,000 or greater 95 percent of the time and less than $100,000 5 percent of the time. See the exhibit "EaR Distribution."

EaR is helpful in comparing the likely effects of different risk management strategies on earnings. However, there are limitations, including the complexity of the calculations and a need to understand the relationship of different variables on an organization's results.[2]

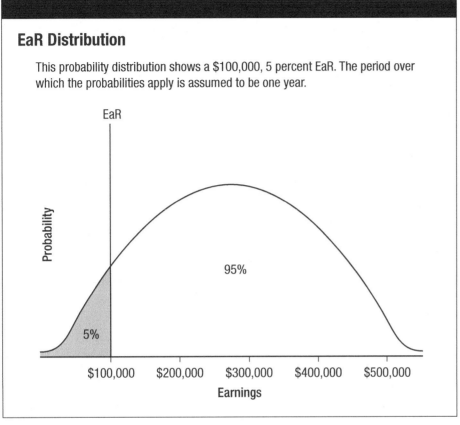

EaR Distribution

This probability distribution shows a $100,000, 5 percent EaR. The period over which the probabilities apply is assumed to be one year.

EaR

Probability

95%

5%

$100,000 $200,000 $300,000 $400,000 $500,000

Earnings

[DA10432]

CATASTROPHE MODELING

Catastrophe models combine mathematical representations of the natural occurrence patterns and characteristics of catastrophes with exposure information, including property replacement values and construction and occupancy types, to provide information concerning the potential for large losses.

Catastrophe models can assess not only potential loss severity but also the probability that a catastrophe will occur. In the United States, the principal causes of loss modeled are hurricanes, earthquakes (ground shaking and fire following), and severe thunderstorms (inclusive of tornado, hail, and straight-line winds). Catastrophe models have also been developed for wildfire, winter storms, flood, and terrorism.

Because catastrophe modeling has become a standard industry practice, it is important to understand how catastrophe models operate, how they are used, and the various issues that can affect their reliability.

How Catastrophe Models Operate

Catastrophe models use insurer-supplied exposure data to produce a range of potential losses that may result from the catastrophes being modeled, along with their associated probability of exceedance (the probability that a loss of a specified size will be equaled or exceeded).

Catastrophe models typically include these three basic components, or modules:

* Hazard
* Engineering
* Financial

The exhibit shows the components of a catastrophe model, along with its inputs and outputs. See the exhibit "Catastrophe Modeling."

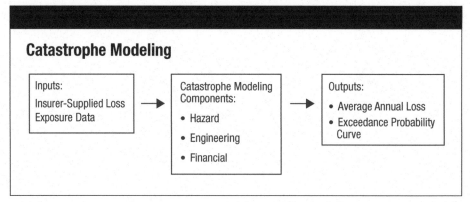

Catastrophe Modeling

Inputs:
Insurer-Supplied Loss Exposure Data

→

Catastrophe Modeling Components:
* Hazard
* Engineering
* Financial

→

Outputs:
* Average Annual Loss
* Exceedance Probability Curve

[DA09278]

Although the computer codes for catastrophe models are generally proprietary, modeling firms provide thousands of pages of detailed documentation in an effort to ensure that model users understand the models and the models' sensitivities, uncertainties, and implications for risk management; as well as that model users understand best practices for using model results. Because both the assumptions behind and results from different catastrophe models vary, a primary insurer often considers information derived from several catastrophe models.

Hazard Component

The first component of a catastrophe model is the hazard component. The hazard component simulates a catastrophic event to determine hazard intensity and is built by teams of scientists, including meteorologists, seismologists, hydrologists, climate scientists, and geophysicists. The hazard component answers these questions:

* Where are future catastrophes likely to occur?
* How large or severe are they likely to be?
* How frequently are they likely to occur?

Large catalogs comprising tens of thousands of computer-simulated catastrophes are generated, representing the broad spectrum of plausible events. For each simulated event, the model calculates the intensity at each location within the affected area. For example, for earthquakes, intensity may be expressed in terms of the degree of ground shaking or the number and intensity of fires spawned by the event; for hurricanes, intensity is expressed in terms of wind speed and storm surge height.

The models incorporate large and detailed databases of geophysical information. For example, windstorm models use high-resolution digital land use and land cover data to calculate the effects of surface friction on wind speed. Earthquake models employ detailed soil data, which determine the degree of seismic wave amplification and the potential for liquefaction at specific sites affected by the event.

Catastrophe models may produce different results because they are based on different theoretical assumptions and variables. For example, over 100 years of data are available on hurricanes, but the early data are not as detailed, sophisticated, or accurate as recent data. Different modeling firms may therefore employ different datasets and consequently develop different theories about the potential frequency and severity of future hurricanes.

Engineering Component

The second component of a catastrophe model is the engineering component. The engineering component uses the intensity information from the hazard component to estimate the extent of structural damage that would occur based on information about the properties that are exposed to a simulated catastrophic event. These estimates incorporate information such as building construction, occupancy, height, age, and building code enforcement. Additional detail, such as roof shape, roof-to-wall connections, and the presence or absence of hurricane shutters can also be used, when available.

Developed by structural engineers, equations called damage functions are used to compute the level of damage that is expected to occur to buildings and their contents and to estimate the time it will take to repair or rebuild affected structures. This last type of damage function is used to produce estimates of business interruption (BI) losses or alternative living expenses (ALE) for residential policies. The catastrophe model's damage functions can incorporate published research, the results of laboratory testing, findings from on-site damage surveys, and detailed claims data provided by insurers.

Another reason that catastrophe models can produce varied results is because they use different engineering research to determine damageability. For example, research and professional opinions vary regarding the effects of hurricane winds and flying debris on different types of structures.

Financial Component

The third component of a catastrophe model is the financial component, wherein estimates of physical damage to buildings and contents are translated into estimates of monetary loss. These estimates, in turn, are translated into insured losses by applying insurance policy conditions to the total damage estimates. In essence, the financial component evaluates the effect of a simulated catastrophe on an insurer's in-force policies and operating results. Depending on the magnitude of the simulated catastrophe, the primary insurer will sustain a range of losses. The financial component usually reflects coverage characteristics of the in-force policies, such as whether they are on an actual cash value (ACV) or a replacement cost basis.

Some catastrophe models include socioeconomic factors, such as the likelihood of fraud or theft following a catastrophe. Demand surge is another factor to consider in calculating the total insured loss. Demand surge occurs when repair costs increase dramatically following a catastrophe because of supply shortages, whether of materials or labor. For example, the price of glass, roof shingles, and plywood could increase significantly in the affected area following a hurricane.

How Catastrophe Models Are Used

Primary insurers use the results of catastrophe models to understand the catastrophe loss potential given their portfolio of in-force policies. Model results are also used as input into pricing decisions, risk selection and underwriting, the design of territories, loss mitigation studies, and risk transfer strategies.

Reinsurers and reinsurance intermediaries use the results of catastrophe models to determine how an existing or proposed reinsurance program will respond under various catastrophe scenarios and to establish a rate for catastrophe reinsurance coverage. Reinsurers also use catastrophe modeling to manage catastrophe exposures assumed from their primary insurer clients and to aid in determining catastrophe retrocessional needs.

Catastrophe models provide detailed output from which various measures of loss potential and risk can be derived. Two key outputs from catastrophe modeling are the average annual loss and the exceedance probability curve.

Average Annual Loss

The average annual loss (AAL) is the long-term average loss expected in any one year for in-force policies for the cause of loss being modeled. AAL is also referred to as the catastrophe loss cost, or pure premium, and is typically expressed as the expected loss per unit of exposure.

When the analysis is performed on a zip code level, the catastrophe model produces AAL values for each zip code. Zip codes with high AAL values are particularly vulnerable to catastrophic loss. Because AAL values reflect all the components of the catastrophe model (hazard, engineering, and financial), AAL values are more effective in identifying concentrations of catastrophe-prone in-force policies than a simple review of the geographic distribution of in-force policies.

AAL analysis has several uses. Catastrophe models can generate policy-level AAL information so that reinsurance rates can be developed. AAL can be allocated between the primary insurer's net retention and the reinsurance program to determine the AAL for each layer in the reinsurance program. If the cause of loss being modeled is the only cause of loss covered by the rein-surance program, a reinsurer could develop a rate by adding its own expense and profit factors to the AAL. A risk load is also often incorporated into the rate to cover the possibility of extreme events generating losses well in excess of the AAL. Reinsurers and primary insurers can also use AAL information to compare the pricing of different reinsurance program proposals.

Exceedance Probability Curve

While AAL is a useful metric, the fundamental outputs of catastrophe models are not single numbers. One of the most commonly used outputs is the exceedance probability (EP) curve, which represents the full spectrum of potential losses and their associated probabilities of occurrence. These prob-abilities are called exceedance probabilities and reflect the probability that a loss of a specified size will be equaled or exceeded.

The exhibit shows an example of an EP curve. The probability that various levels of loss (in millions of U.S. dollars) will be equaled or exceeded in the coming year is shown. Also shown are return periods, in years, as the inverse of the exceedance probability. Exceedance probabilities are assigned by the catastrophe model. For example, there is a 1 percent probability that a $44 million (or higher) catastrophe loss will occur in any given year. Put another way, a loss of $44 million (or higher) is expected every 100 years, on average. Similarly, there is a 0.4 percent probability that a $75 million (or higher) loss will occur in any given year. Expressed in terms of return periods, a $75 mil-lion (or higher) loss is expected every 250 years, on average. See the exhibit "Exceedance Probability Curve."

It is prudent to focus on exceedance probabilities, rather than on return periods, to avoid thinking that "the 100-year loss won't occur in my lifetime" or that if the 100-year loss occurred this year, it won't occur again for another 100 years. In fact, there is a 1 percent probability every year that the 100-year loss will occur.

Based on an exceedance probability analysis, the primary insurer can make informed decisions regarding the size of the reinsurance limit it should purchase.

Exceedance Probability Curve

Exceedance Probability (Percent)	Return Period (Years)	Estimated Loss ($ millions)
0.01	10,000	234
0.05	2,000	146
0.10	1,000	127
0.20	500	104
0.30	333	92
0.40	250	75
0.50	200	67
1.00	100	44
2.00	50	24
3.00	33	17
4.00	25	13
5.00	20	9
10.00	10	3

[DA09279]

Catastrophe Modeling Issues

Although catastrophe modeling has become standard practice for primary insurer pricing, there are some issues about using catastrophe modeling in rate development. Different models from different vendors can produce different outcomes because of variation in the data and assumptions used to build each model. Further, advances in scientific and engineering research can affect model results even if the historical data have not changed.

Catastrophe models also place significant demands on primary insurers' information systems, for a primary insurer's data must be compatible with the catastrophe model's input requirements. Information that the primary insurer must capture to make the best use of catastrophe models can increase the primary insurer's costs. The reliability of model output is only as good as the quality of the exposure data used as input.

Despite these issues, catastrophe modeling is an effective, widely used method for assessing catastrophe risk. In fact, since the inception of modeling in the mid-1980s, applications of the technology have broadened to serve corporate risk managers, investors, mortgage underwriters, government officials, and any others who benefit from an enhanced understanding of their risk. See the exhibit "Applying Big Data to Catastrophe Modeling."

Applying Big Data to Catastrophe Modeling

There are questions about the extent to which human activities contribute to an increase in natural catastrophes. Climate change may cause a rise in sea levels, which increases the risk of storm surge damage, and may contribute to increased frequency and severity of hurricanes. Another question is whether fracking contributes to an increase in earthquakes in some areas.

The National Hurricane Center (NHC) has stated that although it has 160 years of historical hurricane data, this information is not sufficient to predict future hurricane risk. However, big data can be used in three ways to create more accurate catastrophe models.

First, numerous sources of data can now be obtained and analyzed. Insurers can, for example, gather granular information about individual properties in a portfolio, acquire analyses of the effects of climate change and fracking from scientific sources, use information from the NHC to determine the location of the strongest winds relative to the center of a hurricane, or analyze social media analysis for information about ground shaking or sinking in areas near fracking operations.

Second, insurers can use big data technology to analyze enormous amounts of information from multiple sources very quickly, allowing models to respond to changes in climate, engineering, technology, and geopolitical and socioeconomic conditions.

Third, through machine learning, in which computers continually teach themselves to make better decisions based on previous results and new data, the models can continue to improve accuracy as new data is analyzed.

[OV_12098]

SUMMARY

Organizations select modeling methods to simulate, test, and predict outcomes and then use the results to better manage the uncertainty of risk. Empirical probability distributions, theoretical probability distributions, EVT, and regression analysis are four methods of modeling based on historical data. Methods based on expert input include preference among bets, judgments of relative likelihood, and the Delphi technique. The Monte Carlo simulation and fuzzy logic are methods based on combining historical data and expert input.

Organizations use decision tree analysis to compare the consequences, costs, and gains of alternative decisions and to select the most effective strategy to achieve a goal. Organizations use event tree analysis to examine all possible consequences of an accidental event and the effectiveness of existing measures to prevent or control those consequences.

An influence diagram provides a graph of a decision-making process, showing the known information and variables affecting the decision. The diagram consists of three types of nodes. Rectangles represent decisions, diamonds represent costs and benefits, and ovals represent variables affecting outcomes. Arrows show the relationships between nodes. Decision trees are similar to influence diagrams but present more detail, with branches representing each decision component and the alternative options.

Applying uncertainty modeling requires several steps. First, the problem or decision must be analyzed and options proposed. Then, an influence diagram is developed for each proposed option. The next steps are determining the probabilities for each option, followed by consideration of economic and financial factors. The options are then compared based on their respective probabilities and expected outcomes, including economic costs. Finally, a recommendation can be made based on the analysis.

VaR and EaR are metrics used in evaluating financial risk. VaR is used primarily by financial organizations to determine the probability of investments falling below a threshold value. EaR is used by financial and nonfinancial organizations to model the effects of changes in various factors on an organization's earnings.

A catastrophe model typically includes these three generic components: a hazard component, an engineering component, and a financial component. Two key outputs from catastrophe modeling are AAL and the EP curve. AAL is the loss to in-force policies that can be expected in any single year, on average over the long term, from the cause of loss being modeled. The EP curve is the full spectrum of potential losses that can occur along with their associated probabilities. Despite certain issues that exist, catastrophe models are the accepted industry standard for assessing catastrophe risk and providing valuable information on the potential financial effects of catastrophic events.

ASSIGNMENT NOTES

1. Marvin Rausand, "Event Tree Analysis," slide presentation, Department of Production and Quality Engineering, Norwegian University of Science and Technology, October 7, 2005, slide 3,www.ntnu.no/ross/slides/eta.pdf (accessed April 3, 2012).

2. Rick Nason, "Market Risk Management and Common Elements With Credit Risk Management," in Enterprise Risk Management, eds. John Fraser and Betty J. Simkins (Hoboken, N.J.: John Wiley & Sons, Inc., 2010), pp. 249-250.

4

Analyzing Loss Exposures

Educational Objectives

After learning the content of this assignment, you should be able to:

▷ Describe the following methods of loss exposure identification:

- Document analysis

- Compliance review

- Personal inspections

- Expertise within and beyond the organization

▷ Explain why data used in risk management decisions need to be relevant, complete, consistent, and organized.

▷ Explain how to analyze loss exposures considering the four dimensions of loss and data credibility.

Analyzing Loss Exposures

IDENTIFYING LOSS EXPOSURES

For individuals, common property and liability exposures can be identified by a property-casualty insurance producer as part of an assessment of insurance needs. Similarly, individuals' net income loss exposures can be identified by life insurance producers as part of a needs assessment for life and health insurance products. For organizations, loss exposure identification is typically more complex, using a variety of methods and sources of information.

The methods of information that enable an organization to take a systematic approach to identifying loss exposures include these:

- Document analysis
- Compliance review
- Inspections
- Expertise within and beyond the organization

Document Analysis

The variety of documents used and produced by an organization can be a key source of information regarding loss exposures. Some of these documents are standardized and originate from outside the organization, such as questionnaires, checklists, and surveys. These standardized documents broadly categorize the loss exposures that most organizations typically face and are not completed with information that is exclusive to the organization.

Other documents are organization-specific, such as financial statements and accounting records, contracts, insurance policies, policy and procedure manuals, flowcharts and organizational charts, and loss histories. Although the use and function of the various documents may overlap, causing possible duplication in loss exposure identification, reviewing multiple documents is necessary to avoid failing to identify important loss exposures.

In addition to the documents discussed in this section, virtually any document connected to an organization's operations also reveals something about its loss exposures. For example, Web sites, news releases, or reports from external organizations such as A.M. Best or D&B may indicate something about an organization's loss exposures. Although it is not feasible to review every document that refers to an organization, some of these additional sources may be useful.

Risk Assessment Questionnaires and Checklists

Standardized documents published outside an organization, such as insurance coverage checklists and risk assessment questionnaires, broadly categorize the loss exposures that most organizations typically face. A variety of checklists and questionnaires have been published by insurers, the American Management Association (AMA), the International Risk Management Institute (IRMI), the Risk and Insurance Management Society (RIMS), and others.

Although some organizations or trade associations have developed specialized checklists or questionnaires for their members, most are created by insurers and concentrate on identifying insurable hazard risks. Some focus on listing the organization's assets, whereas others focus on identifying potential causes of loss that could affect the organization.

Checklists typically capture less information than questionnaires. Although checklists can help an organization identify its loss exposures, they do not show how those loss exposures support or affect specific organizational goals. Linking loss exposures with the goals they support can be useful in analyzing the potential financial consequences of loss. Therefore, checklists are of limited benefit in the analysis step of the risk management process.

A questionnaire captures more descriptive information than a checklist. For example, as well as identifying a loss exposure, a questionnaire may capture information about the amounts or values exposed to loss. The questionnaire can be designed to include questions that address key property, liability, net income, and at least some personnel loss exposures.

Questionnaire responses can enable an insurance or a risk management professional to identify and analyze an organization's loss exposures regarding real property, equipment, products, key customers, neighboring properties, operations, and so on. Additionally, the logical sequencing of questions helps in developing a more detailed examination of the loss exposures an organization faces.

Both checklists and questionnaires may be produced by insurers (such questionnaires are known as insurance surveys). Most of the questions on these surveys relate to loss exposures for which commercial insurance is generally available.

Risk management or risk assessment questionnaires have a broader focus and address both insurable and uninsurable loss exposures. However, a disadvantage of risk assessment questionnaires is that they typically can be completed only with considerable expense, time, and effort and still may not identify all possible loss exposures.

Standardizing a survey or questionnaire has both advantages and disadvantages. Standardized questions are relevant for most organizations and can be answered by persons who have little risk management expertise.

However, no standardized questionnaire can be expected to uncover all the loss exposures particularly characteristic of a given industry, let alone those unique to a given organization. Additionally, the questionnaire's structure might not stimulate the respondent to do anything more than answer the questions asked; that is, it will elicit only the information that is specifically requested. Consequently, it may not reveal key information. Therefore, questionnaires should ideally be used in conjunction with other identification and analysis methods.

Because even a thoroughly completed checklist or questionnaire does not ensure that all loss exposures have been recognized, experienced insurance and risk management professionals often follow up with additional questions that are not on the standardized document.

Financial Statements and Underlying Accounting Records

Risk management professionals with accounting or finance expertise sometimes begin the loss exposure identification process by reviewing an organization's financial statements, including the balance sheet, income statement, statement of cash flows, and supporting statements. As well as identifying current loss exposures, financial statements and accounting records can be used to identify any future plans that could lead to new loss exposures.

An organization's **balance sheet** is the financial statement that reports the assets, liabilities, and owners' equity of the organization as of a specific date. Owners' equity, or net worth, is the amount by which assets exceed liabilities. Asset entries indicate property values that could be reduced by loss. Liability entries show what the organization owes and enable the risk management professional to explore two types of loss exposures: (1) liabilities that could be increased or created by a loss and (2) obligations (such as mortgage payments) that the organization must fulfill, even if it were to close temporarily as a result of a business interruption.

The **income statement** is particularly useful in identifying net income loss exposures; that is, those loss exposures that reduce revenue or increase expenses.

The **statement of cash flows** (also called the statement of sources and uses of funds) is the financial statement that summarizes the cash effects of an organization's operating, investing, and financing activities during a specific period.

Funds-flow analysis on the statement of cash flows can identify the amounts of cash either subject to loss or available to meet continuing obligations. For example, the statement of cash flows would indicate the amount of cash that is typically on hand to pay for any losses resulting from loss exposures that have been retained by the organization.

Financial statements can reveal that an organization is subject to significant financial risks, such as fluctuations in the value of investments, interest rate volatility, foreign exchange rate changes, or commodity price swings.

Balance sheet

The financial statement that reports the assets, liabilities, and owners' equity of an organization as of a specific date.

Income statement

The financial statement that reports an organization's profit or loss for a specific period by comparing the revenues generated with the expenses incurred to produce those revenues.

Statement of cash flows

The financial statement that summarizes the cash effects of an organization's operating, investing, and financing activities during a specific period.

However, the primary advantage of financial statements from a risk management professional's perspective is that they help to identify major categories of loss exposures.

For example, property loss exposures can be seen in the asset section of the balance sheet. Some liability loss exposures, especially contractual obligations such as loans or mortgages, can be seen in the liabilities section of the balance sheet. The potential effects of net income loss exposures can be seen by comparing revenues with expenses on the income statement.

The major disadvantage of using financial statements for identifying loss exposures is that although they identify most of the major categories of loss exposures (property, liability and net income are identified but personnel loss exposures are not), they do not identify or quantify the individual loss exposures. For example, the balance sheet may show that there is $5 million in property exposed to loss, but it does not specify how many properties make up that $5 million, where those properties are located, or how much each individual property is worth. Moreover, the real and personal property values recorded in financial statements are based on accounting conventions and are not accurate for purposes of insurance or risk management.

Another disadvantage is that financial statements depict past activities—for example, revenue that has already been earned, expenses that have already been incurred, prior valuations of assets and liabilities, and business operations that have already taken place. They are of limited help in identifying projected values or future events. Therefore, even after using financial statements for loss exposure identification, insurance and risk management professionals still need to project what events might occur in the future, determine how these future events could change loss exposures, and analyze and quantify potential losses accordingly.

Contracts

A contract is an agreement entered into by two or more parties that specifies the parties' responsibilities to one another. Analyzing an organization's contracts may help identify its property and liability loss exposures and help determine who has assumed responsibility for which loss exposures. It is often necessary to consult with legal experts when interpreting contracts.

Contract analysis can both identify the loss exposures generated or reduced by an organization's contracts and ensure that the organization is not assuming liability that is disproportionate to its stake in the contract. Ongoing contract analysis is part of monitoring and maintaining a risk management program.

Entering into contracts can either increase or reduce an organization's property and liability loss exposures. For example, a contract to purchase property or equipment will increase the organization's property loss exposures, whereas a contract to sell property or equipment will reduce property loss exposures.

A contract can generate liability loss exposures in two ways. First, the organization can accept the loss exposures of another party through a contract, such as a **hold-harmless agreement** (sometimes referred to as an indemnity agreement). For example, an organization may enter into a hold-harmless agreement with its distributor under which the organization agrees to indemnify the distributor (pay the losses for which the distributor is liable) if the distributor is found liable for a products liability claim. **Indemnification** is the process of restoring an individual or organization to a pre-loss financial condition.

The second way a contract may generate a liability loss exposure is if the organization fails to fulfill a valid contract. For example, if an organization agrees to deliver manufactured goods to a distributor and then fails to deliver those goods, the distributor is entitled to bring a legal claim against the organization. The distributor's claim presents a liability loss exposure for the organization.

Alternatively, an organization can reduce or eliminate liability loss exposures by entering into a contract that transfers its liability to another organization. For example, an organization can enter into a hold-harmless agreement under which the second party agrees to indemnify the organization in the event of a liability claim.

Hold-harmless agreement (or indemnity agreement)
A contractual provision that obligates one of the parties to assume the legal liability of another party.

Indemnification
The process of restoring an individual or organization to a pre-loss financial condition.

Insurance Policies

Although insurance is a means of risk financing, reviewing insurance policies can also be helpful in risk assessment.

Analyzing insurance policies reveals many of the insurable loss exposures that an organization faces. However, this analysis may either indicate the organization is insured for more loss exposures than it really has, or, alternatively, may not show all the loss exposures the organization faces.

As insurance policies typically are standardized forms, an organization does not necessarily face every loss exposure covered by its policies. Furthermore, the organization may face many other loss exposures that either cannot be covered by insurance policies or are covered by policies the organization has chosen not to purchase.

To identify insurance coverage that an organization has not purchased, and therefore potentially identify insurable loss exposures that have not been insured, a risk management professional can compare his or her organization's coverage against an industry checklist of insurance policies currently in effect.

Organizational Policies and Records

Loss exposures can also be identified using organizational policies and records, such as corporate by-laws, board minutes, employee manuals, procedure manuals, mission statements, and risk management policies. For example, policy and procedure manuals may identify some of the organization's property loss exposures by referencing equipment, or pinpoint liability loss exposures by referencing hazardous materials with which employees come into contact. See the exhibit "Internal Documents as Loss Exposures."

Internal Documents as Loss Exposures

Internal documents, in addition to identifying loss exposures, need to be analyzed to determine their appropriateness and consistency with external publications. An organization's internal documents are not typically written in anticipation that they will be viewed outside the organization. However, many internal documents are used during legal proceedings and therefore may present a potential liability loss exposure to the organization. This illustrates the need for internal documents to be consistent with external information the organization releases.

[DA02555]

As well as identifying existing loss exposures, some documents may indicate impending changes in loss exposures. For example, board minutes may indicate management's plans to sell or purchase property, thereby either reducing or increasing its property loss exposures.

One drawback to using policies and records to identify loss exposures is the sheer volume of documents that some organizations generate internally. It may be virtually impossible to have one employee or a group of employees examine every internal document. In these instances, insurance and risk management professionals would need to examine a representative sample of documents. This makes the task manageable, but increases the likelihood that not all loss exposures will be identified.

Flowcharts and Organizational Charts

A flowchart is a diagram that depicts the sequence of activities performed by a particular organization or process. An organization can use flowcharts to show the nature and use of the resources involved in its operations as well as the sequence of and relationships between those operations.

A manufacturer's flowchart might start with raw material acquisition and end with the finished product's delivery to the ultimate consumer. Individual entries on the flowchart, including the processes involved and the means by which products move from one process to the next, can help identify loss exposures—particularly critical loss exposures.

For example, the flowchart might illustrate that every item produced must be spray-painted during the production process. This activity presents a critical property loss exposure, because an explosion at the spray-painting location might disable the entire production line. The simplified flowchart in the exhibit reveals that difficulties with getting the furniture through customs at the Los Angeles Port could disrupt the entire furniture supply chain. See the exhibit "Furniture Manufacturer Flowchart."

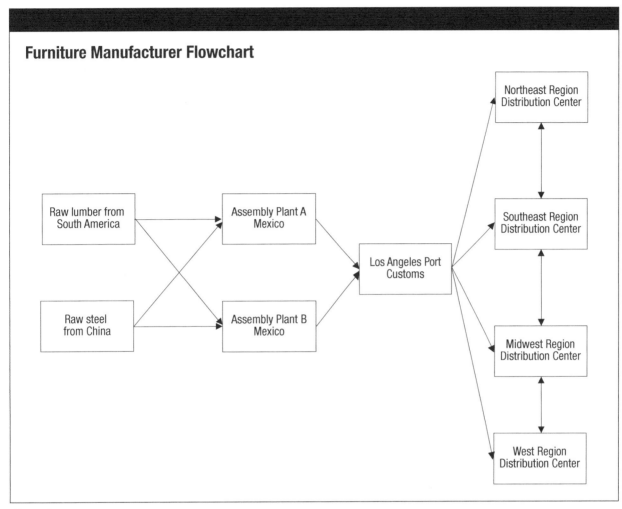

Furniture Manufacturer Flowchart

[DA02556]

Information can also be obtained from organizational charts. An organizational chart depicts the hierarchy of an organization's personnel and can help to identify key personnel for whom the organization may have a personnel loss exposure. This chart can also help track the flow of information through an organization and identify any bottlenecks that may exist. Although organizational charts can be fundamental in properly identifying personnel loss exposures, an individual's place on an organizational chart does not guarantee that he or she is a key employee. The organizational chart does not necessarily reflect the importance of the individual to the continued operation or profitability of the organization.

Loss Histories

Loss history analysis, that is, reviewing an organization's own losses or those suffered by comparable organizations, can help a risk management or an insurance professional to both identify and analyze loss exposures. Loss histories of comparable organizations are particularly helpful if the organization is too small or too new to have a sizeable record of its own past losses, or if the organization's own historical loss records are incomplete.

Any past loss can recur unless the organization has had a fundamental change in operations or property owned. Accordingly, loss histories are often an important indicator of an organization's current or future loss exposures. However, loss histories will not identify any loss exposures that have not resulted in past losses. Therefore, use of loss histories alone is inadequate.

Compliance Review

In addition to document analysis, insurance and risk management professionals may also conduct compliance reviews to identify loss exposures. A compliance review determines an organization's compliance with local, state, and federal statutes and regulations. The organization can conduct most of the compliance review itself if it has adequate in-house legal and accounting resources. Otherwise, it may have to use outside expertise.

The benefit of compliance reviews is that they can help an organization minimize or avoid liability loss exposures. However, a drawback of compliance reviews is that they are expensive and time consuming. Furthermore, because regulations are often changing, remaining in compliance requires ongoing monitoring. As a result, conducting a compliance review simply to identify loss exposures is often impractical. However, because noncompliance is a liability loss exposure, loss exposure identification can be part of the justification of the cost of a compliance review and is an ancillary benefit once a review has been completed.

Personal Inspections

Some loss exposures are best identified by personal inspections, that is, information-gathering visits to critical sites both within and outside an organization. Such visits often reveal loss exposures that would not appear in written descriptions of the organization's operations and therefore should lead to a more complete list of loss exposures.

Personal inspections should ideally be conducted by individuals whose background and skills equip them to identify unexpected, but possible, loss exposures. Additionally, the person conducting the inspection should take the opportunity to discuss the particular operations with front-line personnel, who are often best placed to identify nonobvious loss exposures. Therefore, a personal inspection can overlap with consulting expertise within and beyond the organization.

Expertise Within and Beyond the Organization

Thorough loss exposure identification should include soliciting expertise both inside and outside the organization. Doing so renders a more complete and objective picture of the organization's loss exposures.

Interviews with employees can be conducted to gather information about their jobs and departments. Whereas an inspection can only reveal what is happening during the inspection, interviews can elicit information about what occurred before the inspection, what might be planned for the future, or what could go or has gone wrong that has not been properly addressed.

Interviews should include a range of employees from every level of the organization. Questionnaires can be designed for use in conjunction with these interviews to ensure that they are comprehensive and are eliciting as much information as possible.

To obtain an external perspective, practitioners in fields such as law, finance, statistics, accounting, auditing, and the technology of the organization's industry can be consulted. The special knowledge of experts in identifying particular loss exposures is an invaluable resource.

One area of specialization that often requires such expert services is **hazard analysis**. For example, a business consultant might identify conditions that cause the organization to overlook opportunities for growth. Alternatively, concerns about environmental hazards might require a specialist to take air or water samples and a specialized laboratory to analyze them. Although hazard analysis is focused on loss exposures that have already been identified, the results of the analysis often identify previously overlooked loss exposures. See the exhibit "Identifying Loss Exposures With New Data Analysis Techniques."

Hazard analysis
A method of analysis that identifies conditions that increase the frequency or severity of loss.

Identifying Loss Exposures With New Data Analysis Techniques

New techniques to analyze insurance data are developing rapidly. The Internet of Things (IoT), for example, consists of a network of objects that transmit data to computers that analyze the data. A business can take advantage of the IoT by installing sensors to detect various hazards, such as fire, machinery breakdown, or contaminants. These sensors communicate information about the hazard to the organization's safety department and, if necessary, the appropriate first responders.

Similarly, workers can wear devices with sensors that transmit information about ergonomics to identify and correct improper lifting and other activities that might cause injuries.

Social network analysis, which involves discovering patterns and relationships based on links in a network, along with text mining, which involves language recognition, can help underwriters identify an organization's emerging exposures, including product liability or investor complaints that could turn into lawsuits. For example, by mining social media posts, a computer model could identify descriptions of customers' reactions to certain products as positive or negative.

[OV_12095]

DATA REQUIREMENTS FOR EXPOSURE ANALYSIS

Loss exposure analysis is often based on probability and the statistical analysis of data. The statistical analysis of loss exposures starts with gathering sufficient data in a suitable form. Once these data have been collected, they can be subjected to a variety of probability and statistical techniques that are frequently used by insurance and risk management professionals.

The most common basis of an analysis of current or future loss exposures is information about past losses arising from similar loss exposures. To accurately analyze loss exposures using data on past losses, the data should meet four criteria. They should be relevant, complete, consistent, and organized.

Relevant Data

To analyze current loss exposures based on historical data, the past loss data for the loss exposures in question must be relevant to the current or future loss exposures the insurance or risk management professional is trying to assess. For example, if an organization was trying to assess its auto physical damage loss exposures for the next twelve months, it may examine its auto physical damage losses for the last four or five years and then take into account any changes in the makeup of its auto fleet and the rate of increase for repairs to determine potential losses for the next twelve months.

Although the organization may have auto physical damage records for the last twenty or thirty years, much of that data may no longer be relevant because of advances in auto engineering. Modern cars use different designs and materials that provide more for passenger safety at the expense of increased physical damage to the auto in the event of an accident. Therefore, data from ten years ago may not be relevant to today's auto physical damage loss exposures.

Similarly, relevant data for property losses include the property's repair or replacement cost at the time it is to be restored, not the property's historical or book value. For liability losses, the data should relate to past claims that are substantially the same as the potential future claims being assessed.

Even relatively minor differences in the factual and legal bases of claims can produce substantially different outcomes and costs. Data to analyze personnel loss exposures must relate to personnel with similar experience and expertise as those being considered as future loss exposures. The appropriate data for considering net income loss exposures would depend on the type of loss exposure being analyzed. Those data should involve similar reductions in revenue and similar additional expenses as would those loss exposures under consideration.

Complete Data

Obtaining complete data about past losses for particular loss exposures often requires relying on others, both inside and outside the organization. What constitutes complete data depends largely on the nature of the loss exposure being considered.

Having complete information helps to isolate the causes of each loss. Furthermore, having complete data enables the risk management professional to make reasonably reliable estimates of the dollar amounts of the future losses.

For example, considering loss exposures related to employee injuries would require historical loss data to include information regarding loss amounts, the employee's experience and training, the time of day of the loss, the task being performed, and the supervisor on duty at the time. Similarly, complete data on a property loss to a piece of machinery would include the cost of repairing or replacing any damaged or inoperative machinery, the resulting loss of revenue, any extra expenses, or any overtime wages paid to maintain production.

Consistent Data

To reflect past patterns, loss data must also be consistent in at least two respects. If data are inconsistent in either respect, the future loss exposures could be significantly underestimated or overestimated.

First, the loss data must be collected on a consistent basis for all recorded losses. Loss data are often collected from a variety of sources, each of which may use different accounting methods. Consequently, these data are likely to be inconsistent in their presentation.

For example, one common source of inconsistency results when some of the loss amounts being analyzed are reported as estimates and others are reported as actual paid amounts. Similarly, data will be inconsistent if some amounts are reported at their original cost and others are reported at their current replacement cost.

Second, data must be expressed in constant dollars, to adjust for differences in price levels. Differences in price levels will also lead to inconsistency. Two physically identical losses occurring in different years will probably have different values. Inflation distorts the later loss, making it appear more severe because it is measured in less valuable dollars.

To prevent this distortion, historical losses should be adjusted (indexed) so that loss data is expressed in constant dollars. To express data in constant dollars means that the amounts reported are comparable in terms of the value of goods and services that could be purchased in a particular benchmark year. Price indices are used to adjust data so that they are in constant dollars. See the exhibit "When a Dollar Is Not Worth a Dollar."

When a Dollar Is Not Worth a Dollar

When referring to historical values, a variety of terms are used, such as nominal dollars, current dollars, and real or constant dollars.

Nominal dollars—dollar values at the time of the loss. For example, if a fire destroyed a building in 1995 and it cost $100,000 to repair the building in 1995, then the loss in nominal dollars is $100,000.

Current dollars—dollar values today. This value involves inflating all historical dollar values to today's value by using some measure of inflation (such as the Consumer Price Index). For example, the $100,000 loss in 1995 is actually a $125,000 loss in today's (current) dollars.

Real or constant dollars—dollar values in some base year. This value enables comparison of losses that have occurred in different time periods. The choice of base year does not matter. For convenience, the most recent year is often chosen. For example, suppose losses were reported over the four-year window 2002-2005. To determine real or constant dollars, multiply 2002 values by 1.08 (to account for the 8 percent increase in prices from 2002 to 2005) to convert the 2002 values into 2005 values for comparison. Similarly, 2003 losses would have to be multiplied by 1.06 and 2004 losses by 1.03.

[DA02571]

Organized Data

Even if data are relevant, complete, and consistent, if they are not appropriately organized they will be difficult for the insurance or risk management professional to use to identify patterns and trends that will help to reveal and quantify potential future loss exposures. Data can be organized in a variety of different ways, depending on which is most useful for the analysis being performed.

For example, listing losses for particular loss exposures by calendar dates may be useful for detecting seasonal patterns but may not disclose patterns that could be revealed by listing such losses by size. An array of losses—amounts of losses listed in increasing or decreasing value—could reveal clusters of losses by severity and could also focus attention on large losses, which are often most important for insurance and risk management decisions. Organizing losses by size is also the foundation for developing loss severity distributions or loss trends over time.

ANALYZING LOSS EXPOSURES

Analyzing loss frequency, loss severity, total dollar losses, and timing helps insurance and risk management professionals develop loss projections, and, therefore, also helps them prioritize loss exposures so that risk management resources can be concentrated where they are needed most.

The analysis step of the risk management process involves considering the four dimensions of a loss exposure:

- Loss frequency—The number of losses (such as fires, auto accidents, or liability claims) that occur during a specific period.
- Loss severity—The dollar amount of loss for a specific occurrence.
- Total dollar losses—The total dollar amount of losses for all occurrences during a specific period.
- Timing—The points at which losses occur and loss payments are made. (The period between loss occurrence and loss payment can be lengthy.)

If any of these dimensions of loss exposure analysis involve empirical distributions developed from past losses, the credibility of the data being used needs to be determined. Data credibility is the level of confidence that available data are accurate indicators of future losses.

Loss Frequency

Loss frequency is the number of losses—such as fires, thefts, or floods—that occur during a specific period. Relative loss frequency is the number of losses that occur within a given period relative to the number of exposure units (such as the number of buildings or cars exposed to loss).

For example, if an organization experiences, on average, five theft losses per year, five is the mean of an empirical frequency distribution. If the organization has only one building, then both the loss frequency and the relative frequency of losses from theft is five per year. However, if the organization has five buildings, then the organization still has a loss frequency of five theft losses per year, but the relative frequency is one loss per year per building. Two of the most common applications of relative frequency measures in risk management are injuries per person per hour in workers compensation and auto accidents per mile driven.

Frequency distributions are usually discrete probability distributions based on past data regarding how often similar events have happened. For example, the exhibit contains the frequency distribution of the number of hurricanes that make landfall in Florida during a single hurricane season. One way of describing the frequency of hurricanes is to report a mean frequency of occurrence, such as approximately 1.2 hurricanes making landfall per year. See the exhibit "Skewness of Number of Hurricanes Making Landfall in Florida During One Hurricane Season."

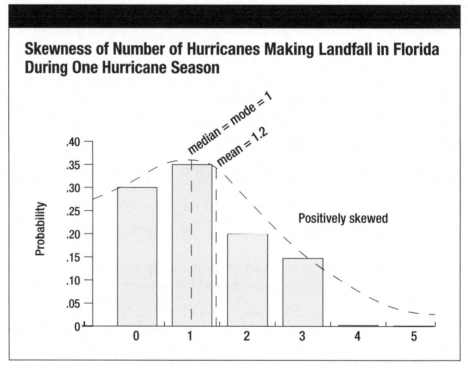

[DA02586]

However, this figure does not incorporate some of the other information available from the entire frequency distribution. For example, the most likely outcome may be one hurricane per year (35.0 percent of the time). However, having zero hurricanes per year is also reasonably likely (30.0 percent of the time), but having five or more hurricanes make landfall in Florida is reasonably unlikely (0.1 percent of the time). Therefore, an insurance or risk management professional should supplement the mean of 1.2 with other information from the frequency distribution, such as the standard deviation (which is approximately 1.04) and skewness measures.

Loss frequency can be projected with a fairly high degree of confidence for some loss exposures in large organizations. For example, a company that ships thousands of parcels each day probably can more accurately project the number of transit losses it will sustain in a year, based on past experience and adjusted for any expected changes in future conditions, than can a company that ships only hundreds of parcels each month.

Most organizations do not have enough exposure units to accurately project low-frequency, high-severity events (such as employee deaths). However, an estimate with a margin for error is better than no estimate at all, as long as its limitations are recognized.

Loss Severity

The purpose of analyzing loss severity is to determine how serious a loss might be. For example, how much of a building could be damaged in a single fire? Alternatively, how long might it take for an organization to resume operations after a fire?

Maximum Possible Loss

Effectively managing risk requires identifying the worst possible outcome of a loss. The maximum possible loss (MPL) is the total value exposed to loss at any one location or from any one event. For example, in the case of fire damage to a building and its contents, the maximum possible loss is typically the value of the building plus the total value of the building's contents.

To determine MPL for multiple exposure units, such as a fleet of cars, an insurance or a risk management professional may consider factors such as whether multiple vehicles travel together (a circumstance that could cause one event, such as a collision, to affect several vehicles at once) or whether several vehicles are stored in the same location (a circumstance that could cause one event, such as a fire, flood, or theft, to affect several vehicles). This helps determine the maximum number of vehicles that could be involved in any one loss and therefore the event's MPL.

Although maximum possible property losses can be estimated based on the values exposed to loss, this estimation is not necessarily appropriate or possible for assessing maximum possible liability losses. In theory, liability losses are limited only by the defendant's total wealth. Therefore, some practical assumptions must be made about the MPL in liability cases to properly assess that loss exposure. Instead of focusing on the defendant's total wealth, a common assumption is that the maximum amount that would be exposed to liability loss 95 percent (or 98 percent) of the time in similar cases is the MPL.

Frequency and Severity Considered Jointly

In order to fully analyze the significance of a particular loss exposure, it is important to consider both severity and frequency distributions and how they interact. One method of jointly considering both loss frequency and loss severity is the Prouty Approach, which identifies four broad categories of loss frequency and three broad categories of loss severity. Another method is more statistically based and involves combining frequency and severity distributions to create a single total claims distribution. See the exhibit "The Prouty Approach."

The Prouty Approach

Loss Severity		Loss Frequency			
		Almost Nil	Slight	Moderate	Definite
Severe		Reduce or prevent / Transfer	Reduce or prevent / Transfer	Reduce or prevent / Retain	Avoid
Significant		Reduce or prevent / Transfer	Reduce / Transfer	Reduce or prevent / Retain	Avoid
Slight		Reduce or prevent / Retain	Reduce / Retain	Reduce or prevent / Retain	Prevent / Retain

[DA02588]

As shown in the exhibit, the Prouty Approach entails four categories of loss frequency:

- Almost nil—Extremely unlikely to happen; virtually no possibility
- Slight—Could happen but has not happened
- Moderate—Happens occasionally
- Definite—Happens regularly

There are three categories of loss severity:

- Slight—Organization can readily retain each loss exposure.
- Significant—Organization cannot retain the loss exposure, some part of which must be financed.
- Severe—Organization must finance virtually all of the loss exposure or endanger its survival.

These broad categories of loss frequency and loss severity are subjective. One organization may view losses that occur once a month as moderate, while another would consider such frequency as definite. Similarly, one organization may view a $1 million loss as slight, while another might view it as severe. However, these categories can help insurance and risk management professionals prioritize loss exposures.

A loss exposure's frequency and severity tend to be inversely related. That is, the more severe a loss tends to be, the less frequently it tends to occur. Conversely, the more frequently a loss occurs to a given exposure, the less severe the loss tends to be.

Loss exposures that generate minor but definite losses are typically retained and incorporated in an organization's budget. At the other extreme, loss exposures that generate intolerably large losses are typically avoided. Therefore, most risk management decisions, such as whether to adopt the risk control and risk financing techniques shown in "The Prouty Approach" exhibit, concern loss exposures for which individual losses, although tolerable, tend to be either significant or severe and have a moderate, slight, or almost nil chance of occurring.

A given loss exposure might generate financially significant losses because of either high individual loss severity or high-frequency, low-severity losses that aggregate to a substantial total. Organizations may be tempted to focus on high-profile "shock events," such as a major fire, a violent explosion, or a huge liability claim. However, smaller losses, which happen so frequently that they become routine, can eventually produce much larger total losses than a single dramatic event. For example, many retail firms suffer greater total losses from shoplifting, which happens regularly, than they do from large fires that might happen once every twenty years. Minor, cumulatively significant losses usually deserve as much risk management attention as large individual losses.

Another way of jointly considering frequency and severity is to combine both frequency and severity distributions into a total claims distribution, which can provide additional information about potential losses that may occur in a given period. Combining distributions can be difficult because as the number of possible outcomes increases, the possible combinations of frequency and severity grow exponentially. See the exhibit "Total Claims Distribution for Hardware Store Shoplifting Losses."

The "Total Claims Distribution for Hardware Store Shoplifting Losses" exhibit presents a simple example of three possible frequencies (0, 1, and 2)

Total Claims Distribution for Hardware Store Shoplifting Losses

Frequency

	Number of Losses	Probability
F0	0	.33
F1	1	.33
F2	2	.34

Severity

	Dollar Loss	Probability
S1	$100	.33
S2	$250	.33
S3	$500	.34

Total Claims Distribution

Dollar Loss	Probability*	Probability Calculation		
$ 0	.33	p(F0)	←	There is only one possible way to have $0 losses: the frequency = 0.
100	.11	p(F1) × p(S1)	←	There is only one possible way to have $100 in losses: one $100 loss.
200	.04	p(F2) × p(S1) × p(S1)	←	There is only one possible way to have $200 in losses: two $100 losses.
250	.11	p(F1) × p(S2)	←	There is only one possible way to have $250 in losses: one $250 loss.
350	.07	[p(F2) × p(S1) × p(S2)] + [p(F2) × p(S2) × p(S1)]	←	There are two possible ways to have $350 in losses: one $100 loss and one $250 loss, or one $250 loss and one $100 loss.
500	.15	[p(F2) × p(S2) × p(S2)] + [p(F1) × p(S3)]	←	There are two possible ways to have $500 in losses: two $250 losses or one $500 loss.
600	.08	[p(F2) × p(S1) × p(S3)] + [p(F2) × p(S3) × p(S1)]	←	There are two possible ways to have $600 in losses: one $100 loss and one $500 loss, or one $500 loss and one $100 loss.
750	.08	[p(F2) × p(S2) × p(S3)] + [p(F2) × p(S3) × p(S2)]	←	There are two possible ways to have $750 in losses: one $250 loss and one $500 loss, or one $500 loss and one $250 loss.
1,000	.04	p(F2) × p(S3) × p(S3)	←	There is only one possible way to have $1,000 in losses: two $500 losses.

*Rounded

[DA02589]

and three possible severities ($100, $250, and $500) that represent shoplifting losses from a hardware store. The frequency and severity distributions for a given year are shown in the exhibit, along with the total claims distribution created by considering all the possible combinations of the frequency and severity distributions.

For example, a 33 percent chance exists of a loss not occurring during the year (frequency = 0). Therefore, in the total claims distribution, a 33 percent chance exists of the total losses being $0. There is only one possible way for a $100 loss to occur: a frequency of 1 and a severity of $100. Therefore, that probability is .11 [.33 (frequency 1) × .33 (severity $100) = .11]. There are two ways that the total claims for the year could equal $500. Either the organization could have one loss of $500, or it could have two losses of $250. Therefore, the probability of a $500 loss is the probability of one $500 loss plus the probability of two $250 losses.

A total claims distribution can be used to calculate the measures of central tendency and dispersion and evaluate the effect that various risk control and risk financing techniques would have on this loss exposure.

Total Dollar Losses

The third dimension to consider in analyzing loss exposures is total dollar losses, calculated by multiplying loss frequency by loss severity. Total dollar losses represent a simplified version of combining frequency and severity distributions and can be used when analyzing frequency and severity distributions that have multiple possible outcomes. See the exhibit "Total Dollar Losses."

Total Dollar Losses

Frequency

	Number of Losses	Probability
F0	0	.03
F1	1	.05
F2	2	.08
F3	3	.10
F4	4	.15
F5	5	.20
F6	6	.15
F7	7	.10
F8	8	.08
F9	9	.05
F10	10	.01

Severity

	Dollar Loss	Probability
S1	$100	.30
S2	$250	.25
S3	$500	.20
S4	$683	.15
S5	$883	.10

Expected value = $383.33.

Expected value = 4.9.

Expected total dollar losses = 4.9 × $383.33 = $1,878.33

Worst case total dollar losses = 9 × $883.00 = $7,950.00

[DA02590]

Expected total dollar losses can be projected by multiplying expected loss frequency by expected loss severity, while worst-case scenarios can be calculated by assuming both high frequency and the worst possible severity. For example, the "Total Dollar Losses" exhibit includes the frequency and severity distributions that were shown in the "Total Claims Distribution for Hardware Store Shoplifting Losses" exhibit if they were expanded to include more possible outcomes.

Combining the frequency and severity distributions in the exhibit would be difficult given the total number of possible combinations. An insurance or risk management professional could make some simpler calculations to determine what the potential total dollar losses may be. In this example, expected total dollar losses would be $1,878.33, and the worst-case scenario could be calculated as $7,950.00, using F9 in the exhibit. (F10 was not used, given its low probability.) These estimates could then be used in managing these loss exposures, such as evaluating whether to insure the loss exposures for the premium an insurer is quoting.

Timing

The fourth dimension to consider in analyzing loss exposures is timing of losses. Risk assessment requires considering not only when losses are likely to occur, but also when payment for those losses will likely be made. The timing dimension is significant because money held in reserve to pay for a loss can earn interest until the actual payment is made. Whether a loss is counted when it is incurred or when it is paid is also significant for various accounting and tax reasons that are beyond the scope of this discussion.

Funds to pay for property losses are generally disbursed relatively soon after the event occurs. In contrast, liability losses often involve long delays between the occurrence of the adverse event, when an occurrence is recognized, the period of possible litigation, and the time when payment is actually made. Damages for disability claims, for example, might be paid over a long period. In some cases, especially those involving environmental loss exposures or health risks, the delay can span several decades. Although this delay increases the uncertainty associated with the loss amount, it allows reserves to earn interest or investment income over a longer period of time.

Data Credibility

After analyzing the four dimensions of a loss exposure, an insurance or risk management professional then evaluates the credibility of the projections of loss frequency, loss severity, total dollar losses, and timing. The term data credibility refers to the level of confidence that available data can accurately indicate future losses. Two related data credibility issues may prevent data from being good indicators of future losses—the age of the data and whether the data represent actual losses or estimates of losses. See the exhibit "Assessing Credibility of Data."

Assessing Credibility of Data

There are several factors, both internal and external, that may influence data credibility for an organization. Internally, changes in the way that an organization operates, such as alterations to manufacturing processes or changes in data collection methods, may significantly reduce the credibility of previously collected data. Externally, events such as natural catastrophes, large liability awards, or terrorist attacks not only alter the data that are collected in that time frame, but also may cause shifts in the operating environment that render previously collected data less credible.

[DA02591]

Ideally, data used to forecast losses are generated in the same environment that will apply to the projected period. However, the environment for most loss exposures changes, even if those changes happen slowly. The changing environment renders more recent data a more credible predictor of future losses than older data. However, because of delays in reporting and paying of claims, more recent data are not always actual losses, but estimates of what the ultimate losses will be.

This leaves insurance and risk management professionals with a dilemma: Is it better to use older data, which are accurate but may have been generated in an environment that is substantially different from that of the period for which they are trying to predict, or to use more recent data and sacrifice some accuracy to maintain the integrity of the environment?

Once the projections are made along the four dimensions of loss exposures, the analysis of the loss exposures will often dictate which type of risk control or risk financing measures should be implemented. See the exhibit "Transportation Losses for a Large Shipper."

For example, the pattern shown in the "Transportation Losses for a Large Shipper" exhibit illustrates the expected transportation losses for a large shipper that has been in business for ten years and that has a steadily increasing volume of transportation services.

The average losses during the coming years might be projected to fall along the line labeled "projected," and the probable maximum loss might be projected to fall along the line labeled "maximum." Probable minimum loss levels might also be projected, as shown by the "minimum" line.

If such projections can be made with a high degree of confidence in the data used for the projections, actual losses would be expected to follow a pattern like the "actual" line on the graph, deviating from the average from one year to the next but in no case exceeding the maximum or falling below the minimum. Because the shipper can reasonably anticipate the degree of uncertainty, it may choose to retain these losses instead of insuring them.

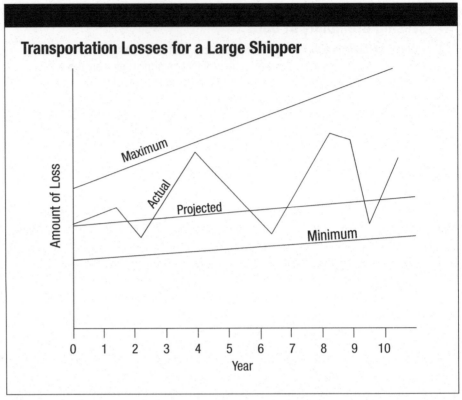

Transportation Losses for a Large Shipper

[DA02592]

Similarly, the "Product Liability Losses for a Large Manufacturer" exhibit represents products liability losses experienced by a large manufacturer. A few losses usually occur each year. However, in Year 4, almost no losses occurred, whereas, in Year 8, at least one major loss occurred. (The losses in Year 8 are so high that total losses exceeded even maximum projections.) It may have been possible to project these losses to a certain extent at lower levels, but possibilities existed for substantial losses above the expected and maximum levels. It might be disastrous to attempt to finance such losses solely out of the organization's operating budget. See the exhibit "Product Liability Losses for a Large Manufacturer."

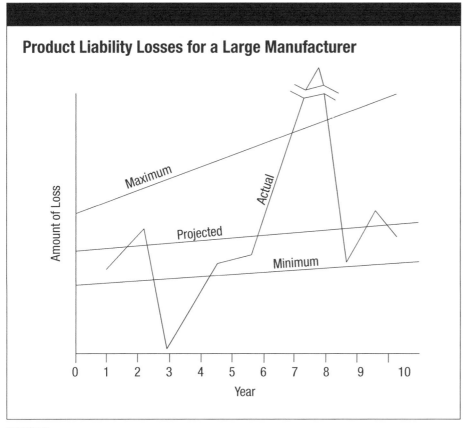

Product Liability Losses for a Large Manufacturer

[DA02593]

SUMMARY

Because identifying loss exposures is the beginning of the risk management process, it should be done thoroughly and systematically. Various methods can be used to identify loss exposures, including document analysis, compliance review, inspections, and expertise within and beyond the organization.

To accurately analyze loss exposures using data on past losses, the data should be relevant, complete, consistent, and organized.

The analysis step of the risk management process involves considering the four dimensions of a loss exposure: loss frequency, loss severity, total dollar losses, and timing.

Loss Reserving Techniques

Educational Objectives

After learning the content of this assignment, you should be able to:

▷ Describe the role of loss reserves, including the relationship over time between incurred losses, paid losses, reserves, and policyholders' surplus.

▷ Explain how case reserves are established for the following categories of loss reserves:

- Reported losses—payment certain

- Reported losses—payment uncertain

- Allocated loss adjustment expenses (ALAEs)

▷ Explain how bulk reserves are established for the following categories of loss reserves:

- Reported losses—payment uncertain

- IBNR reserves

- Loss adjustment expenses, both allocated and unallocated

▷ Describe the following combined methods that can be used to estimate loss reserves:

- Two-part combination method

- Bornhuetter-Ferguson method

- Three-part combination method

Loss Reserving Techniques

LOSS RESERVES

Loss reserves are an important factor in determining the financial condition of insurers. Accurate reserving practices are critical to the stability and solvency of insurers.

Because insurers rely on estimates called **loss reserves**, they have difficulty establishing amounts that accurately reflect future loss and expense payments. However, because losses are a large portion of the liabilities recorded on an insurer's balance sheet, reserve amounts directly affect policyholders' surplus and insurer profitability.

Loss and Loss Adjustment Expense Reserves

Insurers must establish loss reserves to cover the delay between the time a loss occurs and the time the loss is settled and the claim is paid. Once a claim has been reported to the insurer, time is required to investigate the loss to determine whether the incident is covered under the policy and then to negotiate an appropriate settlement. This delay is shorter for most property claims and is usually longer for third-party liability claims, which often involve litigation. For example, a products liability or medical malpractice claim may take several years to settle and close, while a kitchen fire under a homeowners policy is usually closed within a few months.

Loss reserves also include **loss adjustment expense (LAE)** amounts, related either to individual claim files or to the overall claim operation, that cannot be allocated to a specific claim file. The National Association of Insurance Commissioners (NAIC) categorizes these expenses as either Defense and Cost Containment (DCC) or Adjusting and Other (AO).[1] DCC includes expenses related to the defense and litigation of claims. AO includes all other expenses, such as adjusters' salaries and other fees and expenses. Previously, the terms **allocated loss adjustment expense (ALAE)** and **unallocated loss adjustment expense (ULAE)** had been used to categorize loss expenses.

Despite the change in terminology, many insurance professionals continue to use the former terms. DCC expenses are often related to ALAE, and AO expenses are related to ULAE. Because actuarial techniques used to estimate unpaid LAE consider whether an expense can be directly associated with a particular claim, most actuarial literature continues to categorize loss adjustment expenses as either ALAE or ULAE. **Loss adjustment expense reserves**

Loss reserve
An estimate of the amount of money the insurer expects to pay in the future for losses that have already occurred and been reported, but are not yet settled.

Loss adjustment expense (LAE)
The expense that an insurer incurs to investigate, defend, and settle claims according to the terms specified in the insurance policy.

Allocated loss adjustment expense (ALAE)
The expense an insurer incurs to investigate, defend, and settle claims that are associated with a specific claim.

Unallocated loss adjustment expense (ULAE)
Loss adjustment expense that cannot be readily associated with a specific claim.

Loss adjustment expense reserves
Estimates of the future expense that an insurer expects to incur to investigate, defend, and settle claims for losses that have already occurred.

are related to loss reserves and represent estimates of future expenses for settling outstanding claims.

Loss reserve amounts are only one component of an insurer's total loss amount. Loss and LAE reserves are combined with **paid losses** to arrive at an **incurred losses** amount.

Paid losses

Losses that have been paid to, or on behalf of, insureds during a given period.

Incurred losses

The losses that have occurred during a specific period, no matter when claims resulting from the losses are paid.

Incurred but not reported (IBNR) reserves

A reserve established for losses that reasonably can be assumed to have been incurred but not yet reported.

Incurred losses = Paid losses + Loss reserves + Loss adjustment expense reserves

Insurers also establish bulk (or aggregate) reserves to estimate (1) the growth in reported case reserves or an amount for reported losses for which case reserves are inadequate, (2) losses that are assumed to have happened but have not yet been reported, and (3) additional costs of claims that have been reopened after previously being settled and closed. These bulk reserve components are collectively known as **incurred but not reported (IBNR) reserves**.

Establishing reserves for losses that have not yet been reported is more difficult than establishing reserves for known cases. IBNR reserves are generally estimated based on past experience and then modified for current conditions, such as increased claims costs and the current frequency and severity of reported claims.

Life Cycle of Incurred Losses

Accident-year method

A method of organizing ratemaking statistics that uses incurred losses for an accident year, which consist of all losses related to claims arising from accidents that occur during the year, and that estimates earned premiums by formulas from accounting records.

Loss reserves amounts must be reviewed and updated to reflect changes in paid losses and loss expense amounts over time. Insurers periodically update their estimates of incurred losses for past years using different methods. One approach is to update losses using an **accident-year method**, which aggregates incurred losses for a given period (such as twelve months) using all incurred losses for insured events that occurred during that period. Any losses that occurred in previous periods are not included.

For example, accident-year data for the calendar year 20X6 would include all events that occurred in that year. Loss amounts for events that occur in subsequent years would not be included in this amount. As loss payments are made during the accident year, paid losses increase and reserves decrease by an equal amount. Therefore, incurred losses are unchanged. However, incurred losses do change when a reserve is increased or decreased because of new information on a claim or because a new claim is reported. An accident year's accounts can be kept open for many years until all losses that occurred in that year are fully paid.

Ultimate loss

The final paid amount for all losses in an accident year.

Insurers attempt to estimate accurate loss reserves as soon as possible after the end of an accident year. If loss reserves have been accurately estimated, then incurred losses should equal ultimate losses at that point in time. In practice, an accident year's incurred losses are often less than **ultimate loss** amounts for some time after the end of the accident year. Information received after the end of an accident year usually causes loss reserves to increase, also causing incurred losses to increase for the accident year. This situation might occur when an insurer has to make a large payment as a result of a court judgment many years after the date of loss. This payment may not have been anticipated when reserves were originally established, and this causes incurred losses to increase for the accident year. The increase or decrease of incurred losses over time is called **loss development**.

For example, actuaries can review the life cycle of incurred losses related to a single accident year. Based on this review, it is determined that incurred losses increased from zero months to seventy-two months after the start of the accident year, at which point incurred losses equaled the ultimate loss amount. The review also indicates that losses for the accident year were not fully paid until 108 months after the start of the accident year. See the exhibit "Life Cycle of Incurred Losses for a Single Accident Year."

Loss development

The increase or decrease of incurred losses over time.

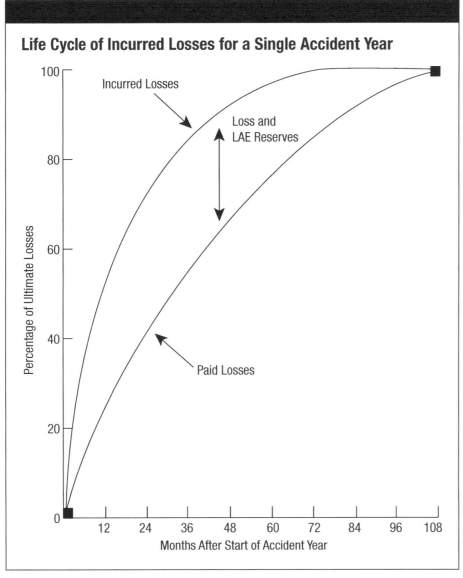

Life Cycle of Incurred Losses for a Single Accident Year

Incurred Losses

Loss and LAE Reserves

Paid Losses

Percentage of Ultimate Losses

Months After Start of Accident Year

[DA06229]

Implications of Inadequate Loss Reserves

Loss amounts are a key element on insurers' financial statements, and accurate claim reserving is critical to maintaining the insurer's financial strength. Underestimating or overestimating the final cost of claims can distort an insurer's financial condition. Continued underreserving of claims over several years can lead to insolvency or bankruptcy for an insurer. Establishing and maintaining adequate loss reserves is important for the insurer's financial health because reserves directly affect the insurer's ability to maintain existing business and to grow in the future.

In their review of insurer financial statements, state regulators focus on the continued solvency of the insurer and its ability to pay claims in the future. Regulators are, therefore, also concerned about the adequacy of loss reserves and about insurers with a history of understating loss reserves. Insurers that consistently overstate loss reserves may also be of concern to regulators because doing so may lead to unwarranted rate increases over time and to overpriced insurance products. Continued overstating of loss reserves could result in tax penalties relating to the taxes that would otherwise apply to the resulting deferred income.

Past claims payments are also the basis of future rates. As part of ratemaking, actuaries base future rates not only on the amount paid on both open and closed claims, but on the amount reserved for open claims and IBNR claims. Consistent and accurate loss reserving translates into insurance rates that accurately reflect future loss potential.

Challenges to Establishing Adequate Loss Reserves

One internal cause of inadequate loss reserves is errors on the part of claims personnel. These errors can occur in several ways, such as when initial reserves are determined based on incomplete or inaccurate information. Reserve inaccuracy can also be the result of a lack of expertise on the claims representative's part or an unwillingness to reevaluate the claim and adjust the loss reserve amount where appropriate. Lack of training for claims representatives or frequent turnover in the claims department can result in underreserving or overreserving of losses as well. Furthermore, management changes, changes in reserving guidelines, or restructuring of reinsurance programs can affect the adequacy of loss reserves.

Because reserves should reflect the ultimate cost of a claim and not the claim's present value, they should account for the claim's future settlement value. For example, a medical malpractice claim could take many years to settle and close. During that time, external factors such as inflation may increase medical costs, or new and expensive medical technology may be developed. Whenever possible, the reserves for such claims should anticipate those increased costs.

Other external causes of inadequate loss reserves include changes in legislation or regulation, which could, for example, increase workers compensation benefits. Judgments in court cases can lead to new case law and open emerging areas of coverage, such as environmental or construction defects claims. Because related claims would not previously have been contemplated under existing coverage forms, claims personnel would need to review claims files to determine whether to establish reserves.

Relationship Between Loss Reserves and Surplus

The difference between any organization's assets and its liabilities indicates its net worth. For insurers, this net worth is designated as policyholders' surplus. This means that all of an insurer's net worth is available to satisfy claims before any owner is entitled to funds. Loss reserves are one of the largest liabilities on an insurer's balance sheet and are shown under the "Losses" element. Loss adjustment expense reserves are included within the "Loss Adjustment Expenses" element of the balance sheet.

If reserves are too low, the difference between assets and liabilities will result in an overstated policyholders' surplus amount. Underreserving will also result in an overstated underwriting profit for that year. As claims are settled in the future and reserves are adjusted, future underwriting profits may decrease. Once inadequate reserves are properly recognized and the liabilities amount is corrected on the balance sheet, policyholders' surplus will be reduced. When reserve amounts are set too high, policyholders' surplus will be understated and will need to be increased once the reserves are properly recognized. This is a critical issue for insurers because policyholders' surplus is vital to insurer financial strength. See the exhibit "Principal Elements of an Insurer Balance Sheet."

Principal Elements of an Insurer Balance Sheet

Assets	Liabilities
Bonds	Losses
Stocks	Loss Adjustment Expenses
Cash	Unearned Premiums
Premium Balances	**Surplus and Other Funds**
Reinsurance Recoverables	Surplus as Regards Policyholders

[DA06230]

For example, an insurer with $10 million in reserves and policyholders' surplus of $5 million has a ratio of reserves to policyholders' surplus of 2 to 1. An error of 10 percent in estimating reserves would cause an error of 20 percent in the stated policyholders' surplus. If reserves were initially established at $10 million and later adjusted to $11 million, the effect on policyholders' surplus would be a 20 percent decrease, from $5 million to $4 million. See the exhibit "Effect of Understated Reserves on Policyholders' Surplus."

Effect of Understated Reserves on Policyholders' Surplus

Table 1—Primary Insurer Balance Sheet

Assets		Liabilities	
Cash	$25,000,000	Unearned Premiums	$10,000,000
		Reserves	10,000,000
		Policyholders' Surplus	5,000,000
Total Assets	$25,000,000	Total Liabilities and Surplus	$25,000,000

Table 2—Primary Insurer Balance Sheet With 10 Percent Adjustment to Reserves

Assets		Liabilities	
Cash	$25,000,000	Unearned Premiums	$10,000,000
		Reserves	11,000,000
		Policyholders' Surplus	4,000,000
Total Assets	$25,000,000	Total Liabilities and Surplus	$25,000,000

[DA06231]

METHODS FOR ESTABLISHING CASE RESERVES

To accurately report their financial position, insurers must estimate reserves as precisely as possible. However, estimating reserves is difficult because, in most cases, the amount that the insurer will eventually pay for a claim is uncertain. For example, the insurer may not know all the facts about the underlying claim when estimating its reserves.

Case reserve

A loss reserve assigned to an individual claim.

Bulk reserves

Reserves established for the settlement of an entire group of claims.

There are two general methods for establishing reserves for losses and loss adjustment expenses— **case reserves** and **bulk reserves**. For some categories of claims, reserves can be set using either the case or bulk reserve method. For example, in instances in which the amount of payment is uncertain for reported losses, loss reserves could be set for each individual loss (case) or for the whole group of losses (bulk).

With case reserves specifically, the primary insurer's claims department usually sets reserves. A claims file is established for each reported loss and includes an estimate of the ultimate loss that will be paid to the claimant. The claims representative's estimate of the ultimate loss, less any payments already made, makes up the case loss reserve for the file. Allocated loss adjustment expense reserves can also be established for each individual claim.

Case reserves can be established for these categories of loss reserves:

- Reported losses–payment certain
- Reported losses–payment uncertain
- Allocated loss adjustment expenses (ALAEs)

Reported Losses—Payment Certain

The reserve for reported losses for which the amount of payment is certain is the easiest of the loss reserves to calculate. Because the claimant and the insurer have already agreed on the amount of the payment, calculating this type of reserve is simply a matter of adding the agreed settlement amounts for all claims. Calculating reserves in the other categories is more complex.

Reported Losses—Payment Uncertain

More expertise is necessary to determine the amount to reserve for reported losses for which the amount of payment is uncertain. The insurer must estimate the ultimate loss using known information about the claim, historical loss data for similar claims, and the judgment of the individual making the estimate. If the claimant later reports additional facts that will affect the value of the claim, the insurer must adjust the reserve accordingly.

Three methods are commonly used to determine the case loss reserves for reported losses when the amount of payment is uncertain:

- Judgment method
- Average method
- Tabular method

Judgment Method

The first method of determining case loss reserves is the judgment method. With the **judgment method**, a claims representative estimates the value of each claim based mostly on professional experience. This method does not involve any statistical analysis.

Judgment method
A method to establish a case loss reserve based largely on experience with similar claims.

One weakness of the judgment method is that the accuracy of its results depends on the quality and extent of the claims representative's experience. Two people may estimate vastly different figures for the same loss. Even reserves established by the same person for similar losses could vary from time to time.

Average Method

The second method for determining case loss reserves is based on statistical data and is generally called the **average method** or the factor method. Through this method, the case reserve for specific categories of claims is set at

Average method
A method to establish a case reserve by using an average amount for specific categories of claims.

an average amount that is based on an analysis of past claims and is trended for inflationary changes, changes in amounts insured, and other factors that may cause future payments to differ from past payments.

The average method is most suitable for types of insurance in which claims are relatively frequent, reported and paid promptly, and not subject to extreme variations. Automobile physical damage is an example of a type of insurance with these characteristics. For example, every auto collision claim may be reserved at a value of $1,500, and that value is not changed until the claim is paid. The insurer may feel that setting more accurate reserves on this type of claim is not worth the expense associated with the extra effort.

Under the average method, reserves for some individual claims are inadequate, and reserves for other claims are excessive. However, if the average is accurate, the aggregate loss reserve accurately reflects the ultimate loss amounts for all outstanding claims.

If used alone, the average method may produce inadequate reserves for those types of liability insurance that have a wide variation in claims amounts and long delays in settlements (such as medical malpractice insurance and product liability insurance). In these cases, the average method and the judgment method are sometimes used together. Using this combined reserving approach, an average value is assigned to each claim as soon as it is reported. For example, every auto bodily injury claim may initially be reserved for an average value of $10,000. In sixty days, or as soon as additional information becomes available on the claim, the reserve is adjusted, based on judgment.

Tabular Method

Tabular method

A case reserving method that establishes an average amount for all claims that have similar characteristics in terms of the claimant's age, health, and marital status.

The third method of determining case loss reserves is the **tabular method**. This method is useful for calculating case loss reserves for lost income benefits under workers compensation insurance or for calculating structured settlement amounts under liability insurance.

The tabular method uses rates and factors from one or more actuarial tables to calculate the present value of future loss payments. This present value amount becomes the case loss reserve for those payments. These tables are examples of those that can be used:

• Morbidity tables, showing the likelihood of sickness or injury

• Mortality tables, showing the likelihood of death

• Annuity tables, showing the likelihood of survival

• Remarriage tables, showing the likelihood of remarriage by a widow or widower [2]

Each case loss reserve calculated by the tabular method can be considered an average reserve for all claims with the same characteristics (for example, claimants with the same age, health, and marital status). Consequently, the tabular method is likely to yield an appropriate total reserve for a large number of individual claims—even though the case reserve for any given claim can vary substantially from the amount ultimately paid for that claim. The primary weakness of the tabular method is that its applicability is limited to situations in which a fixed amount of benefits is paid over a period of time, such as a person's life; however, in these types of situations, it is the preferred method. See the exhibit "Calculating Case Reserves by Using the Tabular Method: An Example."

Calculating Case Reserves by Using the Tabular Method: An Example

Suppose a lost income benefit of $300 per week for life is payable to a fifty-year-old permanently disabled male worker. A case loss reserve for this benefit can be calculated by using mortality tables and present value factors. Mortality tables can be used to derive one-year probabilities of survival at each age. Because this person is disabled, the factors in the mortality table may need to be adjusted to reflect the mortality rates for disabled persons. Special mortality tables for this purpose have been developed. Using present value factors and the results of the mortality table values, actuaries can calculate the present value factor for an annual annuity of $1 payable to this person for life. Assume this present value factor is 16.412. The case reserve is calculated by multiplying the present value factor by the annual benefit amount. In this example, the case reserve would be $256,027 ($300 per week × 52 weeks × 16.412).

[DA09061]

Allocated Loss Adjustment Expenses (ALAEs)

Case reserves for ALAE can be established by using the judgment method or by adding a fixed percentage to each case loss reserve. The judgment method of establishing case reserves for ALAE suffers from the same weaknesses as the judgment method of establishing case loss reserves. For some types of insurance, simply adding a percentage to each loss reserve can produce accurate aggregate reserves for ALAE.

Correcting Case Reserves

At any point in time, the total case reserves for reported losses are likely to be inadequate because they tend to develop, or increase, over time.

One method for correcting inadequate total case reserves is to increase the case reserve for each claim. The simplest way to do this is to add the same percentage to each. These increases are often called "additional case reserves."

A more time-consuming method of correcting understated case reserves is to review each open claims file, increasing only those reserves that are inadequate. This approach assumes that either the reviewers can more accurately determine loss reserve amounts than those who established the original claim reserve or more information has become available on the claim.

For their own financial reporting purposes, reinsurers may supplement the primary insurer's case reserves. A reinsurer's claims personnel may review the primary insurer's claim files and add amounts that they feel are necessary to account for loss development. The reinsurer's total case reserves would then consist of the primary insurer's case reserves and the reinsurer's additional case reserves.

METHODS FOR ESTABLISHING BULK RESERVES

An insurer usually cannot identify specific claims with inadequate or excessive case reserves or predict which claims will reopen. Therefore, insurers make a general provision for additional reserves, called bulk reserves. For some types of insurance, the bulk reserves can be a substantial part of an insurer's total liabilities.

Typically determined by an actuary, bulk reserves can be established for these categories of loss reserves:

- Reported losses—payment uncertain
- Incurred but not reported (IBNR) reserves
- Loss adjustment expenses, both allocated and unallocated

Reported Losses—Payment Uncertain

Reserves for reported losses when the amount of payment is uncertain can be calculated on a bulk basis by subtracting the amount already paid for losses from a certain percentage of total earned premium. For example, an actuary may estimate general liability losses at 70 percent of an earned premium of $13 million, or $9.1 million. However, if $3 million has already been paid on these losses, then this amount is subtracted from the reserve, reducing the reserve from $9.1 million to $6.1 million.

IBNR Reserves

Incurred but not reported (IBNR) losses are losses that have occurred but have not yet been reported to the insurer. Because these losses have occurred, IBNR reserves are established and reflect estimates of unknown future loss payments. The IBNR loss category also includes a reserve for reported losses that are expected to develop; that is, the final payment for these losses is expected to exceed the amount for which they are currently reserved. (This component of IBNR is sometimes called IBNER: incurred but not enough reserved.)

For liability insurance, IBNR reserves are difficult to estimate because tremendous uncertainty exists regarding the number and size of losses yet to be reported and the development of reported losses.

A primary insurer usually has a liability for IBNR losses. Because estimating the number and average size of individual claims that may be reported late is difficult, IBNR reserves are, by their nature, a bulk reserve. IBNR reserves are residual reserves because, at any point in time, they equal the difference between incurred losses and ultimate losses. This formula shows the relationship:

IBNR reserves = Ultimate losses – Reported incurred losses

Three basic methods of estimating IBNR reserves exist, along with many acceptable alternative approaches:

- Loss ratio method
- Percentage method
- Loss triangle method

Loss Ratio Method

The first method of estimating IBNR reserves is the loss ratio method. This method assumes that the ultimate loss ratio will equal the loss ratio that was considered when calculating premium rates. Therefore, if the premium rates assumed a loss ratio of 80 percent, the ultimate losses are assumed to equal 80 percent of earned premiums. Deducting paid and reserved amounts for reported losses from the ultimate loss amounts yields the IBNR reserve.

The loss ratio method may be useful in the early stages of developing IBNR reserves for long-tail liability insurance. However, the loss ratio method should be used only for the first year or two after losses are incurred. More sophisticated and responsive methods should be used as soon as the actual reported losses provide an adequate basis for projecting IBNR reserves.

One weakness of the loss ratio method is that the actual loss ratio seldom equals the anticipated loss ratio. In fact, the difference between them can be substantial. If the actual loss ratio is less than the anticipated loss ratio, the loss ratio method results in redundant reserves. If the actual loss ratio is greater than the anticipated loss ratio, the method results in inadequate reserves. Furthermore, if the premium rates charged were inadequate (as evidenced by an underwriting loss), the reinsurer needs to recognize the inadequate subject premium rates used by the primary insurer when calculating the anticipated loss ratio.

Despite these weaknesses, the loss ratio method is often used in the early stages of development for long-tail liability insurance because, during this time, the loss triangle method is not completely reliable. After twenty-four months, the loss triangle method is likely to be more reliable than the loss ratio method.

Percentage Method

The second method of estimating IBNR reserves is the percentage method. This method uses historical relationships between IBNR reserves and reported losses to develop percentages that are used in IBNR forecasts. For example, if the IBNR losses were 30 percent of total incurred losses over a period of years, IBNR losses for a particular year may be estimated at 30 percent of incurred losses for that year. In its application, the percentage method develops a separate percentage for each accident year. If the trend (upward or downward) in the percentage of IBNR losses is measurable, the percentage used for projecting IBNR losses should reflect that trend.

The number of months necessary for losses to develop to their ultimate level varies depending on the type of insurance. The percentage method is acceptable for estimating property loss reserves because they can be estimated with reasonable accuracy soon after they are reported. It is likely to be less accurate for liability loss reserves, which typically take longer to develop.

The exhibit shows an IBNR calculation using the percentage method. In this example, IBNR losses are assumed to equal 20 percent of reported losses for the most recent accident year—twelve months of development (twelve months after the start of the policy year), 10 percent for the prior accident year—twenty-four months of development, and 5 percent for the next prior accident year—thirty-six months of development. Losses are assumed to be fully developed at forty-eight months after the start of the accident year. The IBNR reserve for each accident year is calculated by multiplying the reported losses for that accident year by the IBNR factor. The total IBNR reserve for the four accident years is $1,723,258. See the exhibit "Calculation of IBNR Reserve for X4 From Hypothetical Data Using the Percentage Method."

Calculation of IBNR Reserve for X4 From Hypothetical Data Using the Percentage Method

Historical Accident Year	Reported Losses ($)	Evaluation Point (Months of Development)	IBNR Factor	IBNR Reserve ($)
X1	4,725,679	48	0.00	0
X2	4,887,963	36	0.05	244,398
X3	4,878,845	24	0.10	487,885
X4	4,954,876	12	0.20	990,975
Total	$19,447,363			$1,723,258

[DA09067]

Loss Triangle Method

The third method for estimating IBNR reserves is the loss triangle method, which is also known as the loss development method, the chain link method, the chain ladder method, and the link ratio method. The loss triangle method uses historical loss data to calculate loss development factors with which to estimate IBNR reserves. This method is commonly used to determine IBNR reserves for liability insurance, particularly liability insurance that requires many years to fully develop. The loss triangle method is subject to wide variability in the first year or two of loss development and is more complex than the other reserving methods already presented. As with all loss reserving methods, this method will not produce reliable results unless the historical data and the actuarial assumptions are accurate.

A loss triangle is a display of historical loss data in the shape of a triangle. The data usually consist of the total reported losses for each historical year, although other data can be used, such as losses paid, number of claims paid, or average claim size. The nature of the estimates derived from a loss triangle depends on the data used in the triangle. The data in a reported losses triangle are used to project the development of total loss amounts for each historical year. IBNR loss reserves can then be derived based on this projected loss development. Because loss triangles analyze historical loss development patterns to forecast future loss development, a major assumption of the loss triangle method is that the historical pattern of development will continue.

The loss data used in a loss triangle may or may not include allocated loss adjustment expense (ALAE) information. If the loss data include ALAE, then the forecasted loss amounts will also include it. (In some cases, separate loss triangles are used to estimate ALAE.)

These are the four major steps for calculating IBNR reserves from a loss triangle:

1. Organize historical data in a loss triangle format
2. Calculate twelve-month loss development factors from the loss triangle
3. Calculate ultimate loss development factors from the twelve-month development factors
4. Use ultimate loss development factors to calculate the IBNR reserve

The first step in the loss triangle method is to organize historical data in a loss triangle format. A simplified loss triangle using the severity of reported losses is shown in the exhibit. This loss triangle is based on incurred losses not including ALAE, and it assumes that ultimate losses can be accurately estimated at seventy-two months after the start of an accident year. See the exhibit "Loss Triangle Based on Incurred Losses ($000)."

Each row of data in the "Loss Triangle Based on Incurred Losses ($000)" exhibit shows historical estimates of the incurred loss amounts for the accident year shown at the left end of the row. For example, the first row shows data for accident year X1. On December 31, X1 (twelve months after the

Loss Triangle Based on Incurred Losses ($000)

Accident Year	Months of Development (after beginning of accident year)					
	12	24	36	48	60	72 Ultimate
X1	10,000	10,200	10,300	10,350	10,375	10,375
X2	12,000	12,300	12,500	12,600	12,650	12,650
X3	14,000	14,500	14,750	14,850	14,900	
X4	16,000	16,600	16,900	17,050		
X5	18,000	18,800	19,200			
X6	20,000	21,000				
X7	22,000					

[DA09068]

start of the X1 accident year), the primary insurer estimated its incurred losses for accident year X1 to be $10,000,000. On December 31, X2 (twenty-four months after the start of the X1 accident year), the estimate for X1 accident-year losses had increased to $10,200,000. By December 31, X6 (seventy-two months after the start of the X1 accident year), the estimate for X1 losses had reached $10,375,000. At that point, the primary insurer assumed that the incurred losses reserves for accident year X1 had reached their ultimate value.

The lowest diagonal of the table, running from $22,000,000 on the left to $12,650,000 on the right, shows the estimate for each year's losses as of December 31, X7, the latest year for which data are available. On December 31, X8, another diagonal of severity data should be added below the figures in the table.

The second step in the loss triangle method is to calculate twelve-month loss development factors from the loss triangle. The exhibit uses data in the "Loss Triangle Based on Incurred Losses ($000)" exhibit to calculate loss development factors based on changes in incurred losses over successive twelve-month periods. These factors are called twelve-month loss development factors (also known as age-to-age loss development factors and link ratios). For example, the first factor for X1 (1.020) shows the change in the company's estimates of X1 accident-year losses from December 31, X1, to December 31, X2. It was calculated by dividing the twenty-four month figure for X1 by the twelve-month figure for X1 ($10,200,000 ÷ $10,000,000 = 1.020). Each of the other figures in this exhibit's triangle was calculated in the same manner. The X7 year has no twelve-month loss development factor because two successive estimates are required to calculate a loss development factor, and only one estimate is available. See the exhibit "Calculating Twelve-Month Loss Development Factors."

Calculating Twelve-Month Loss Development Factors

Accident Year	Twelve-Month Loss Development Factors				
	12 to 24	24 to 36	36 to 48	48 to 60	60 to Ultimate
X1	1.020	1.010	1.005	1.002	1.000
X2	1.025	1.016	1.008	1.004	1.000
X3	1.036	1.017	1.007	1.003	
X4	1.038	1.018	1.009		
X5	1.044	1.021			
X6	1.050				
Average	1.036	1.016	1.007	1.003	1.000
5-Year Average	1.039	1.016	1.007	1.003	1.000
3-Year Average	1.044	1.019	1.008	1.003	1.000
Selected	1.044	1.019	1.008	1.003	1.000

[DA09069]

The lower section of the "Calculating Twelve-Month Loss Development Factors" exhibit shows the derivation of twelve-month loss development factors that are used to estimate ultimate loss amounts for each historical accident year. The row labeled "Average" shows the average of all of the twelve-month loss development factors above it. The next row shows the average of the twelve-month factors for the five most recent years above it.[3] The third row shows the average of the twelve-month loss development factors for the three most recent years.

The last row in the "Calculating Twelve-Month Loss Development Factors" exhibit, labeled "Selected," shows the twelve-month factors that an analyst may choose. Selecting twelve-month factors is a matter of judgment. In the exhibit, the averages show an increasing trend. That is, the three-year average is greater than the five-year average, and, in the first column, the five-year average is greater than the overall average. Therefore, an analyst would probably select the largest of the three averages, without modification. See the exhibit "Selecting Twelve-Month Loss Development Factors."

The third step in the loss triangle development method is to calculate **ultimate loss development factors** from the twelve-month loss development factors. The exhibit shows the calculation of ultimate loss development factors. Each selected factor from the "Calculating Twelve-Month Loss Development Factors" exhibit is multiplied by the other selected factors to its right to calculate an ultimate loss development factor. See the exhibit "Calculating Ultimate Loss Development Factors."

Ultimate loss development factor

A factor that is applied to the most recent estimate of incurred losses for a specific accident year to estimate the ultimate incurred loss for that year.

Selecting Twelve-Month Loss Development Factors

The selection process involves comparing the average factors for various periods, such as those used in the "Calculating Twelve-Month Loss Development Factors" exhibit. The time periods used reflect the types of claims being estimated. The following approach may be helpful in selecting a factor:

- If the three averages show an increasing trend, select the largest factor.
- If the three averages show a decreasing trend, select the smallest factor.
- If the three averages do not show a trend, select the factor intermediate in value.

A selected factor can be adjusted if, in the actuary's opinion, it is inconsistent with the loss data or other adjacent factors. For example, most actuaries would expect each twelve-month loss development factor to be smaller than the factor immediately preceding it because as losses age, loss development tends to slow down. For example, for X1, the twenty-four-to-thirty-six-month factor (1.010) is lower than the twelve-to-twenty-four-month factor (1.020).

[DA09070]

Calculating Ultimate Loss Development Factors

Time Period	Ultimate Loss Development Factor
60 Months to Ultimate	$1.000 = 1.000$
48 Months to Ultimate	$1.003 \times 1.000 = 1.003$
36 Months to Ultimate	$1.008 \times 1.003 \times 1.000 = 1.011$
24 Months to Ultimate	$1.019 \times 1.008 \times 1.003 \times 1.000 = 1.030$
12 Months to Ultimate	$1.044 \times 1.019 \times 1.008 \times 1.003 \times 1.000 = 1.076$

[DA09071]

The fourth step in the loss triangle method is to use ultimate loss development factors to calculate the IBNR reserve. Multiplying the ultimate loss development factor from the "Calculating Ultimate Loss Development Factors" exhibit by the latest evaluation of losses for each year ("Loss Triangle Based on Incurred Losses ($000)" exhibit) gives an estimate of ultimate losses for each accident year, as shown in column 5 of the exhibit. The IBNR reserve (column 6) is calculated by subtracting incurred and reported losses (column 2) from estimated ultimate losses (column 5). See the exhibit "Calculating IBNR Reserves Using Loss Development Factors."

The data in the "Loss Triangle Based on Incurred Losses ($000)" exhibit are consistent, making it easy for the analyst to arrive at reasonable loss development factors. Most loss triangles are less consistent and include anomalous data items.

Calculating IBNR Reserves Using Loss Development Factors

(1) Historical Accident Year	(2) Incurred and Reported Losses ($000)	(3) Months of Development	(4) Ultimate Loss Development Factor	(5) Estimated Ultimate Losses ($000)	(6) IBNR Reserve ($000)
X1	10,375	72	1.000	10,375	0
X2	12,650	72	1.000	12,650	0
X3	14,900	60	1.000	14,900	0
X4	17,050	48	1.003	17,101	51
X5	19,200	36	1.011	19,411	211
X6	21,000	24	1.030	21,630	630
X7	22,000	12	1.076	23,672	1,672
Total	$117,175			$119,739	$2,564

[DA09072]

Such anomalies may result from chance variations in loss frequency or severity, from changes in rules of law, or from delays in adjusting claims. They may also result from conscious decisions made by claim personnel to increase or decrease the level of case reserves, as well as from changes to the level of case reserves resulting from shifting responsibilities in the claims handling process.

Systematic increases in loss reserves over time indicate a consistent practice of carrying inadequate case reserves. These systematic increases create larger than normal loss development factors.

After a period of systematic increases in loss reserves, knowing whether the reserves are still inadequate, or whether they are now correct, is difficult. However, the typical assumption is that the reserves are still inadequate. The loss triangle itself does not indicate the adequacy of loss reserves. That determination requires a careful analysis of individual claims files or, in many cases, additional data on individual claims.

Loss Adjustment Expenses

Bulk reserves can be used for both ALAE and unallocated loss adjustment expense (ULAE).

Allocated Loss Adjustment Expense

Bulk reserves for ALAE can be estimated by applying a percentage factor to either earned premiums or incurred losses. The percentage factor is determined by analyzing the insurer's experience. For example, if experience shows that ALAE averages 25 percent of incurred losses, then 25 percent is applied to current incurred losses to estimate the reserve for ALAE.

One disadvantage of this method of estimating ALAE is that the calculation assumes no changes have occurred that affect the factor. If changes have occurred, the factor must be adjusted. Another disadvantage results from the manner in which losses are usually settled. Small losses, especially those settled without payment, are usually settled more quickly than large losses. Consequently, total loss reserves at any given time are likely to include a disproportionate number of large losses. Because large losses usually involve proportionately more ALAE than small losses, the percentage method may underestimate the ALAE reserve. Calculating ALAE using the loss triangle method may overcome this problem.

Unallocated Loss Adjustment Expense

By definition, ULAE cannot be attributed to specific claims. Consequently, the reserve for such expenses must be estimated on a bulk basis. The reserve for ULAE is usually estimated as a percentage of the sum of incurred losses and ALAE. The insurer determines the percentage based on experience.

Because ULAE consists of budgeted items, the total amount to be paid in a given year is easy to estimate at the beginning of the year. However, some of the ULAE paid in a given year is related to losses incurred in earlier years, particularly for long-tail liability insurance. Allocating current expenses to prior accident years is common, but such allocations may distort current accident year expense.

COMBINED METHODS OF LOSS RESERVING

No single reserving method can produce the best loss reserve estimates in all situations. Every reserving method is based on certain underlying assumptions, which may or may not be satisfied in a given situation. Thus, several methods should be considered, when possible; in many cases, the various methods of loss reserving are combined to leverage their strengths and improve the accuracy of loss reserve estimates.

These combined methods, among others, can be used to estimate loss reserves:

- Two-part combination method
- Bornhuetter-Ferguson method
- Three-part combination method

Two-Part Combination Method

To realize the advantages of both the loss ratio method and the loss triangle method, some actuaries have suggested that a weighted average of the two methods be used with weights varying by the number of months after the start of the policy year. The exhibit shows a set of weights that may be used for estimating liability loss reserves. See the exhibit "Weights for Combining the Loss Ratio Method and the Loss Triangle Method."

Weights for Combining the Loss Ratio Method and the Loss Triangle Method

Months of Development (after start of accident year)	Weights	
	Loss Ratio Method	Loss Triangle Method
12	100%	0%
24	50%	50%
36	25%	75%
48	10%	90%
60 or more	0%	100%

[DA09062]

At the end of the accident year (twelve months of development), the reserve would be based entirely on the loss ratio method because the reported loss data are not mature enough to estimate ultimate losses using the loss triangle method. Starting at twenty-four months of development, the loss reserve can be partially based on the loss triangle method. At sixty months of development and thereafter, the reserve is based solely on the loss triangle method.

The weights shown in the "Weights for Combining the Loss Ratio Method and the Loss Triangle Method" exhibit are based on judgment. Different weights could be selected for different types of insurance.

Bornhuetter-Ferguson Method

A variation of the two-part combination method that does not rely on judgmental weights is called the Bornhuetter-Ferguson method. The Bornhuetter-Ferguson method estimates the incurred but not reported (IBNR) reserve using expected losses and an IBNR factor. It is frequently used when the losses reported to the insurer are not sufficiently mature to use the loss triangle method. Immature loss data occurs because of the delay between the time a loss occurs and when it is reported to the insurer. This delay is more pronounced for liability insurance than for property insurance.

Likewise, reinsurers experience an even longer delay in loss reporting because they establish reserves only after the primary insurer does. Losses arising out of casualty excess of loss treaties generally suffer the most delay. The reinsurer's reported losses can be zero for the first two or three years before retentions are exceeded and primary insurers report known claims to their reinsurers.

One weakness of the Bornhuetter-Ferguson method is the level of inherent subjectivity that is involved in selecting IBNR factors, which can be estimated using a variety of techniques applied to industry data or historical insurer data. Even small changes in assumptions can cause wide variations in IBNR reserves and thereby net income, sometimes changing a profit to a loss, or vice versa.

The exhibit illustrates how the Bornhuetter-Ferguson method is used to calculate IBNR loss reserves for a casualty excess of loss treaty. The ultimate earned premiums (column 2) are multiplied by an initial expected loss ratio (column 3) to yield initial expected losses (column 4). Then an expected percentage of unreported losses (column 5)—an estimate of losses that have occurred but have not yet been reported to the reinsurer—derived from loss development factors is multiplied by the initial expected losses (column 4) to yield expected IBNR reserves (column 6). See the exhibit "Bornhuetter-Ferguson Method—Casualty Excess of Loss Treaty."

Bornhuetter-Ferguson Method—Casualty Excess of Loss Treaty

(1)	(2)	(3)	(4)	(5)	(6)
Accident Year	Ultimate Earned Premiums ($000)	Initial Expected Loss Ratio	Initial Expected Losses ($000)	Expected Percentage of Unreported Losses (%)	IBNR Reserves ($000)
X0	13,940	0.70	9,758	14.5	1,415
X1	13,940	0.75	10,455	17.8	1,861
X2	13,940	0.85	11,849	22.5	2,666
X3	19,110	0.95	18,155	30.8	5,592
X4	15,870	1.10	17,457	42.3	7,384
X5	15,870	1.15	18,251	56.3	10,275
X6	19,110	0.85	16,244	72.7	11,809
X7	31,310	0.80	25,048	82.5	20,665
Total	$143,090		$127,217		$61,667

Column 2 is obtained by applying the loss triangle method to earned premiums.

The expected loss ratios in column 3 are adjusted for the premium adequacy level for each year relative to the current year.

Column 5 is derived from loss development factors.

Data provided by Jerome E. Tuttle, FCAS, FCIA, CPCU, ARM, ARe, AIM, Senior Vice President & Senior Pricing Actuary, Platinum Underwriters Reinsurance, Inc. [DA09063]

For example, in the "Bornhuetter-Ferguson Method—Casualty Excess of Loss Treaty" exhibit, in the year X5, the ultimate earned premium is estimated to be $15,870,000. Because of inadequate pricing in X5, the initial expected loss ratio (column 3) is 1.15. Multiplying the two figures yields initial expected losses (column 4) of $18,250,500. The $18,250,500 is multiplied by 56.3 percent (column 5), which is the projected percentage of losses that have been incurred but not yet reported to the reinsurer under the treaty, to yield the indicated IBNR reserves for X5 under the treaty of $10,275,032 (column 6).

Three-Part Combination Method

The three-part combination method combines the loss ratio method, the loss triangle method, and case loss reserves. This combination therefore requires three sets of weights. The weights are set so that they place most or all of the emphasis on the loss ratio method in the first year. Thereafter, the loss ratio method is phased out, and the loss triangle method is phased in. Subsequently, the loss triangle method is phased out, and more weight is placed on case loss reserves. Finally, when all losses have been reported and only a few remain open, the reserve is based entirely on case loss reserves.

This emphasis on case loss reserves is based on the belief that in the final stages of development, case reserves are likely to be more accurate than bulk reserves. The exhibit shows a set of weights that may be used for a three-part combination. The weights are based on judgment. See the exhibit "Sample Weights for the Three-Part Combination Method."

Sample Weights for the Three-Part Combination Method

Months of Development	Loss Ratio Method (%)	Loss Triangle Method (%)	Case Reserves (%)
12	100	0	0
24	50	50	0
36	25	75	0
48	0	100	0
60	0	100	0
72	0	100	0
84	0	100	0
96	0	100	0
108	0	90	10
120	0	75	25
132	0	50	50
144	0	25	75
156 or more	0%	0%	100%

SUMMARY

Insurers establish loss reserves to reflect amounts that will be needed in the future to pay claims that have occurred but are not yet closed. Inadequate loss reserves can lead to overstating or understating an insurer's profitability.

Case reserves are reserves established for the settlement of an individual claim. They can be established for three categories of loss reserves: reported losses–payment certain, reported losses–payment uncertain, and allocated loss adjustment expenses. The three general methods of establishing case loss reserves when the amount of payment is uncertain are the judgment method; the average, or factor, method; and the tabular method.

Bulk reserves are reserves established for settling an entire group of claims. They can be established for three categories of loss reserves: reported losses–payment uncertain; IBNR reserves; and loss adjustment expenses, both allocated and unallocated. The three basic methods of establishing IBNR reserves are the loss ratio method, the percentage method, and the loss triangle method.

Methods of loss reserving can be combined to leverage the strengths of two or more methods. Combination methods include the two-part combination method, the Bornhuetter-Ferguson method, and the three-part combination method.

ASSIGNMENT NOTES

1. National Association of Insurance Commissioners, Accounting Practices and Procedures Manual, vol. III, Statutory Issue Paper no. 55 (Washington, D.C.: National Association of Insurance Commissioners, 2009), p. IP-55-2.
2. (1) The remarriage table is used only if the provisions of the insurance policy state that benefits are terminated by remarriage.
3. Because of the abbreviated nature of this exhibit, the average of all years and the average for five years are the same except for the first column. This would not usually be the case in practice.

6

Ratemaking Techniques

Educational Objectives

After learning the content of this assignment, you should be able to:

▹ Describe the insurer goals of ratemaking and the ideal characteristics of rates.

▹ Describe the components of an insurance rate and common ratemaking terms.

▹ Explain how the following factors can affect ratemaking:

- Estimation of losses

- Delays in data collection and use

- Change in the cost of claims

- Insurer's projected expenses

- Target level of profit and contingencies

▹ Describe the following ratemaking methods:

- Pure premium

- Loss ratio

- Judgment

▹ Describe each of the following steps in the ratemaking process:

- Collect data

- Adjust data

- Calculate the indicated overall rate change

- Determine territorial and class relativities

- Prepare and submit rate filings to regulatory authorities as required

6

▷ Explain how the following ratemaking factors vary by type of insurance:

- Experience period
- Trending
- Large loss limitations
- Credibility
- Increased limits factors

Ratemaking Techniques

6

INSURER RATEMAKING GOALS

Insurance ratemaking is challenging, because when rates are developed, the amounts of fortuitous future losses and their associated expenses are unknown. In light of this uncertainty, insurers try to develop rates that meet their goals.

With the ratemaking process, insurers strive to be profitable while also meeting all insurance policy obligations. An ideal insurance rate has a number of different characteristics, including some that are contradictory.

Ratemaking Goals

From the insurer's perspective, the primary goal of **ratemaking** is to develop a rate structure that enables the insurer to compete effectively while earning a reasonable profit on its operations. To accomplish this, the rates must result in premiums that adequately cover all losses and expenses and that leave a reasonable amount for profits and contingencies.

This ratemaking goal complements the underwriting goal, which is to develop and maintain a profitable book of business. To be profitable, the insurer must have adequate rates. However, to maintain its book of business, the insurer's rates must be competitive. These goals can easily conflict with each other. The rate chosen by an insurer is often a compromise between maximizing profit and maintaining (or expanding) market share.

To be approved, rates must comply with applicable regulations. Rate regulation is generally based on having rates that are adequate, not excessive, and not unfairly discriminatory.

Ideal Characteristics of Rates

Ideally, rates should have five characteristics:

- Be stable
- Be responsive
- Provide for contingencies
- Promote risk control
- Reflect differences in risk exposure

Rates do not always have all of these characteristics. Also, some characteristics conflict with others, and compromises are often necessary. For example,

Ratemaking
The process insurers use to calculate insurance rates, which are a premium component.

rate stability could conflict with the characteristic of responsiveness, which suggests that rates should change promptly in response to external factors that affect losses.

Stable

Stable rates are highly desirable because changing rates is expensive. It takes a fair amount of time and expense to calculate rate indications, get needed approval, and implement them. Generally, rates are changed no more than annually. Rates should also be stable in the sense of not changing drastically from one rate change to the next. Sudden large rate changes cause dissatisfaction among customers and sometimes lead to regulatory or legislative actions.

Responsive

Rates should include the best possible estimates of losses and expenses that will arise from the coverage. Because external conditions change over time, the most recent claim experience ought to predict future experience better than older experience. For this reason, most insurers and advisory organizations review their rates at least annually.

Provide for Contingencies

Future events cannot be predicted accurately, and the insurer has a responsibility to pay all valid claims even if costs are higher than estimated. Rates should provide for contingencies, such as unexpected variations in losses and expenses. This provision will also provide greater security that the insurer will be able to meet its obligations to potential claimants.

Promote Risk Control

Ratemaking systems help to promote risk control by providing lower rates for policyholders who exercise sound risk control. For example, policyholders who install burglar alarm systems receive a reduction in their crime insurance rates. Lower fire insurance rates are charged to policyholders who install automatic sprinkler systems at their premises. However, policyholders who engage in activities that tend to result in more losses, such as persons who use their cars for business, generally pay higher rates.

Reflect Differences in Risk Exposure

A rate is a charge for the exposure to risk. If insureds have attributes that make them more or less susceptible to a risk, using a flat rate means that some will be overcharged and others will be undercharged. For example, the fire insurance rate should not be the same for a wood-frame building as for a steel and concrete building; an ideal rate reflects these differences. Moreover, if the rate could not reflect differences in exposure, the insurer would end up with only higher-risk insureds, a process called anti-selection. Using the preceding example again, owners of wood-frame buildings would gladly pay an "average" rate for fire insurance, while owners of steel buildings would find another insurer who would credit them for the lower risk. The first insurer would end up with only wood-frame insureds, and the average rate would be insufficient for that group. Because insurers have the ability to collect and analyze detailed data on each insured, they can incorporate exposure differences into the rates more accurately.

RATE COMPONENTS AND RATEMAKING TERMS

A rate is the basis for the premium charged by an insurer. To understand why a certain premium or rate is charged, the components that make up a rate must be understood. Knowledge of the components and terminology used in ratemaking will serve as a foundation to understanding the ratemaking process.

This section reviews the components of an insurance rate and discusses common ratemaking terms.

Rate Components

An insurance **rate** consists of three components:

Rate
The price per exposure unit for insurance coverage.

- An amount needed to pay future claims and loss adjustment expenses (prospective loss costs)
- An amount needed to pay future expenses, such as acquisition expenses, overhead, and premium taxes (expense provision)
- An amount for profit and contingencies (profit and contingencies factor)

The first component of an insurance rate is related to the prospective **loss costs** developed by advisory organizations or by insurers with large pools of loss data. The second and third components are related to an expense multiplier. Once the insurance rate is calculated, it is multiplied by the appropriate number of exposure units to produce a **premium**.

Loss costs
The portion of the rate that covers projected claim payments and loss adjusting expenses.

Premium
The price of the insurance coverage provided for a specified period.

Ratemaking Terms

These are common terms used in the ratemaking process:

Exposure base (sometimes just exposure) is a variable that approximates the loss potential of a type of insurance. For property coverage, the exposure base is the value being insured; for product liability, the exposure is sales.

Earned exposure unit is the exposure unit for which the insurer has provided a full period of coverage. The periods are typically measured in years.

Pure premium is the amount included in the rate per exposure unit required to pay losses. This component is also sometimes called the loss cost.

Pure premium
The average amount of money an insurer must charge per exposure unit in order to be able to cover the total anticipated losses for that line of business.

Expense provision

The amount that is included in an insurance rate to cover the insurer's expenses and that might include loss adjustment expenses but that excludes investment expenses.

Underwriting expenses

Costs incurred by an insurer for operations, taxes, fees, and the acquisition of new policies.

Expense provision is the amount added to the pure premium required to pay expenses. Such expenses include acquisition expenses; general expenses; premium taxes; and licenses and fees paid to government, regulatory, and advisory organizations. This component is sometimes referred to as **underwriting expenses**.

Loss adjustment expenses (LAE) are the expenses associated with adjusting claims. These expenses are often split into either allocated or unallocated LAE. Some allocated loss adjustment expenses, such as legal fees to defend a claim, may be included in the pure premium instead of in the expense provision. An example of loss adjustment expenses included in the expense provision is the cost of an insurer's in-house claims adjusters.

Insurers add a loading for profit and contingencies. This loading protects the insurer against the possibility that actual losses and expenses will exceed the projected losses and expenses included in the insurance rate. If excessive losses or expenses are not incurred, the funds generated by the loading produce additional profit for the insurer.

Investment Income

A property-casualty insurer performs two distinct operations: insurance operations and investment operations. The insurance operations write policies, collect premiums, and pay losses. The result of the insurance operations is called **underwriting profit**. The investment operations use the funds generated by the insurance operations to buy or sell bonds, stocks, and other investments to earn an investment profit. The return from these investments is called investment income.

Underwriting profit

Income an insurer earns from premiums paid by policyholders minus incurred losses and underwriting expenses.

Historically, property-casualty insurers did not consider their investment returns directly when calculating insurance rates. They may, however, have considered investment returns informally when determining allowances for profits and contingencies. Today, insurers commonly consider investment results explicitly in their rate calculations. Some states even require that investment income be considered explicitly. Sophisticated models are available that can be used to include investment returns in the insurance rate.

The investment return earned by an insurer depends largely on the types of insurance written, the loss reserves, and associated unearned premium reserves. Property losses are usually paid relatively quickly, while liability losses often are not paid until years after losses occur. Consequently, an insurer's loss reserves for liability insurance are usually much greater than its loss reserves for an equivalent amount of property insurance. Because the assets that support the loss reserves are invested to produce income for the insurer, investment returns have a much larger effect on liability insurance rates than property insurance rates.

FACTORS THAT AFFECT RATEMAKING

Various factors have considerable effect on the rate that is set for a particular insurance coverage.

Estimating future events and costs in the real world is subject to uncertainty. These areas of uncertainty affect ratemaking:

- Estimation of losses
- Delays in data collection and use
- Change in the cost of claims
- Insurer's projected expenses
- Target level of profit and contingencies

Estimation of Losses

The key to developing insurance rates that are adequate to pay future claims is estimating the amount of losses for those claims. Past loss experience is generally used as a starting point to estimate future losses. Ratemaking is based on estimating losses from past coverage periods and then adjusting those losses for future conditions. For example, adjustments could be made to past loss experience for anticipated future inflation or for changes in benefits mandated by legislation.

However, past loss experience may not be completely known because not all covered losses are paid immediately. At any point in time, many claims have been incurred but not yet paid. The difference between the estimated amount that will ultimately be paid for claims and the actual loss amount paid to date is the loss reserves. Insurers face the challenge of estimating ultimate losses for past experience as accurately as possible because of the difficulty of estimating future payments.

Insurance rates are based partly on incurred losses. Incurred losses include both paid losses and outstanding loss reserves. Loss reserves are estimates of future payments for covered claims that have already occurred, whether the claims are reported or not. Insurers are legally required to set aside funds for these future payments; these are shown as liabilities on their balance sheets. Because loss reserves are estimates of future events, they are somewhat imprecise. Nonetheless, rates are based partly on such estimates. Therefore, if loss reserve estimates are too low, rates will probably be too low. If loss reserves are too high, rates will probably be too high.

To illustrate, assume that rates for auto liability insurance are calculated based on losses that occurred in the most recent three-year period. The insurer's past experience indicates that 25 percent of losses are paid in the year the accident occurs, 50 percent are paid in the second year, and 25 percent are paid in the third year. The exhibit shows the losses for each year in the three-year period, with Year 1 being the earliest year and Year 3, the most recent year. See the exhibit "Hypothetical Auto Liability Loss Experience at Year 3 End."

Hypothetical Auto Liability Loss Experience at Year 3 End

Year	(1) Paid Losses	(2) Loss Reserves	(3) Incurred Losses
1	$10,000,000	$0	$10,000,000
2	7,500,000	2,500,000	10,000,000
3	2,500,000	7,500,000	10,000,000
Total	$20,000,000	$10,000,000	$30,000,000

[DA03362]

The exhibit shows this information:

- The paid losses in Column (1) are the amounts paid from January 1 of Year 1 up to and including December 31 of Year 3. The insurer has already paid this money to claimants.
- The loss reserves shown in Column (2) are the insurer's best estimates, as of December 31 of Year 3, of the amounts it will pay in the future for losses that occurred during each one-year period. Because all losses that occurred in Year 1 have been paid, no loss reserve exists for Year 1.
- Column (3), which is incurred losses for a given period, is the sum of Columns (1) and (2).

If the insurer in this exhibit insured 100,000 cars each year during this three-year period, it provided 300,000 car-years of protection. A car-year represents the loss exposure of one car insured for one year. If the 300,000 car-years are divided into the $30 million of incurred losses, the insurer needs a pure premium—the amount needed to pay losses—of $100 per car per year ($30,000,000 ÷ 300,000 = $100) to pay its losses during this past three-year period. This example includes not only paid losses but also loss reserves.

If the pure premium indicated by this experience period were used to develop rates for a future year, any inadequacy in past loss reserves would also make future rates inadequate, assuming conditions remain the same. Using the preceding example, assume that the loss reserves were underestimated by 15 percent; that is, the company had only $8,500,000 in loss reserves at the end of Year 3 instead of $10,000,000. The total incurred losses for the years would then be $28,500,000, and the calculated pure premium would be only $95 per car per year ($28,500,000 ÷ 300,000). Rates based on underestimated losses could lead to underwriting losses and possibly even insolvency.

In theory, an insurer could avoid this problem by waiting for all claims to be paid before using loss experience to calculate rates. When all claims incurred during a given period have been paid, there is no need for loss reserves. In practice, however, waiting would create problems. If the rate filing were delayed for several years to permit all claims to be settled, then factors such as inflation, changes in traffic conditions, and so forth would have a greater chance of changing the loss exposure. The effects of these factors might be greater than the effects of errors in estimating loss reserves.

Delays in Data Collection and Use

Responsiveness is a desirable ratemaking characteristic. Because conditions are constantly changing, any delay between when data are collected and when they are used tends to reduce rate accuracy. A delay inevitably occurs between when losses are incurred and when they are reflected in rates charged to customers. The delay can span several years. During this period, economic or other factors can increase or decrease the rates the insurer should charge if the premium is to reflect the expected losses.

The delay in reflecting loss experience in rates stems from several sources, including these:

- Delays by insureds in reporting losses to insurers
- Time required to analyze data and prepare a rate filing
- Delays in obtaining state approval of filed rates
- Time required to implement new rates
- Time period during which rates are in effect, usually a full year

When a rate is in effect for a full year, the last policy issued under that rate could be issued 365 days (one year) after the effective date of the rate filing, and the policy's coverage under that rate continues until policy expiration, yet another year later. See the exhibit "Policy Year Time Frame."

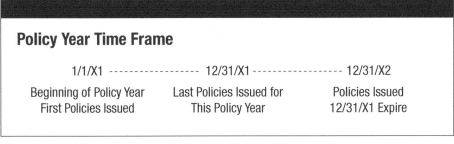

Policy Year Time Frame

1/1/X1	12/31/X1	12/31/X2
Beginning of Policy Year First Policies Issued	Last Policies Issued for This Policy Year	Policies Issued 12/31/X1 Expire

[DA03368]

The "Chronology of a Rate Filing" exhibit shows a reasonably typical schedule for developing, approving, and implementing new rates for auto insurance. The exhibit assumes that the insurer is basing its new rates on its loss experience for a prior three-year period, called the **experience period**. Data from the

Experience period
The period for which all pertinent statistics are collected and analyzed in the ratemaking process.

experience period are collected and analyzed in the ratemaking process. See the exhibit "Chronology of a Rate Filing."

Chronology of a Rate Filing

1/1,	Year 1	Start of experience period, first loss incurred
12/31,	Year 1	
12/31,	Year 2	
12/31,	Year 3	End of experience period
3/31,	Year 4	Start of data collection and analysis
7/1,	Year 4	Rates filed with regulators
9/1,	Year 4	Approval of rates received
1/1,	Year 5	New rates initially used
12/31,	Year 5	Rates no longer used
12/31,	Year 6	Last loss incurred under this rate filing

[DA03369]

The experience period in the exhibit begins on January 1 of Year 1. Data are collected for the three-year period beginning on that date and ending on December 31 of Year 3. The analysis phase of the ratemaking process begins three months after the end of the experience period. Some insurers wait longer to start the ratemaking process in order to permit loss data to mature because many claims incurred during the experience period would not yet have been reported to the insurer within three months.

The exhibit assumes that the new rates will become effective on January 1 of Year 5, one year after the end of the experience period. They will remain in effect until December 31 of Year 5, two years after the end of the experience period. However, the policies issued on December 31 of Year 5 will remain in force until December 31 of Year 6. Consequently, the last claim under these rates will be incurred three years after the end of the experience period, and six years after the beginning of the experience period, when the first losses on which the rate calculation was based occurred.

Some insurers shorten this process slightly by filing new rates every six months or issuing six-month policies. Others follow a longer cycle.

Change in Cost of Claims

Both loss severity and loss frequency affect an insurer's loss experience during any given period. Economic inflation or deflation during the inevitable delay also affects the average cost of a loss (severity). Finally, legislative or regulatory changes such as modification in rules governing claim settlement can affect the number of losses (frequency). Rates calculated without regard to these factors could prove to be grossly inadequate or grossly excessive.

These factors are difficult to quantify, but they clearly affect losses. Some factors that affect the size and frequency of losses cannot be identified or measured directly, but their aggregate effect on losses can be determined with reasonable accuracy by **trending**. The effects of historical changes can be used to adjust the experience used in the ratemaking analysis. In addition, the rates must include a provision for changes that may arise during the period rates will be in effect. For example, in the "Chronology of a Rate Filing" exhibit, the end of the experience period used is December 31, Year 3. However, the claims under the new rates will not start occurring until January 1, Year 5, and may occur as late as December 31, Year 6. Therefore, the filing made on July 1, Year 4, must make allowance for as much of two-and-a-half years of additional (estimated) trend.

Trending

A statistical technique for analyzing environmental changes and projecting such changes into the future.

Insurer's Projected Expenses

Insurance rates are also based on the insurer's projected expenses. Like losses, expenses can change over time, and any projected changes must be considered in the ratemaking process. Rather than past expenses, it is sometimes more relevant to use judgment or budgeted expenses, especially when conditions change dramatically. For example, if a new agent commission plan was introduced, past commission expense would not necessarily be a good estimate of the costs for new policies.

Ratemakers are also challenged to allocate general administrative expenses properly among different types of insurance. Changes in the allocation of these expenses may need to be reflected in the rates.

Target Level of Profit and Contingencies

The insurer must decide what provision for profit and contingencies should be included in the rate. Consideration is given to the overall desired rate of return, including likely returns from **investment income** versus underwriting profit, respectively. An insurer's target profit may also depend on other factors. For example, an insurer may initially accept a lower profit (and thus charge lower rates) for a new insurance product in order to build a customer base.

Investment income

Interest, dividends, and net capital gains received by an insurer from the insurer's financial assets, minus its investment expenses.

RATEMAKING METHODS

While there can be a myriad of data, adjustments, and other inputs to the ratemaking process, there are actually just a few methods for adjusting an existing rate or developing a new rate.

Insurers commonly use three ratemaking methods:

- Pure premium method
- Loss ratio method
- Judgment method

The three methods are compared in the exhibit. See the exhibit "Ratemaking Methods."

Ratemaking Methods

Method	Data Required	Uses
Pure premium method	• Incurred losses • Earned exposure units • Expense provision • Profit and contingencies factor	To develop rates from past experience (cannot be used without past experience)
Loss ratio method	Actual loss ratio, calculated from: • Incurred losses • Earned premiums Expected loss ratio, calculated as: 100%—Provision for expenses, profit, and contingencies	To modify existing rates (cannot be used without existing rates; cannot be used to determine rates for a new type of insurance)
Judgment method	Rates based on experience and judgment	To develop rates when data are limited (requires skilled judgment)

[DA03381]

Pure Premium Ratemaking Method

Pure premium method

A method for calculating insurance rates using estimates of future losses and expenses, including a profit and contingencies factor.

The first ratemaking method is the **pure premium method**. This method uses loss per exposure based on past experience as the basis for the rate. While this method relies on past experience, it is independent of any current rates.

The pure premium method has four steps. The first step is to calculate the pure premium. The pure premium (the amount needed to pay losses and, depending on the line of business, allocated loss adjustment expenses) is calculated by dividing the dollar amount of incurred losses by the number of earned exposure units.

$$\text{Incurred losses} = \$4 \text{ million}$$

$$\text{Earned car-years} = 100{,}000$$

$$\text{Pure premium} = \frac{\text{Incurred losses}}{\text{Earned car-years}}$$

$$\text{Pure premium} = \frac{\$4{,}000{,}000}{100{,}000} = \$40$$

The second step in the pure premium method is to estimate expenses per exposure unit based on the insurer's past expenses (except investment expenses and possibly loss adjustment expenses). Whatever loss adjustment expenses are included in the pure premium are excluded from the expenses. Investment expenses are not directly reflected in rate calculations. If expenses are $1.7 million, then expenses per exposure unit are as shown:

$$\frac{\$1{,}700{,}000}{100{,}000} = \$17$$

The third step is to determine the profit and contingencies factor. In this example, a factor of 5 percent is used. A provision for net investment income is generally included within the profit provision.

$$\text{Rate per exposure unit} = \frac{\text{Pure premium} + \text{Expenses per exposure unit}}{1 - \text{Profit and contingencies factor}}$$

$$= \frac{\$40 + \$17}{1 - 0.05}$$

The final step is to add the pure premium and the expense provision and divide by one minus the profit and contingencies factor. For example, if the pure premium is $40, the expenses per exposure unit are $17, and the profit and contingencies factor is 5 percent, the formula would be this:

$$\text{Rate per exposure unit} = \frac{\text{Pure premium} + \text{Expenses per exposure unit}}{1 - \text{Profit and contingencies factor}}$$

$$= \frac{\$40 + \$17}{1 - 0.05}$$

$$= \frac{\$57}{0.95}$$

$$= \$60$$

The rate per exposure unit of $60 is equal to the pure premium of $40 (the amount required to pay losses) plus an additional $17 (the amount required to pay expenses) and $3 (for profit and contingencies).

Some insurers separate their expenses into two components: fixed expenses and variable expenses. Fixed expenses are stated as a dollar amount per exposure unit. Variable expenses are stated as a percentage of the rate. For example, the insurer in the preceding example might decide that its cost for issuing a policy and collecting the premium is $2.50 per car-year, regardless of premium size, rating class, or rating territory. Its other underwriting expenses, such as commissions and premium tax, vary by premium size. The variable expenses equal 12 percent of the final premium. The rate per exposure unit in this case would be this:

$$\text{Rate per exposure unit} = \frac{\text{Pure premium} + \text{Fixed expenses per exposure unit}}{1 - \text{Variable expense percentage} - \text{Profit and contingencies factor}}$$

$$= \frac{\$40 + \$2.50}{1 - 0.12 - 0.05}$$

$$= \frac{\$42.50}{0.83}$$

$$= \$51 \text{ (rounded)}$$

The new rate per exposure unit of $51 is equal to the sum of pure premium of $40 (the amount required to pay losses or loss costs), fixed expenses of $2.50, variable expenses of $6 (rounded), and $2.50 (rounded) for profit and contingencies.

Loss Ratio Ratemaking Method

Loss ratio method

A method for determining insurance rates based on a comparison of actual and expected loss ratios.

The second ratemaking method is the **loss ratio method**. In its simplest form, the loss ratio method uses two loss ratios—the actual loss ratio and the expected loss ratio of the insurer during the selected experience period:

1. $\text{Actual loss ratio} = \dfrac{\text{Incurred losses}}{\text{Earned premiums}}$

2. $\text{Expected loss ratio} = 100\% - \text{Expense provision}$

In this method, profit and contingencies are included in the expense provision because the method modifies a current insurance rate. The expected loss ratio plus the provision for expenses, profit, and contingencies always add up to 100 percent.

This is the loss ratio ratemaking equation in its simplest form:

$$\text{Rate change} = \frac{\text{Actual loss ratio} - \text{Expected loss ratio}}{\text{Expected loss ratio}}$$

If the rate change percentage is negative, it indicates a rate reduction. If positive, it indicates a rate increase. For example, if the actual loss ratio equals 54 percent and the expected loss ratio equals 60 percent, then the rate change is a decrease of 10 percent.

$$\frac{\text{Actual loss ratio} - \text{Expected loss ratio}}{\text{Expected loss ratio}} = \frac{(0.54 - 0.60)}{0.60}$$

$$= \frac{-0.06}{0.60}$$

$$\text{Rate change} = -0.10 = -10\%$$

In this case, the insurer's actual loss ratio was better than expected. Based only on this information, it appears that the insurer could lower its rates and still make the desired profit on business subject to these rates. Lower rates would probably also attract additional business, which would produce greater profits.

The loss ratio ratemaking method cannot be used to calculate rates for a new type of insurance, because neither an actual loss ratio for the calculation nor an old rate to adjust is available. For a new type of insurance, either the pure premium method or the judgment method must be used.

Judgment Ratemaking Method

The third and oldest ratemaking method is the **judgment ratemaking method**. Though its use is no longer as widespread as it once was, this method is still used for some types of insurance, such as ocean marine insurance, some inland marine classes, aviation insurance and situations when limited data are available, as with terrorism coverage. Although the judgment ratemaking method might use limited or no loss experience data, an experienced underwriter or actuary generally has a sense of what rates have produced desired results in the past. See the exhibit "Using Big Data for Ratemaking."

Judgment ratemaking method

A method for determining insurance rates that relies heavily on the experience and knowledge of an actuary or an underwriter who makes little or no use of loss experience data.

Using Big Data for Ratemaking

Insurers are using big data, defined as data that is too large to be gathered and analyzed by traditional methods, in various ways to improve the accuracy of their ratemaking. Because of new data analytic techniques, insurers can now identify many more rating variables for personal lines rates. Vehicle telematics provide information on a customer's actual driving behaviors. Some insurers have direct access to states' departments of motor vehicles and can rapidly mine data on customers' and applicants' driving records. Insurers can use various sources of data, such as weather and geological databases, to rate homeowners policies by peril.

Big data can also be used in commercial ratemaking. Data regarding weather, geological features, and satellite imagery can help evaluate property risks. Text mining and social media analysis can indicate potential product liability, malpractice, or directors' and officers' exposures.

[OV_12089]

RATEMAKING PROCESS OVERVIEW

Ratemaking can involve a number of complex technical issues. An understanding of the process involved reveals the importance and contribution of each step in the ratemaking process.

When creating or revising insurance rates, an insurer's staff, or an advisory organization on behalf of the insurer, follows a series of steps:

1. Collect data
2. Adjust data
3. Calculate overall indicated rate change
4. Determine territorial and class relativities
5. Prepare rate filings and submit to regulatory authorities as required

An insurer follows a similar process when reviewing loss costs, rather than rates. The provisions for expense and for profit and contingencies are excluded from the process, but all other adjustments and parts of the process are unchanged.

For companies that rely on loss cost filings made by **advisory organizations**, the ratemaking process involves calculating and filing an appropriate **loss cost multiplier**.

Advisory organization

An independent organization that works with and on behalf of insurers that purchase or subscribe to its services.

Loss cost multiplier

A factor that provides for differences in expected loss, individual company expenses, underwriting profit and contingencies; when multiplied with a loss cost, it produces a rate.

Collect Data

To obtain and maintain usable data, each insurer must code data when transactions occur. Some coding is prescribed by advisory organizations, but many insurers collect more data than advisory organizations require. Information about specific policies is collected most conveniently when policies, endorsements, and invoices are issued. Claim data are collected when claims are reported, reserves are established or changed, checks or drafts are issued, or claims are closed.

Before collecting ratemaking data, the insurer must determine the kinds of data needed. The data fall into three general categories:

- Losses, both paid and incurred (including any loss adjustment expenses to be included in the pure premium)
- Earned premium and/or exposure information
- Expenses, including a profit and contingencies factor

If rates are to vary by rating class and/or territory, data must be identified for each class and territory. For example, if an insurer is considering establishing a new class of business, it would first identify experience for this class separately so there would be data to calculate a separate class rate.

Ideally, the incurred losses, earned premiums, and earned exposure units should be based on the same group of policies. Because this is not always practical, approximation techniques are used. For example, sometimes it is most practical to compare premiums during one twelve-month period with losses for a slightly different twelve-month period, even if these two periods do not involve exactly the same policies.

Different aggregations of data may be used, depending on the line of business. For example, loss payments for a single claim could be made over several successive calendar years. Consequently, the **calendar-year method** is unsuitable for collecting ratemaking data for liability and workers compensation insurance, because the delay in loss payment can be long and the loss reserves can be large relative to earned premiums. For those types of insurance, either the **policy-year method** or accident-year method should be used.

For fire, inland marine, and auto physical damage insurance, losses are paid relatively quickly, and loss reserves tend to be small relative to earned premiums. Consequently, the calendar-year method may be satisfactory for ratemaking data collection, although it is still not as accurate as the other two methods. See the exhibit "Using Vehicle Telematics for Automobile Ratemaking."

Calendar-year method

A method of collecting ratemaking data that estimates both earned premiums and incurred losses by formulas from accounting records.

Policy-year method

A method of collecting ratemaking data that analyzes all policies issued in a given twelve-month period and that links all losses, premiums, and exposure units to the policy to which they are related.

Using Vehicle Telematics for Automobile Ratemaking

Vehicle telematics provide insurers with a wealth of data regarding customers' actual driving behaviors. Speed, braking frequency, miles driven, daily routes, and even the number of left turns are all factors that can be used in setting rates.

However, using telematics is voluntary for consumers, and insurers typically offer discounts to customers who choose to participate. Generally, it is the most careful drivers with the best driving records who participate in telematics programs.

[OV_12096]

Adjust Data

After data have been collected, they must be adjusted. Adjustment is necessary because the raw exposure, premium, and loss data reflect conditions from present and past periods, whereas the rates being developed will be used in the future.

Actuaries use several ways of adjusting premium and loss data:

- Adjust premium to current rate level
- Adjust historic experience for future development
- Apply trending to losses and premium

Adjust Premiums to Current Rate Level

If rates charged in the experience period were written at different rate levels, premiums will need to be adjusted to the current level.

The ideal way to adjust premiums to current rate level is to calculate the premium for each policy in the experience period at current rate level. For example, the 20X1 personal auto premiums at 20X4's rate level would be calculated by pricing each auto insured in 20X1 at 20X4 rates. However, re-rating every exposure requires storing, retrieving and using every rating factor for each policy of each exposure, possibly making this method economically unfeasible. An alternative is to adjust historic premiums in total to current levels.

As an illustration of this approach, assume that a book of business has $100 of losses each year. In Year 1, a premium of $200 is charged, but the insurer decreases rates by 20 percent in each of the next two years. Therefore, an insured that paid $1,000 premium in the first year would pay only $640 after the two rate decreases. If the insurer had a 50 percent loss ratio the first year, 63 percent the second year, and 78 percent the third year, it would be inappropriate to project the coming year's loss ratio as the average of those loss ratios. The 50 percent loss ratio in Year 1 was based on premiums that would not be charged as of Year 3, so it should not be used directly for ratemaking. The premium that had been charged must be adjusted to what would be charged in Year 3, the most recent year. See the exhibit "Effect of On-Level Premium Adjustment."

Effect of On-Level Premium Adjustment

Year	(1) Developed Losses	(2) Collected Premium	(3) = (1)/(2) Collected Loss Ratio	(4) Rate Level Index	(5) On-Level Factor	(6) = (2)×(5) On-Level Premium	(7) = (1)/(6) On-Level Loss Ratio
1	$100	$200	50%	1.00	0.64	$128	78%
2	$100	$160	63%	0.80	0.80	$128	78%
3	$100	$128	78%	0.64	1.00	$128	78%

[DA06289]

On-level factor

A factor that is used to adjust historical premiums to the current rate level.

Column 4 in the table shows the rate level relative to Year 1. This rate level index reflects the assumption that rates decreased 20 percent from the prior year in both Year 2 and Year 3. The **on-level factor** in Column 5 adjusts rate levels for each year to the most recent period's rate levels. It equals the rate level index for the most recent period (Year 3) divided by the rate level index for each year. At the most recent year's rate level, each year's losses would have produced a 78 percent loss ratio.

Premiums may also have to be adjusted for different levels of coverage purchased. For example, an automobile liability insurer finds that it is now selling much more of its $100,000 per accident limits than the $25,000 limit it had in the past. The premiums (and perhaps losses) need to be adjusted for this change in coverage provided.

Adjust Historic Experience for Future Development

When policy-year or accident-year experience is used to predict future results, one must remember that the experience might not be complete. There may still be open claims that require future payment or the possibility of a late-reported claim for which the insurer is liable. The insurer must estimate the values of these future payments and add it to the payments to date in order to estimate the ultimate losses of each period.

For example, at the end of a year, payments for medical malpractice claims that occurred during that year may be only 10 percent of the ultimate payment. Because of the complexity and long discovery period of such claims, even the incurred losses tend to increase over time. Conversely, for automobile physical damage, an insurer's net loss payments might decrease over time as it collects salvage and subrogation recoveries on claims it has paid.

The future development of the losses can be estimated by several actuarial methods. The most common method used is applying **loss development factors** to the current experience. With any method, the goal is to estimate the final, total cost to pay all the claims within each year. These projections are then used as the basis for estimating the losses that will be incurred in the proposed policy period.

Loss development factor

An actuarial means for adjusting losses to reflect future growth in claims due to both increases in the incurred amount for reported losses and incurred but not reported (IBNR) losses.

Apply Trending to Losses and Premium

Another way losses are adjusted for ratemaking is through trending. Trending is the review of historic environmental changes and projecting such changes into the future. Examples of such changes would be inflation of claim costs, the increasing safety of newer cars, or changes in legal liability.

Trend adjustments can come from various sources. In some instances, external indexes such as the Consumer Price Index or one of its components may be used in trending. The most frequently used source of trends is historical experience. This experience can be reviewed by an insurer using its own data or by a statistical agent, such as Insurance Services Office, Inc. (ISO) or the National Council on Compensation Insurance (NCCI), using the combined experience of numerous companies. The trend adjustment commonly uses historical experience to project past trends into the future. Loss trending is usually reviewed in separate severity and frequency components.

These trends can be projected into the future using an exponential trending method. **Exponential trending** assumes that data being projected will increase or decrease by a fixed percentage each year as compared with the previous year. For example, claim frequency will increase 1.3 percent each year, or claim severity will increase 8.2 percent each year. Exponential trends have a

Exponential trending

A method of loss trending that assumes a fixed percentage increase or decrease for each time period.

compounding effect over time. For example, price inflation would be expected to follow an exponential trend. See the exhibit "Claim Severity Trend Calculation."

Claim Severity Trend Calculation

(1)	(2)	(3)	(4)	(5)
		Developed	= (3)/(2)	
	Developed	Number of	Average Claim	Change From
Accident Year	Losses	Claims	Severity	Prior Year
20X1	$11,000,000	9,167	$1,200	
20X2	$10,287,750	7,913	$1,300	8.3%
20X3	$11,112,000	7,880	$1,410	8.5%
20X4	$10,659,000	6,995	$1,524	8.1%
20X5	$11,275,000	6,860	$1,644	7.9%
			Average	8.2%

The losses and claims are the estimated final values for each accident year, projected using development factors or other methods.

[DA06290]

Losses may need to be adjusted to current conditions if other significant external changes have affected loss payouts in recent years. For example, workers compensation insurance benefits are established by statute. If legislation or a court decision changes these benefits, past losses must be adjusted to current benefit levels.

Premiums may also need to be trended to reflect changing conditions. For example, the amount of homeowners insurance purchased tends to change with the value of the home. If home prices have risen, more premiums might be collected on the same house just because of its increase in value. Trending factors would be applied to adjust for past and future changes in premium due to these external factors.

Calculate Overall Indicated Rate Change

The purpose of adjustments, development, and trending is to bring prior experience to a level comparable to the future rate's policy period. Based on the adjusted experience, an overall rate indication is calculated. In some cases, a new rate is calculated directly. However, in most cases, the indication shows a change from the current rate level, for example, an overall 2.7 percent increase.

Several different methods, such as the **loss ratio method** and the pure premium method, can be used to produce an indication. These methods depend on the amount and type of experience available.

Determine Territorial and Class Relativities

If rates vary by territory and/or class, they are reviewed after the calculation of the overall rate change. Further analysis is performed to determine territorial and/or class relativities. These relativities reflect the extent to which various subsets of insureds in a state deserve rates that are higher or lower than the statewide average rate. For example, in a territory with many congested highways, auto insurance rates might be 8.6 percent higher than the statewide average rate, while in a rural territory rates might be 20.2 percent lower. Similarly, a frame-constructed building has a different exposure to fire loss than a fire-resistive steel and concrete building, so different rates are warranted.

Territorial relativities can be determined by comparing the estimated loss ratio (or pure premium) for each geographic territory to the statewide average loss ratio (or pure premium). This comparison produces factors that are applied to the statewide average rate to reflect experience in each geographic territory. If a given territory has limited experience, its territorial loss ratios are likely to vary widely. Differences from the overall average rate must be supported by credible experience. If a class has only a few exposures, even very good (or very poor) experience will produce only minimal difference from the average rate; because of the limited exposures, the difference could be a result of mere chance.

Class relativities are used to develop rates for each rating class. Class relativities are determined similarly to territorial relativities. Once class relativities have been determined, the insurer can prepare a rate table showing rates for each territory and each rating class.

Prepare and Submit Rate Filings

After data have been collected and adjusted, and after any territorial and class relativities have been determined, rate filings must be prepared. A rate filing is a document submitted to state regulatory authorities. The form for and the amount of information required in a filing vary by state.

Generally, the filing must include at least these seven items:

- Schedule of the proposed new rates
- Statement about the percentage change, either an increase or a decrease, in the statewide average rate
- Explanation of differences between the overall statewide change in rate and the percentage change of the rates for individual territories and/or rating classes (if any)

Loss ratio method

A loss reserving method that establishes aggregate reserves for all claims for a type of insurance.

- Data to support the proposed rate changes, including territorial and class relativities
- Expense provision data
- Target profit provision included in the rates, if applicable, and any supporting calculations
- Explanatory material to enable state insurance regulators to understand and evaluate the filing

Depending on state law, formal approval of the filing by regulators might not be required. In some states, approval must be obtained before the rates are used. In other states, formal approval is not required by law, but many insurers prefer to obtain approval before use to avoid the possibility of having to withdraw the rates if regulators decide that rates do not meet statutory requirements.

Actuaries are best qualified to answer any technical questions that the regulators might raise. However, some insurers prefer to delegate most of the contact with regulators to the legal department or filing specialists and to involve actuaries only as needed.

If an advisory organization files rates or loss costs on behalf of an insurer, it handles any follow-up or negotiations. Generally, companies that use an advisory organization are assumed to adopt the filings made by that organization automatically. When loss costs are filed by an advisory organization, the insurer is responsible for filing its expense provisions, which would yield its final rates.

RATEMAKING FACTOR VARIANCES FOR DIFFERENT TYPES OF INSURANCE

Ratemaking can vary widely by type of insurance. These variations can result from the characteristics of loss exposures, regulatory requirements, and other factors.

Major differences between ratemaking for different lines of business can be found in experience period, trending, large loss limitations, credibility, and increased limits factors.

Experience Period

Using an experience period of one to three years is common for auto insurance and other types of liability insurance. For fire insurance, a five-year experience period is used almost universally because it is required by law in many states. The experience for each of the five years is usually not given equal weight. The experience for the most recent years is given greater weight to promote rate responsiveness.

The experience period used for other property causes of loss, such as wind, is even longer—frequently twenty years or more. The purpose of such a long experience period is to avoid the large swings in rates that would otherwise result when a major hurricane, a series of major tornadoes, or another natural catastrophe strikes an area.

Three factors can be considered in determining the appropriate experience period: (1) legal requirements, if any; (2) the variability of losses over time; and (3) the credibility of the resulting ratemaking data. The second and third factors are related to some degree.

Trending

Trending practices also vary by type of insurance. Trending may be based on experience or external indices. Moreover, trending may be needed for premiums as well as losses.

For property insurance, loss claim frequency is low and generally stable, so trending may be restricted to claim severity. However, the average claim is not used to measure claim severity because the average property insurance claim may be distorted by infrequent large claims. Consequently, an external composite index, composed partly of a construction cost index and partly of the consumer price index, is used for trending.

For liability insurance, separate trending of claim severity and claim frequency is common because of the different factors that affect them. Economic inflation or deflation over the course of payments can affect the average cost of a claim (severity). Legislative, regulatory or other external changes, such as modification in rules governing claim settlement, can affect the number of losses (frequency).

In some lines, such as fire insurance, trending both losses and premiums is necessary. Losses are trended partly to reflect any effects of inflation on claim costs. For example, inflation can elevate property values, and people tend to increase the amount of property insurance purchased to reflect the increased values. This increases insurer premium revenue. Increases in amounts insured tend to lag somewhat behind inflation during certain periods. Consequently, insurers trend both losses and premiums and offset the growth in premiums against the growth in losses. Premiums are also trended in other types of insurance for which the exposure units are affected by inflation. Examples include workers compensation (which uses payroll as its exposure base) and some general liability insurance (which uses sales).

A special trending problem exists in workers compensation insurance. Because the benefits for such insurance are established by statute, legislation or a court decision can change the benefits unexpectedly. A law amendment factor is used to adjust rates and losses to reflect statutory benefit changes. Actuaries can estimate with reasonable accuracy the effects of a statutory benefit change on the losses that insurers will incur under their policies. Unlike other trending, rate changes in statutory benefits might apply to outstanding policies as well as new and renewal policies.

For equipment breakdown insurance, inspection and risk control services are a significant portion of the rate, often exceeding the pure premium component. In this case, trending is applied to the risk control expenses because they constitute such a large portion of the rate.

Large Loss Limitations

Unusual rate fluctuations could result from occasional large losses, whether from large individual losses or from an accumulation of smaller losses from a single event, such as a hurricane. In liability insurance, these fluctuations are controlled by using only basic limit losses in calculating incurred losses. **Basic limit** losses are losses capped at some predetermined amount, such as $100,000.

Basic limit

The minimum amount of coverage for which a policy can be written; usually found in liability lines.

A similar practice is followed in workers compensation insurance ratemaking. Individual claims are limited to a specified amount for ratemaking purposes. Another limitation applies to multiple claims arising from a single event. Both limitations vary over time and by state.

Loss limitations also apply in ratemaking for property insurance. For example, when a large single loss occurs in fire insurance, only part of it is included in ratemaking calculations in the state in which it occurred. The balance is spread over the rates of all the states. The amount included in the state depends on the total fire insurance premium volume in that state, so it varies substantially by state.

Catastrophe model

A type of computer program that estimates losses from future potential catastrophic events.

Most losses from catastrophic events, such as hurricanes, are excluded from ratemaking data and replaced by a flat catastrophe charge in the rates. The amount of the catastrophe charge is determined by catastrophe data collected over a long time period to smooth the fluctuations that would otherwise result. A **catastrophe model**, which incorporates past experience with scientific theory, is often used to calculate an appropriate charge for these potential losses.

Commercial insurers may also be required to quote a separate charge applicable to the terrorism loss exposure. Because past loss experience with terrorism losses in the United States has been extremely limited, terrorism ratemaking presents a special challenge.

Credibility

Credibility

The level of confidence an actuary has in projected losses; increases as the number of exposure units increases.

Credibility is a measure of the predictive ability of data. In ratemaking, the credibility of past loss data is important in projecting future losses. Fully credible ratemaking data have sufficient volume to provide an accurate estimate of the expected losses for the line, state, territory, and/or class being reviewed. The volatility of the loss data determines how much volume is needed to be fully credible—the higher the volatility, the more data are required to provide a reasonable projection of future losses. For example, a smaller amount of automobile liability experience is needed for full credibility than for fire insurance, because the larger number of claims per exposure and smaller average claim size leads to more stable results.

Credibility assumptions vary by type of insurance. In auto insurance, advisory organizations and some larger insurers consider the statewide loss data to be fully credible. That assumption might be inappropriate for some small insurers who base their rates solely on their own loss data. For territories and classes with loss data that the advisory organization determines are not fully credible, rates are calculated as a weighted average of the indicated rate for the territory or class and the statewide average rate for all classes and territories combined. The **credibility factor** is used as the weight in the weighted average. It indicates the amount of weight to give to the actual loss experience for the territory or class as compared with an alternative source—in this case, the statewide average loss experience. A credibility factor is a number between 0 (no credibility) and 1 (full confidence).

For property insurance, because of the low average claim frequency, advisory organizations might determine that even the statewide loss data are not fully credible. In that case, a three-part weighted average could be used, combining the state loss data for the rating class, regional (multistate) loss data of the rating class, and state loss data for a major group encompassing several rating classes. Again, credibility factors are used as weights.

The pure premiums for workers compensation insurance developed by the National Council on Compensation Insurance (NCCI) are composed of pure premium charges for medical and indemnity costs. Separate credibility standards exist for each of these categories.

Credibility factor

The factor applied in ratemaking to adjust for the predictive value of loss data and used to minimize the variations in the rates that result from purely chance variations in losses.

Increased Limits Factors

Liability insurance coverage is provided at various limits of coverage. Actuaries use a number of ratemaking techniques for pricing coverage amounts in excess of the basic limit. Although it would be possible to develop separate rates for each limit of liability coverage offered, that approach would require credible ratemaking experience at each limit, as well as significant, often duplicative, efforts.

The most common approach to establishing rates for coverage greater than the basic limit is to develop **increased limits factors**. A base rate is first developed using losses capped at the basic limit. Increased limits factors can then be applied to the basic limit rate. For example, the additional charge to increase the general liability limit to $2 million for any one occurrence might be expressed as 70 percent of the basic coverage limit rate, producing an increased limits factor of 1.70.

Increased limit factor

A factor applied to the rates for basic limits to arrive at an appropriate rate for higher limits.

Charges to increase liability limits can, and frequently do, exceed 100 percent of the charge for basic coverage limits. Several reasons exist for the large increased limits factors for several lines of business, such as general liability and auto liability. First, the additional coverage purchased by the customer can be much higher than the basic limit. For example, in personal auto liability, the basic limit might be $50,000 per accident, but the customer purchases $1 million in coverage to protect his or her assets. Although loss severity does not increase uniformly with increased coverage limits, the exposure to loss is substantially greater at higher limits. Second, higher limits can also require a portion of the coverage to be reinsured, with the additional expense of reinsurance included in the rate. Finally, because large losses occur less frequently than small losses and take longer to settle, the variability of losses in higher coverage layers is greater than for the basic limit losses, and the credibility is lower. This greater variability requires a greater **risk charge** at higher levels of coverage.

Risk charge

An amount over and above the expected loss component of the premium to compensate the insurer for taking the risk that losses may be higher than expected.

SUMMARY

Ratemaking is an important component of the overall insurance mechanism. From the insurer's perspective, rates should enable the insurer to be competitive and earn a reasonable profit. Insurers are also concerned about stability, responsiveness, and reflection of differences in risk exposure, as well as the potential to promote risk control. Rates should provide for unanticipated contingencies, such as actual losses being greater than projected. Ratemaking goals often conflict with each other, requiring compromise.

An insurance rate consists of three components: (1) an amount needed to pay losses and loss adjustment expenses (prospective loss costs); (2) an amount needed to pay expenses, such as acquisition expenses, overhead, and premium taxes (expense provision); and (3) an amount for profit and contingencies (profit and contingencies factor).

Common terms used in the ratemaking process are exposure, earned exposure unit, pure premium, expense provision, loss adjustment expenses, profit and contingencies, and investment income.

Ratemaking is based on estimating losses from past coverage periods and then adjusting those losses for future conditions. However, past loss experience may not be completely known because not all covered losses are paid immediately. Because conditions are constantly changing, any delay between when data are collected and when they are used tends to reduce rate accuracy.

Other factors that affect ratemaking include changes in the cost of claims, the insurer's projected expenses, and the target level of profit and contingencies.

There are three ratemaking methods: the pure premium method, the loss ratio method, and the judgment method. The pure premium method involves calculating a pure premium, the amount needed to pay losses, and then adding an expense provision and applying a profit and contingencies factor. The loss ratio method determines a new rate by modifying an old rate, using a comparison of actual and expected loss ratios. The judgment method is used when little or no loss experience data are available for ratemaking, and it relies heavily on the knowledge and experience of an actuary or underwriter.

The complexities of real-world ratemaking arise from variations in policyholders and loss exposures as well as from time-related changes in the insurance environment. The ratemaking process includes these steps:

1. Collect data
2. Adjust data
3. Calculate overall indicated rate change
4. Determine territorial and class relativities
5. Prepare rate filings and submit them to regulatory authorities as required

Ratemaking factors can vary significantly by type of insurance. These variations can result from the characteristics of loss exposures, regulatory requirements, and other factors. Some of the factors that can vary among types of insurance include these:

• Experience period
• Trending
• Large loss limitations
• Credibility
• Increased limits factors

7

Risk Control

Educational Objectives

After learning the content of this assignment, you should be able to:

▷ Describe the six categories of risk control techniques in terms of the following:

- Whether each reduces loss frequency, reduces loss severity, or makes losses more predictable

- How each can be used to address a particular loss exposure

- How they differ from one another

▷ Describe root cause analysis and the steps in the root cause analysis process.

▷ Explain how an organization can use failure mode and effects analysis (FMEA) to assess and mitigate risk.

▷ Explain how an organization can use fault tree analysis (FTA) to determine the causes of a risk event.

Risk Control

RISK CONTROL TECHNIQUES

To select the most appropriate risk management techniques, insurance and risk management professionals consider the various techniques available so that they can then determine which of those techniques most effectively address an organization's or individual's loss exposures.

All risk management techniques fall into one of two categories: risk control or risk financing. The focus of this section is on **risk control**. Risk control techniques can be classified using these six broad categories:

- Avoidance
- Loss prevention
- Loss reduction
- Separation
- Duplication
- Diversification

Each of the techniques in these six categories aims to reduce either loss frequency or severity, or make losses more predictable. See the exhibit "Target of Risk Control Techniques."

Avoidance

The most effective way of managing any loss exposure is to avoid the exposure completely. If a loss exposure has successfully been avoided, then the probability of loss from that loss exposure is zero.

The aim of **avoidance** is not just to reduce loss frequency, but also to eliminate any possibility of loss. Avoidance should be considered when the expected value of the losses from an activity outweighs the expected benefits of that activity. For example, a toy manufacturer might decide not to produce a particular toy because the potential cost of products liability claims would outweigh the expected revenue from sales, no matter how cautious the manufacturer might be in producing and marketing the toy.

Avoidance can either be proactive or reactive.

Proactive avoidance seeks to avoid a loss exposure before it exists, such as when a medical student chooses not to become an obstetrician because he or

Risk control
A conscious act or decision not to act that reduces the frequency and/or severity of losses or makes losses more predictable.

Avoidance
A risk control technique that involves ceasing or never undertaking an activity so that the possibility of a future loss occurring from that activity is eliminated.

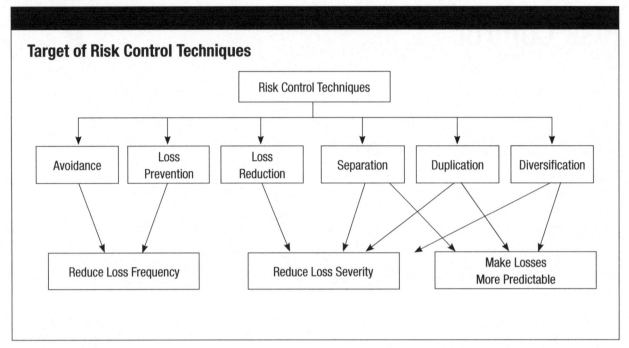

Target of Risk Control Techniques

[DA02648]

she wants to avoid the large professional liability (malpractice) claims associated with that specialty.

Reactive avoidance seeks to eliminate a loss exposure that already exists, such as when manufacturers of hand-held hair dryers stopped using asbestos insulation in their dryers once the cancer-causing properties of asbestos became known.

Reactive avoidance, that is, discontinuing an existing activity, avoids loss exposures from future activities but does not eliminate loss exposures from past activities. For example, the hair dryer manufacturer may avoid claims from consumers who purchase the hair dryers produced after asbestos is no longer used, but would remain legally liable for associated harm suffered by prior consumers.

Because loss exposures do not exist in a vacuum, avoiding one loss exposure can create or enhance another. For example if an individual is concerned about dying in an airplane crash, he or she can choose not to travel by air. However, by avoiding air travel, the individual increases the loss exposure to injury or death from the other means of transport chosen in its place.

Complete avoidance is not the most common risk control technique and is typically neither feasible nor desirable. Loss exposures arise from activities that are essential to individuals and to organizations. Therefore, it is not possible to avoid these core activities. For instance, if a manufacturer's principal product is motorcycle safety helmets, it could not stop selling them in order to avoid liability loss exposures. Similarly, an organization cannot decline to occupy office space in order to avoid property loss exposures. Nonfinancial concerns also can render avoidance impossible. For example, a municipality cannot arbitrarily stop providing police protection or water to its inhabitants in order to avoid the associated liability loss exposures.

Loss Prevention

Loss prevention is a risk control technique that reduces the frequency of a particular loss. For instance, pressure relief valves on a boiler are intended to prevent explosions by keeping the pressure in the boiler from reaching an unsafe level. The valve is a type of loss prevention, not avoidance, because a boiler explosion is still possible, just not as likely.

To illustrate a loss prevention measure, consider a hypothetical manufacturing company, Etchley Manufacturing (Etchley). Etchley has 500 employees working at a single plant. The workers' compensation loss history for this plant shows a significant number of back injuries. Etchley is considering hiring a back injury consultant to host a series of educational seminars for its employees. The consultant estimates that, based on the results of his past seminar series, Etchley will see a 20 percent reduction in the frequency of back injuries. See the exhibit "Example of a Loss Prevention Measure: Etchley Manufacturing."

Loss prevention
A risk control technique that reduces the frequency of a particular loss.

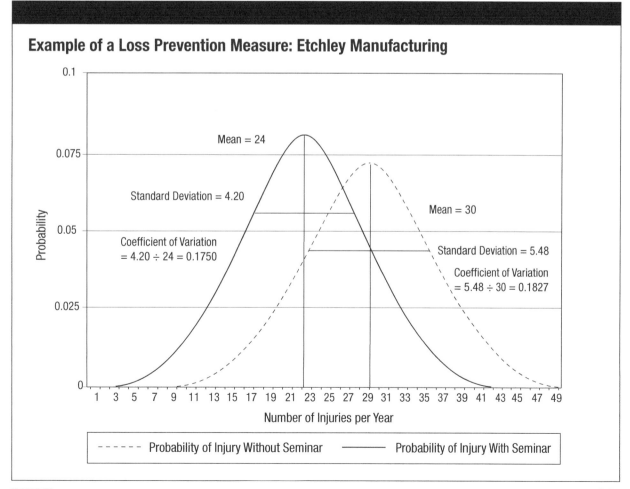

Example of a Loss Prevention Measure: Etchley Manufacturing

Mean = 24
Standard Deviation = 4.20
Coefficient of Variation = 4.20 ÷ 24 = 0.1750

Mean = 30
Standard Deviation = 5.48
Coefficient of Variation = 5.48 ÷ 30 = 0.1827

Probability (y-axis)
Number of Injuries per Year (x-axis)

------ Probability of Injury Without Seminar   ———— Probability of Injury With Seminar

[DA02649]

The chart in the exhibit shows the frequency distributions of back injuries both with and without the educational seminar in order to demonstrate the estimated effect of this loss prevention measure. The frequency distribution without the educational seminar has a mean of 30, a standard deviation of 5.48 and a coefficient of variation of 0.1827.

The frequency distribution with the educational seminar has a lower mean of 24, a lower standard deviation of 4.20, and a lower coefficient of variation of 0.1750. Based on these figures, not only would the consultant's educational seminar reduce the expected frequency of back injuries, it would also reduce their variability from year to year, which would allow Etchley to budget more effectively for those injuries that do occur.

Loss prevention measures that reduce frequency may also affect the loss severity of the specified loss exposures. For example, as a result of the educational seminar, both the number of back injuries that occur and their severity may be reduced.

Generally, a loss prevention measure is implemented before a loss occurs in order to break the sequence of events that leads to the loss. Because of the close link between causes of loss and loss prevention, determining effective loss prevention measures usually requires carefully studying how particular losses are caused. See the exhibit "Preventing Employee Injuries With Wearables and Sensor Data."

Preventing Employee Injuries With Wearables and Sensor Data

New developments in technology and data analytics can provide risk managers with information from sensors and wearables to help prevent workplace accidents and injuries.

Sensors can provide data from machinery regarding how well it is functioning and from devices that monitor air quality, temperature, or other environmental conditions. The data from the sensors is transmitted to a computer that uses a data analysis technique to determine whether operations are proceeding safely.

Wearables are clothing or devices with sensors. Pants and shirts with sensors can transmit ergonomic data to a computer. If an employee is using unsafe body mechanics, training can correct this and help prevent an injury.

[OV_12097]

For example, according to Heinrich's domino theory, as described in the exhibit, most work-related injuries result from a chain of events that includes an unsafe act or an unsafe condition. Workplace safety efforts have therefore focused on trying to eliminate specific unsafe acts or unsafe conditions to break this chain of events and prevent injuries.

As is the case with avoidance, a loss prevention measure may reduce the frequency of losses from one loss exposure but increase the frequency or severity of losses from other loss exposures. For example, a jewelry store that installs security bars on its windows would likely reduce the frequency of theft. These same bars, however, might make it impossible for firefighters to enter the building through the windows or might trap employees inside the store if a fire occurs. See the exhibit "Heinrich's Domino Theory."

Heinrich's Domino Theory

In 1931, H. W. Heinrich published the first thorough analysis of work injuries caused by accidents. He determined that work injuries were actually a result of a series of unsafe acts and/or mechanical or physical hazards (dominoes) that occurred in a specific order. Furthermore, he concluded that if any one of these dominoes could be removed from the chain, the work injury could be prevented. Heinrich's theory included the following five dominoes: (1) social environment and ancestry, (2) the fault of persons, (3) personal or mechanical hazards, (4) the accident, and (5) the injury. For example, if risk control measures could minimize mechanical hazards, the domino chain would be broken and fewer injuries would occur. Many of the principles that Heinrich outlined in his publication became the basis of modern risk control measures.

H.W. Heinrich, Industrial Accident Prevention, 4th edition (New York: McGraw-Hill, 1959). [DA02650]

Loss Reduction

Loss reduction is a risk control technique that reduces the severity of a particular loss. Automatic sprinkler systems are a classic example of a loss reduction measure; sprinklers do not prevent fires from starting, but can limit or extinguish fires that have already started. Some loss reduction measures can prevent losses as well as reduce them.

For example, using burglar alarms is generally considered a loss reduction measure because the alarm is activated only when a burglary occurs. However, because burglar alarms also act as a deterrent, they can prevent loss as well as reduce it.

As an example of a loss reduction measure, assume the consultant Etchley hired to conduct the educational seminars suggested that Etchley provide back braces for all of its employees because back braces help prevent back injuries and reduce the severity of back injuries that do occur.

The exhibit contains the original severity distribution for Etchley and the new severity distribution with all employees using back braces. As with most severity distributions, the severity distribution for back injuries is not symmetrical, but skewed. Most back injuries are grouped in the left-hand portion of the distribution (lower severity values), with some very serious injuries grouped as outliers to the right. This positively skewed distribution pulls the tail of the distribution to the right and increases the mean.

Loss reduction
A risk control technique that reduces the severity of a particular loss.

Note the difference between the means and modes with and without back braces. The use of back braces lowers the average severity (mean) by $15,792 ($29,800 – $14,008 = $15,792) as well as the severity of the injuries that would occur most often (mode) by $5,000 ($8,000 – $3,000 = $5,000).

The two broad categories of loss reduction measures are pre-loss measures, applied before the loss occurs, and post-loss measures, applied after the loss occurs. The aim of pre-loss measures is to reduce the amount or extent of property damaged and the number of people injured or the extent of injury incurred from a single event.

For example, Etchley's use of back braces is a pre-loss measure erecting fire-walls to limit the amount of damage and danger that can be caused by a single fire is also a pre-loss measure. See the exhibit "Example of a Loss Reduction Measure: Etchley Manufacturing."

Example of a Loss Reduction Measure: Etchley Manufacturing

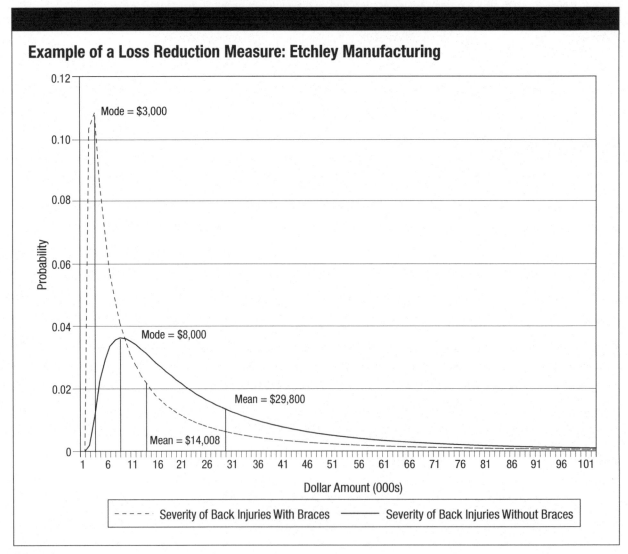

Post-loss measures typically focus on emergency procedures, salvage operations, rehabilitation activities, public relations, or legal defenses to halt the spread or to counter the effects of loss. An example of a post-loss loss reduction measure is to temporarily move an organization's operations to a new location following a fire so that operations can continue while the main premises is repaired, thus reducing loss severity.

Disaster recovery planning is a specialized aspect of loss reduction. A **disaster recovery plan**, also called catastrophe recovery plan or contingency plan, is a plan for backup procedures, emergency response, and post-disaster recovery to ensure that critical resources are available to facilitate the continuity of operations in an emergency situation. For many organizations, disaster recovery planning is especially important in addressing the risks associated with those systems without which the organization could not function. Disaster recovery plans typically focus on property loss exposures and natural hazards, not on the broader array of risks and associated loss exposures that may also threaten an organization's survival.

Disaster recovery plan
A plan for backup procedures, emergency response, and post-disaster recovery to ensure that critical resources are available to facilitate the continuity of operations in an emergency situation.

Separation

Separation is appropriate if an organization can operate with only a portion of these separate units left intact. If one unit suffers a total loss, the portion of the activity or assets at the other unit must be sufficient for operations to continue. Otherwise, separation has not achieved its risk control goal.

Separation
A risk control technique that isolates loss exposures from one another to minimize the adverse effect of a single loss.

Separation is rarely undertaken for its own sake, but is usually a byproduct of another management decision. For example, few organizations build a second warehouse simply to reduce the potential loss severity at the first warehouse. However, if an organization is considering constructing a second warehouse to expand production, the risk control benefits of a second warehouse could support the argument in favor of the expansion.

The intent of separation is to reduce the severity of an individual loss at a single location. However, by creating multiple locations, separation most likely increases loss frequency. For example, using two distantly separated warehouses instead of one reduces the maximum possible loss at each individual location, but increases loss frequency, because two units are exposed to loss. The insurance or risk management professional should be confident that the benefits of reduced loss severity from separation more than offset the increased loss frequency.

As an example of separation, consider a hypothetical organization, Ryedale Shipping Company (Ryedale), which has to decide between these options for shipping its clients' products:

- Option A—use one central warehouse
- Option B—use two warehouses

Under Option A, the central warehouse would contain $500,000 worth of merchandise and have a 5 percent chance of experiencing a fire in any given year. For simplicity, assume that only one fire per year can occur and that if a fire occurs, all of the warehouse's merchandise is completely destroyed. Under Option B, the two warehouses would each have the same probability of a fire (5 percent), but would each house $250,000 worth of merchandise. For simplicity, assume that the two locations are independent of one another. See the exhibit "Example of Separation: Ryedale Shipping Company."

Example of Separation: Ryedale Shipping Company

Option A

	Central Warehouse
Value of merchandise	$500,000
Probability of a fire	.05

Severity distribution (maximum loss in a fire)	$500,000
Probability of a fire in the central warehouse	.05
Expected loss (.05 × $500,000)	$25,000

Option B

	Warehouse 1 (W1)	Warehouse 2 (W2)
Value of merchandise	$250,000	$250,000
Probability of a fire	.05	.05

Severity distribution (maximum loss in a fire)	$250,000
Probability of fire at W1 and fire at W2 (.05 × .05)	.0025
Probability of fire in W1 but not W2 [.05 × (1 − .05)]	.0475
Probability of fire in W2 but not in W1 [(1 − .05) × .05]	.0475
Probability of one fire in either W1 or W2 (.0475 + .0475)	.095
Probability of zero fires (1 − .05) × (1 − .05)	.9025
Expected loss [(.0025 × $500,000) + (.095 × $250,000)]	$25,000

[DA02652]

The exhibit shows the severity distributions for these options and how the expected loss is calculated.

Under Option A, the severity distribution is just the single outcome of a loss of $500,000. There are two possible outcomes in any one year: a fire at the central warehouse or no fire at the central warehouse. Given a probability of fire of .05 (5 percent), Ryedale would expect a $500,000 loss 5 percent of the time and a $0 loss 95 percent of the time. Therefore, the expected loss in any given year is $25,000 (.05 × $500,000 = $25,000).

Under Option B, only $250,000 worth of merchandise is at risk in any one fire. Therefore, having two warehouses reduces Ryedale's severity distribution from $500,000 to $250,000.

Increasing the number of warehouses increases the number of possible outcomes. One of these situations will occur:

- No fire at either location.
- There will be a fire at the first warehouse (W1) but not at the second warehouse (W2).
- There will be a fire at W2 but not at W1.
- There will be a fire at both W1 and W2.

The probability of each of these possible outcomes is shown in the exhibit. Given a probability of fire of .05, Ryedale would expect these outcomes:

- $500,000 loss (fires at both W1 and W2) 0.25 percent of the time
- $250,000 loss at W1 4.75 percent of the time
- $250,000 loss at W2 4.75 percent of the time
- $0 loss 90.25 percent of the time

The expected loss remains $25,000, but the likelihood of suffering a $500,000 loss has fallen from 5 percent to 0.25 percent, whereas the likelihood of suffering a $250,000 loss has increased from 0 percent to 9.5 percent.

This results in a total claims distribution for Option B that has a lower standard deviation than the total claims distribution for Option A. The standard deviation of losses under Option A would be $108,973, and the standard deviation for Option B falls to $77,055.18, which makes losses under Option B more predictable than Option A.

Duplication

Duplication is a risk control technique that uses backups, spares, or copies of critical property, information, or capabilities and keeps them in reserve. Examples of duplication include maintaining a second set of records, spare parts for machinery, and copies of keys.

Duplication differs from separation in that duplicates are not a part of an organization's daily working resources. Duplication is only appropriate if an entire asset or activity is so important that the consequence of its loss justifies the expense and time of maintaining the duplicate.

For example, an organization may make arrangements with more than one supplier of a key raw material. That alternative supplier would be used only if a primary supplier could not provide needed materials because of, for example, a major fire at the primary supplier's plant.

Duplication

A risk control technique that uses backups, spares, or copies of critical property, information, or capabilities and keeps them in reserve.

Like separation, duplication can reduce an organization's dependence on a single asset, activity, or person, making individual losses smaller by reducing the severity of a loss that may occur. Duplication is not as likely as separation to increase loss frequency because the duplicated unit is kept in reserve and is not as exposed to loss as is the primary unit. For example, a duplicate vehicle that is ordinarily kept garaged is not as vulnerable to highway accidents as the primary vehicle.

Duplication is likely to reduce the average expected annual loss from a given loss exposure because it reduces loss severity without increasing loss frequency. Similar to separation, duplication can also make losses more predictable by reducing the dispersion of potential losses.

There are several measures an organization can implement that are similar to duplication and that incorporate nonowned assets.

One option is for an organization to contractually arrange for the acquisition of equipment or facilities in the event that a loss occurs. For example, a plant that manufactures aircraft can pay an annual fee for a contract in which a supplier agrees to deliver within thirty days the hydraulic tools and scaffolding required to continue operations in a rented hangar if the manufacturer's assembly plant incurs a loss. In this way, the aircraft manufacturer can continue operations with minimal business interruptions and avoid the expense associated with the ownership or storage of the duplicate equipment.

Diversification

Diversification

A risk control technique that spreads loss exposures over numerous projects, products, markets, or regions.

Although **diversification** closely resembles the risk control techniques of duplication and separation, it is more commonly applied to managing business risks, rather than hazard risks.

Organizations engage in diversification of loss exposures when they provide a variety of products and services that are used by a range of customers.

For example, an insurer might diversify its exposures by type of business and geographically by selling both personal and commercial insurance and both property-casualty and life insurance in multiple regions. Investors employ diversification when they allocate their assets among a mix of stocks and bonds from companies in different industry sectors. An investor might diversify investments by purchasing stock in a bank and stock in a pharmaceutical manufacturer. Because these are unrelated industries, the investor hopes that any losses from one stock might be more than offset by profits from another.

As with separation and duplication, diversification has the potential to increase loss frequency, because the organization has increased the number of loss exposures. However, by spreading risk, diversification reduces loss severity and can make losses more predictable.

Organizations implement risk control techniques and the measures that support them to address one or more specific loss exposures. Each measure should be tailored to the specific loss exposure under consideration. Furthermore, the application of risk control techniques should serve to support an organization's overall goals, pre-loss and post-loss risk management goals, and risk control goals.

INTRODUCTION TO ROOT CAUSE ANALYSIS

Determination of an accident's root cause allows organizations to discern the cause of a harmful event and prevent such events from recurring.

When an accident occurs in the workplace, the cause may initially appear obvious. For example, if a customer slips on a restaurant floor, a cursory examination might reveal that the wet floor is the cause. A more thorough analysis, however, would focus on why the floor was wet. It would explore whether an employee failed to follow procedures that called for only mopping floors before and after hours, whether the employee was properly trained, and so forth. Determining the answers to these and other questions leads to the **root cause** of the accident. This can help restaurant management implement procedural changes to prevent future customer slips.

Events that affect the safety of an organization's workplace, its employees' health, the environment, or its product's quality, reliability, and production are of concern to risk managers and an organization's management. **Root cause analysis (RCA)** is used to determine the underlying cause of a harmful event.

Root cause

The event or circumstance that directly leads to an occurrence.

Root cause analysis (RCA)

A systematic procedure that uses the results of the other analysis techniques to identify the predominant cause of the accident.

The Nature of Root Cause Analysis

Root causes have four basic characteristics:

- A root cause is expressed as a specific underlying cause, not as a generalization. For example, "Employee did not follow directions" cannot be the root cause of an accident. The RCA would address why the employee did not follow directions. As another example, identifying operator error or equipment failure as a root cause of an event is not sufficient because management cannot address such vague causes. The root cause of such an event should be expressed as something specific, such as "operator removed machine guard."

- A root cause can be reasonably identified. In the machine guard example, it would be necessary to know why the operator removed the machine guard. Was it because it was not working properly? Did the supervisor demand faster production and the guard hampered that? Did the employee want to get the work done faster so he could leave work early? Answers to these and other questions help identify the root cause.

- A root cause must be expressed as something that can be modified. For example, weather conditions or an earthquake could not be considered root causes because such events are beyond human control. In the machine guard example, the root cause could conceivably be maintenance of the machine or personnel problems. If an employee was injured because a lightning strike caused a power failure, the lightning strike could not be considered a root cause because management cannot control the weather. However, the root cause could be the absence of a backup generator.

- A root cause must produce effective recommendations for prevention of future accidents that stem from the root cause. Identifying and mitigating the actions, inactions, conditions, or behaviors that caused a harmful event can prevent reoccurrence of the event. By addressing the root cause of a problem, risk managers can help prevent future incidents.

Harmful events generally are associated with one of three basic causes of loss: physical, human, or organizational. Physical cause is defined as a failure of a tangible or material item, such as a vital part on a manufacturer's production line breaking. When human error or inaction lies at the root of an accident, it is considered to be a human cause of loss (for example, the maintenance department did not perform the proper maintenance on the manufacturer's production line). Organizational causes of loss stem from faulty systems, processes, or policies (such as procedures that do not make it clear which maintenance employee is responsible for checking and maintaining the manufacturer's production line). See the exhibit "Root Cause Analysis Approaches."

Root Cause Analysis Approaches

Root cause analysis (RCA) encompasses a variety of tools, philosophies, and processes. There are several broadly defined RCA approaches, identified according to their basic approach or field of origin:

- Safety-based RCA originated from accident analysis and occupational safety and health.
- Production-based RCA evolved from quality control procedures for industrial manufacturing.
- Process-based RCA is similar to production-based RCA, but it also includes business processes.
- Failure-based RCA stems from failure analysis and is used primarily in engineering and maintenance.
- Systems-based RCA combines these four approaches with change management, risk management, and systems analysis concepts.

[DA08696]

Steps in the Root Cause Analysis Process

The RCA process is a systematic way to determine root cause. See the exhibit "Steps in the Root Cause Analysis Process."

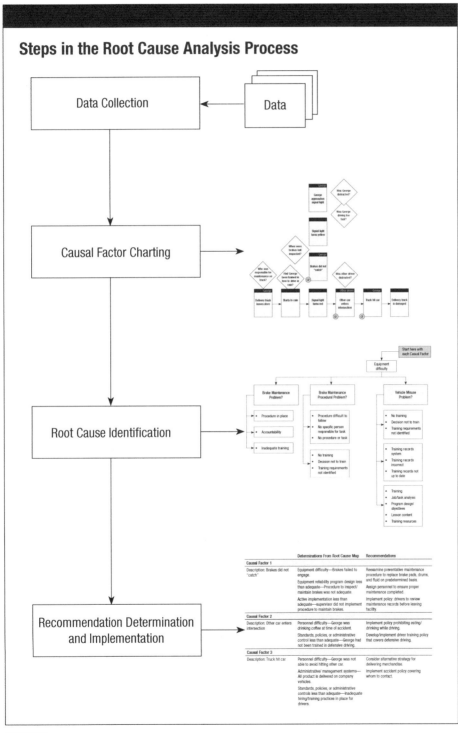

The first step in the RCA process is data collection. Root causes associated with an event cannot be identified without complete information about the surrounding circumstances, facts, and causes.

Causal factors
The agents that directly result in one event causing another.

The second step in the process is **causal factors** charting. This provides the structure to organize and analyze the data gathered during the investigation. It also helps to identify gaps and deficiencies in knowledge as the investigation progresses. Usually, the most readily apparent causal factor is given the most attention during the charting process, but more than one causal factor can be associated with an event. For example, an employee is injured on a manufacturer's production line. Was the injury a result of lax maintenance, the employee removing a machine guard, inadequate training, or all of these?

Step three of the RCA process is root cause identification. Mapping or flow-charting can help determine the underlying reason(s) for each causal factor identified in step two. For example, if equipment difficulty is identified as a causal factor, the map or flowchart is used to identify whether the difficulty was caused by equipment design, reliability, installation, misuse, or some other cause (in which case additional flowcharting is used until the causal factor is determined).

Step four of the RCA process is recommendation determination and implementation. After a root cause has been identified, attainable recommendations for preventing its recurrence are then generated. It is important to implement these attainable recommendations for two reasons. First, if they are not implemented, the effort necessary to perform the RCA process has been wasted. Second, the event(s) that caused the RCA to be performed is likely to occur again. The recommendations determined by the RCA process should be tracked to completion.

RCA is typically used after an event has occurred. However, it also can be used to predict events that could harm the organization. By using RCA in this fashion, organizations can learn to solve problems before they become major events, rather than just reacting to them as they occur.

Root Cause Analysis Example

George drives a delivery truck for New Space furniture store. He was recently hired by New Space but previously worked in the same role for another furniture store. While making a delivery on a rainy afternoon, he encountered a yellow traffic light at an intersection. He applied the truck's brakes, but, according to George's statement, they failed to "catch." His truck slid through the intersection after the light turned red, striking another vehicle. The delivery truck sustained a dented front fender and flat tire. The other vehicle sustained greater damage and was declared a total loss by the driver's insurance company. Both drivers were uninjured. The risk manager for New Space must determine the causal factor(s) and the root cause(s) associated with George's accident.

The first step is to collect data by taking statements from George, the other driver, witnesses, and first responders. They investigated the accident scene to determine road conditions. The delivery truck brakes were examined by a mechanic to determine if they were functioning properly.

The next step is to chart the causal factors. By starting with what is known to be true, investigators can work backward to determine the causal factors. See the exhibit "Causal Factor (CF) Charting."

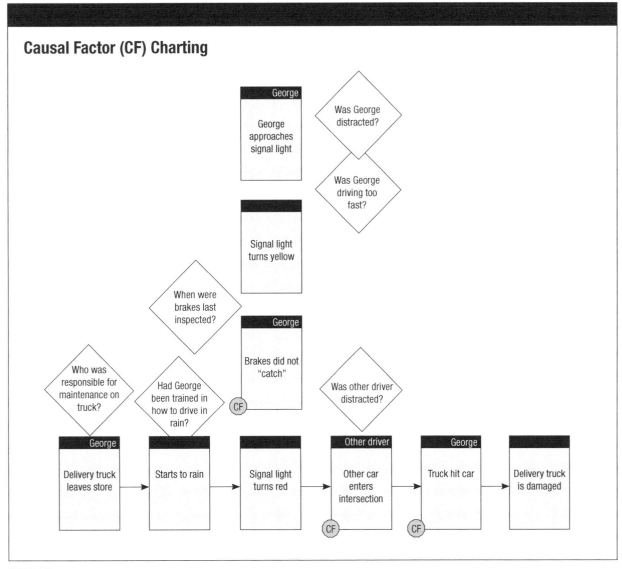

Causal Factor (CF) Charting

[DA08693]

After all causal factors have been identified, root causes are investigated. Each causal factor is inserted into a root cause map to determine its root cause. See the exhibit "Root Cause Mapping."

Root Cause Mapping

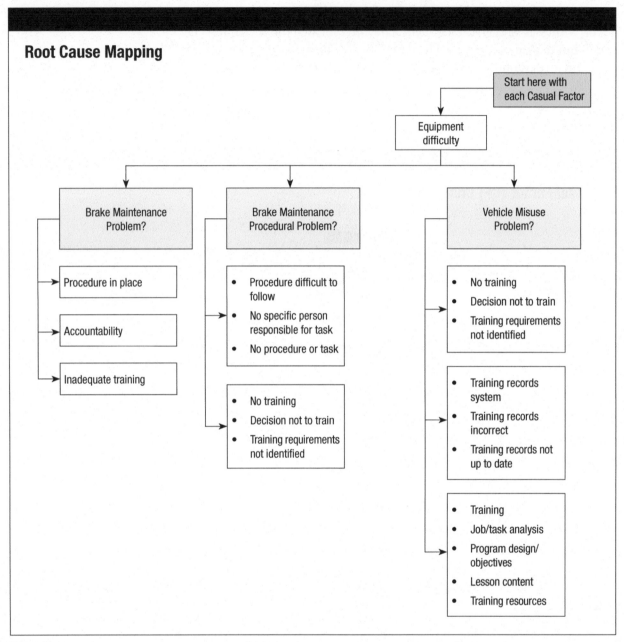

[DA08694]

The fourth step in the process is to develop recommendations that management can implement to prevent the event from recurring. See the exhibit "Root Cause Summary Table."

Root Cause Summary Table

	Determinations From Root Cause Map	Recommendations
Causal Factor 1		
Description: Brakes did not "catch"	Equipment difficulty—Brakes failed to engage. Equipment reliability program design less than adequate—Procedure to inspect/maintain brakes was not adequate. Active implementation less than adequate—Supervisor did not implement procedure to maintain brakes.	Reexamine preventative maintenance procedure to replace brake pads, drums, and fluid on predetermined basis. Assign personnel to ensure proper maintenance completed. Implement policy—Drivers to review maintenance records before leaving facility.
Causal Factor 2		
Description: Other car enters intersection	Personnel difficulty—George was drinking coffee at time of accident. Standards, policies, or administrative control less than adequate—George had not been trained in defensive driving.	Implement policy prohibiting eating/drinking while driving. Develop/implement driver training policy that covers defensive driving.
Causal Factor 3		
Description: Truck hit car	Personnel difficulty—George was not able to avoid hitting other car. Administrative/management systems—All product is delivered on company vehicles. Standards, policies, or administrative controls less than adequate—Inadequate hiring/training practices in place for drivers.	Consider alternative strategy for delivering merchandise. Implement accident policy covering whom to contact.

[DA08695]

FAILURE MODE AND EFFECTS ANALYSIS (FMEA)

An organization can use failure mode and effects analysis (FEMA) to prioritize its risks and maximize its risk control resources.

Failure mode and effects analysis (FMEA) is a root cause analysis technique used predominately in product development and operations management. Its objective is to identify **failure modes** and perform **effects analysis**.

Determining a failure mode's effect on a process requires identifying the effect's location in the system under analysis. FMEA identifies a system's **indenture levels** for this purpose. For example, a system's first indenture level

Failure mode and effects analysis (FMEA)

An analysis that reverses the direction of reasoning in fault tree analysis by starting with causes and branching out to consequences.

Failure mode

The manner in which a perceived or actual defect in an item, process, or design occurs.

Effects analysis

The study of a failure's consequences to determine a risk event's root cause(s).

Indenture level

An item's relative complexity within an assembly, system, or function.

Local effect

The consequence of a failure mode on the operation, function, or status of the specific item or system level under analysis.

Next-higher-level effect

The consequence of a failure mode on the operation, function, or status of the items in the indenture level immediately above the indenture level under analysis.

End effect

The consequence of a failure mode on the operation, function, or status of the highest indenture level.

(Level 1) is the system itself. The next indenture level (Level 2) represents the system segments, with the prime items designated as Level 3. Level 4 represents subsystems, components are at Level 5, subassemblies or circuit cards are at Level 6, and parts are at Level 7.

A failure mode with an effect on the same level that is being analyzed produces a **local effect**. A failure mode that affects the next-higher level produces a **next-higher-level effect**; one that affects the highest indenture level produces an **end effect**.

FMEA's primary goal is to ensure customer safety and production of quality products through these outputs:

- Improvement in the design of procedures and processes
- Minimization or elimination of design characteristics that contribute to failure
- Development of system requirements that reduce the likelihood of failures
- Identification of human error modes and their effects
- Development of systems to track and manage potential future design problems

FMEA may be applied to services as well as products and processes. These are examples of types of FMEA:

- Concept—used in the early design stages to analyze systems or subsystems
- Design—used to analyze products prior to production
- Process—used in manufacturing and assembly processes
- Equipment—used to analyze machinery and equipment design before purchase
- Service—used in service industry processes before release to determine impact on customers
- System—used in global system functions
- Software—used for software functions

Steps in the FMEA Process

Ideally conducted by teams as opposed to an individual, FMEA is used in the design stage to avoid future failures and subsequently for process control. Essentially, it can be used to prevent a harmful event or reduce its severity. See the exhibit "Steps in the FMEA Process."

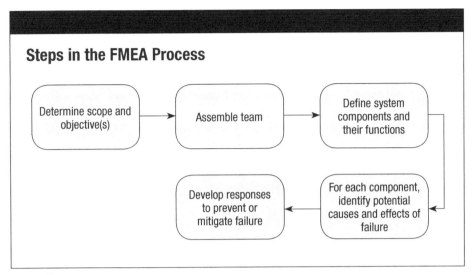

Steps in the FMEA Process

[DA08788]

FMEA can be followed by a **criticality analysis**. These four categories of failures are used in criticality analysis:

- Category 1—failure resulting in excessive unscheduled maintenance
- Category 2—failure resulting in delay or loss of operational availability
- Category 3—failure resulting in potential mission failure
- Category 4—failure resulting in potential loss of life

For example, an explosion caused by defective static controls aboard a truck may be classified as a Category 4 failure, while the driver's temporary illness may be classified as a Category 1 or 2 failure. These categories can be used either subjectively to establish priorities among hazards and their controls or objectively to measure how a risk management professional can alter the expected criticality of a system failure.

One method used to perform a criticality analysis is the calculation of a **risk priority number (RPN)** for each identified failure. RPN determines the relative risk of a particular FMEA item. These are its components:

- Consequence rankings (C)—rate the severity of the effect of the failure
- Occurrence rankings (O)—rate the likelihood that the failure will occur (failure rate)
- Detection rankings (D)—rate the likelihood that the failure will not be detected before it reaches the customer

The rankings for consequence, occurrence, and detection are usually on a one-to-five or one-to-ten scale, depending on the criteria for the organization and process. The highest number on the scale is assigned to the most severe, most likely to occur, or hardest to detect events. See the exhibit "Typical Criteria for the Rankings of Consequence, Occurrence, and Detection."

Criticality analysis

An analysis that identifies the critical components of a system and ranks the severity of losing each component.

Risk priority number (RPN)

The product of rankings for consequence, occurrence, and detection used to identify critical failure modes when assessing risk within a design or process.

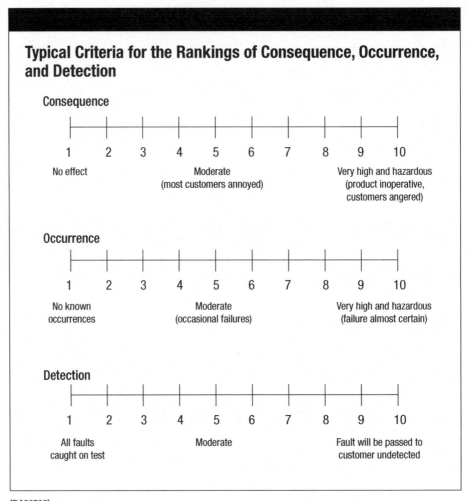

Typical Criteria for the Rankings of Consequence, Occurrence, and Detection

Consequence

1   2   3   4   5   6   7   8   9   10

No effect   Moderate   Very high and hazardous
              (most customers annoyed)   (product inoperative,
                                          customers angered)

Occurrence

1   2   3   4   5   6   7   8   9   10

No known   Moderate   Very high and hazardous
occurrences   (occasional failures) (failure almost certain)

Detection

1   2   3   4   5   6   7   8   9   10

All faults   Moderate   Fault will be passed to
caught on test   customer undetected

[DA08789]

To calculate the RPN, the rankings for consequences, occurrences, and detection are multiplied. The resulting product is then compared with RPNs associated with other failures. The failure associated with the highest RPN usually is addressed first. However, the failure associated with the highest RPN is not always the most critical. That is, it may not necessarily have the greatest **criticality**. See the exhibit "Criticality Example."

Once the most critical failures have been identified, the team or risk management professional should develop a plan of action and implement it by assigning specific actions (remedies) to specific personnel. The remedies should include eliminating the failure mode, minimizing the severity (consequences), reducing the occurrence, and improving detection. After remedies have been applied, revised RPNs can be calculated to determine their effectiveness.

Criticality

A product of the risk priority number elements of consequence and occurrence used to determine the relative risk of a failure mode and effects analysis item.

Criticality Example

C = Consequence rankings

O = Occurrence rankings

D = Detection rankings

C	×	O	×	D	=	RPN
10		10		2		200
3		10		10		300

While the second RPN is higher, the first would require more immediate attention because it has consequence (10) and criticality (10 × 10 = 100) numbers that are far greater than the second. As a general rule, any RPN with a high C-value should be given top priority; any C × O combination that results in a high number is given next priority. C × O, severity of the failure mode consequences times the probability of occurrence, represents how critical that failure is to the failure of the entire system or process (the criticality of the failure).

[DA08790]

FMEA Example

A vending machine company performed an FMEA on individual soda vending machines in various parts of the city. The team performing the FMEA noticed that RPN and criticality prioritized causes of failure were different. According to RPN, "Machine out of sodas" and "Not enough change in machine" were the top two risks. Criticality ranked "Malfunction in money dispensing mechanism" and "Correct change light malfunction" as the most critical.

The organization found that it only took either a high consequence or occurrence along with a high detection rating to generate a high RPN. Because criticality does not include the detection rating, it returned different priorities. The team would need to use its experience and judgment to determine appropriate priorities for action. See the exhibit "FMEA Example."

FMEA Example

Function	Potential Failure Mode	Potential Effect(s) of Failure	C	Potential Cause(s) of Failure	O	Current Process Controls	D	R P N	C R I T
Dispense soda when correct amount of money is inserted in machine	Does not dispense soda	Customer very annoyed	6	Machine out of sodas	7	On regular delivery route	9	378	42
		Discrepancy in machine tallying system		Malfunction in soda dispensing mechanism	2	On regular delivery route	9	108	12
				Power outage	2	None	10	120	12
	Gives too much change	Discrepancy in machine tallying system	7	Malfunction in money dispensing mechanism	7	Alert to company	4	196	49
		Loss of property/ expense for repairs		Damage to machine by customer/ vandalism	2	None	10	140	14
	Gives too little/no change	Customer dissatisfied	6	Change stuck together	2	Alert to company	5	60	12
		Discrepancy in machine tallying system		"Correct change" light malfunction	8	Alert to company	6	288	48
				Not enough change in machine	5	None	10	300	30

[DA08791]

Advantages and Disadvantages

These are the advantages of using FMEA:

- It is widely applicable to many different system modes.
- When used early in the design phase, it can reduce costly equipment modifications.
- It can improve the quality, reliability, and safety of a product or process, as well as improve an organization's image and competitiveness by possibly reducing scrap in production.
- It emphasizes problem prevention by identifying problems early in the process and eliminating potential failure modes.

These are the disadvantages associated with FMEA:

- When used as a top-down tool, FMEA may only identify major failure modes in a system.
- Other analysis methods might be better suited for this type of analysis. When used as a bottom-up tool, it can complement other methods, such as **fault tree analysis (FTA)**, and identify more failure modes resulting in top-level symptoms.
- Analyzing complex multilayered systems can be difficult and tedious with FMEA, and studies that are not adequately controlled and focused can be time-consuming and costly.

Fault tree analysis (FTA)
An analysis that takes a particular system failure and traces the events leading to the system failure backwards in time.

FAULT TREE ANALYSIS (FTA)

Fault tree analysis is a tool risk management professionals can use to determine the underlying causes of a risk event.

Fault tree analysis (FTA) uses the deductive method of moving from the general to the specific to examine conditions that may have led to or influenced a risk event. It can be used to identify potential accidents and to predict the most likely system failures. FTA identifies various ways of "breaking" the fault tree; that is, it interrupts the sequence of events leading to system failure so that the failure itself can be prevented.

The Nature of Fault Tree Analysis (FTA)

The "Fault Tree for Hand Injury to Press Operator" exhibit depicts a fault tree for a harmful event. This harmful event (the injury) appears at the top of the fault tree, and the events necessary to produce it appear as branches. This is known as the fault tree's top event. The tree's branches are connected by "and" gates (shaped like beehives) and "or" gates (shaped like fish tails). These gates represent the causal relationships between events, which are depicted as rectangles within the tree. For example, the "and" gate directly below the injury found in rectangle A indicates that event A can occur only if all four events in rectangles B, C, D, and E occur first. If any one of those four events does not occur, the hand injury to the press operator also cannot occur. See the exhibit "Fault Tree for Hand Injury to Press Operator."

In contrast, an "or" gate signifies that any one of the events leading to the gate is sufficient to cause that event. For example, the operator's hand will be under the die (rectangle C) either if the operator is arranging a piece under the die (rectangle H) or if the operator is inattentive or distracted (rectangle I). To break a fault tree at an "or" gate, none of the events below the gate can be allowed to occur. In this example, to prevent the operator's hand from being under the die, the operator must remain alert and must always use some tool (other than his or her hands) to arrange pieces under the die.

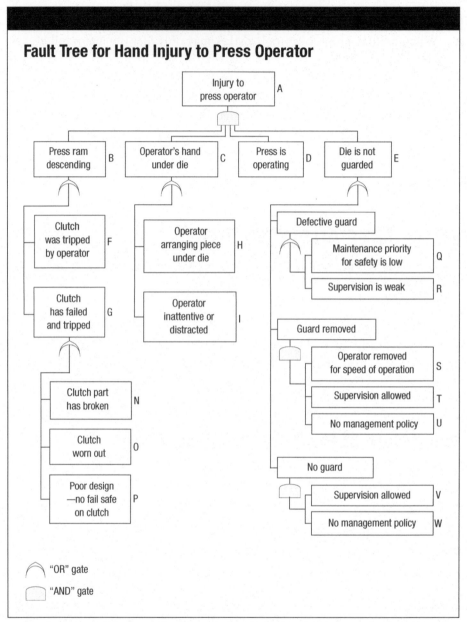

Fault Tree for Hand Injury to Press Operator

Source: Dan Peterson, Techniques of Safety Management: A Systems Approach, 4th edition (Des Plaines, Ill.: American Society of Safety Engineers, 2003), p. 161. [DA01461]

Adding Probabilities to a Fault Tree

A fault tree also can be used to calculate the probability of the risk event if the probabilities of the causal events are known. An "and" gate requires calculating the joint probability that all the events immediately below it will occur. If the probabilities of events in rectangles S, T, and U of the "Fault Tree for Hand Injury to Press Operator" exhibit are .15, .20, and .30, respectively, then the probability of the guard being removed may be calculated in this manner:

$$p(S \text{ and } T \text{ and } U) = p(S) \times p(T) \times p(U)$$

$$= .15 \times .20 \times .30$$

$$= .009$$

An "or" gate requires calculating the probability that any one or more of the events directly below it will occur. This probability is also the probability that the chain of events will proceed through that gate to the next higher branch of the tree, bringing the harmful event that much closer. The "or" gate connecting rectangles H and I to rectangle C in the exhibit indicates that if the probabilities H and I are .40 and .20, and if these two events are not mutually exclusive, then the probability of one or the other (or both) of them occurring is the sum of the probabilities of either one of them occurring alone minus the probability of their both occurring together. This produces these results:

$$p(H \text{ or } I \text{ or both}) = p(H) + p(I) - p(H \text{ and } I)$$

$$= .40 + .20 - (.40 \times .20)$$

$$= .60 - .08$$

$$= .52$$

Application to Loss Control

Because fault tree analysis identifies the events leading to a harmful event, it naturally suggests loss prevention measures. The distinctions between "and" and "or" gates provide some guidance in choosing among loss prevention alternatives. For example, in the "Fault Tree for Hand Injury to Press Operator" exhibit, to prevent a clutch from failing (rectangle G), all three of the conditions in rectangles N, O, and P must be prevented because the "or" gate above these three events indicates that any one of them is sufficient to cause a clutch to fail. Conversely, a press will lack a guard (the "No guard" rectangle at the bottom right of the fault tree) only if the conditions in both rectangles V and W exist. Consequently, preventing either one of these two conditions (through active supervision or through a strong management policy on such guards) will prevent the removal of a guard.

To encourage sound loss control decisions, a fault tree must be as complete and accurate as possible. An incomplete fault tree may entirely omit a chain of events that would make loss control measures applied to some other tree branch ineffective. For example, if a branch of events leading directly to the harmful event in rectangle A of the "Fault Tree for Hand Injury to Press Operator" exhibit were unintentionally omitted from the fault tree, then risk control measures to prevent events B through E would not be sufficient to prevent the harmful event represented by rectangle A. See the exhibit "Five Steps of Fault Tree Analysis."

Five Steps of Fault Tree Analysis

To ensure that a fault tree includes all necessary and sufficient events and is useful as a risk management tool, risk management professionals should follow five steps:

1. Identify a specific harmful event to construct the fault tree. Be as specific as possible so that events contributing to the failure can be fully described.

2. Diagram, in reverse order, the events that led to the harmful event.

3. Determine whether the events leading to any other event on the fault tree are connected by an "and" gate or by an "or" gate.

4. Evaluate the fault tree to determine possible system improvement.

5. Make suggestions to management about risk control measures that can treat the hazards identified in the fault tree.

[DA08707]

Assumptions and Limitations

To properly use fault tree analysis, risk management professionals must recognize its underlying assumptions:

- All components exist in only one of two conditions—success or failure (operational or not operational).

- Any system component's failure is independent of any other component's failure.

- Each failure has an unchanging probability of occurrence. Moreover, to keep fault tree analysis manageable, many fault trees limit the number of potential causes of failure they examine, perhaps overlooking other causes. However, despite this simplified approach, fault tree analysis can aid in evaluating a harmful event.

The limitations of fault tree analysis also should be recognized:

- If a high degree of certainty does not exist concerning the probabilities of the underlying or base events, the probability of the top event may also be uncertain.

- Important pathways to the top event might not be explored if all causal events are not included in the fault tree.

- Because a fault tree is static, it may need to be reconstructed in the future if circumstances or procedures change.

- Human error is difficult to characterize in a fault tree.

- "Domino effects" or conditional failures are not easily included in a fault tree.

SUMMARY

Risk control is a conscious act or decision not to act that reduces the frequency and severity of losses or makes losses more predictable. Risk control techniques prevent losses, reduce the severity of losses, and speed recovery following a loss.

Risk control techniques can be categorized into one of six broad categories:

- Avoidance
- Loss prevention
- Loss reduction
- Separation
- Duplication
- Diversification

The root cause analysis process involves four steps:

1. Data collection
2. Causal factor charting
3. Root cause identification
4. Recommendation determination and implementation

FMEA is a root cause analysis technique used predominantly in product development and operations management. Its ultimate objective is to identify the most critical system failures that can cause the most damaging consequences. Once this is known, a plan of action can be developed and implemented.

FTA traces the events leading to the failure to their underlying causes. When these causes are identified, the risk management professional can determine the probability of their occurrence and apply the loss control techniques that will be most beneficial in preventing the harmful event.

Analyzing Business Performance

Educational Objectives

After learning the content of this assignment, you should be able to:

▷ Associate key performance indicators (KPIs) with these organizational
traits:

- Critical success factors

- Risk tolerance

▷ Describe key risk indicators in terms of the following:

- Purpose

- Sources

- Key characteristics

- Uses

▷ Describe the business process life cycle and business process risk.

Analyzing Business Performance

8

KEY PERFORMANCE INDICATORS

An organization's goals and objectives are met by establishing and attaining measurable standards for the many activities it pursues.

A **key performance indicator (KPI)** measures progress toward an organization's goals, provides an attainable standard for a specific activity, and gives the focus or direction the activity is to take. KPIs help gauge the results of activities critical to the success of an organization. Each organization will establish a level of adherence that will be tolerated in meeting its KPIs.

For an organization, a KPI measures the performance of a specific activity at a predetermined level or amount. It measures the progress an organization has made toward attaining its goals within a specific amount of time. For example, profitability that provides a competitive return on capital is an important objective for automotive manufacturers. After a customer purchases a vehicle, the vehicle may develop problems that are covered under the manufacturer's warranty, and the manufacturer will pay for the necessary repairs to fix the vehicle. A KPI related to achieving sufficient profitability could be "less than 10 percent of new cars sold will require more than $1,000 in warranty work in the first year of ownership," which measures the number of cars and the cost of warranty work. Most KPIs are lagging in nature, meaning they measure what has occurred rather than predicting what will occur. See the exhibit "Examples of KPIs Based on Ratios."

Critical Success Factors and KPIs

A **critical success factor (CSF)** is a vital component for a company moving forward; it can be the difference between achieving or failing to achieve a goal. A CSF is not the same as a KPI; a KPI measures an activity that signals the achievement of a CSF. See the exhibit "CSFs and KPIs."

CSFs and KPIs are interrelated. Just as a CSF helps refine a strategic objective to present a more concise and specific intention, a KPI refines a CSF and measures activities that signal whether a CSF has been achieved. A CSF answers the question, "What will make our organization a success?" and a KPI answers the question "What shows we are a success?"

Key performance indicator (KPI)

Financial or nonfinancial measurement that defines how successfully an organization is progressing toward its long-term goals.

Critical success factor (CSF)

An element, necessary for an organization's success, that is derived from a strategic objective.

Examples of KPIs Based on Ratios

Financial indicators

- Operating margin: operating income divided by net sales
- Net margin: net income divided by net sales
- Return on assets: net income divided by average assets
- ERM risk index: average risk exposure levels across ERM program areas

Staffing indicators

- Revenue productivity index: income divided by staffing head count
- Employee retention: percentage change in base period head count after employee turnover

Operations indicators

- Inventory turnover: cost of goods sold divided by average inventory
- Capacity utilization: actual unit output divided by potential unit output

[DA10445]

CSFs and KPIs

Critical Success Factor	Key Performance Indicator
Safe transport of customer valuables	Reduce transport breakage claims by 5%
High employee morale	Reduce employee turnover by 5%
Customer-focused website	Increase customer interactions with website

[DA10446]

KPIs and Risk Tolerance

Having KPIs established for CSFs is not enough to ensure progress toward organizational goals. For each KPI, there is a tolerance level for how much deviation from the standard established in the KPI will be acceptable. For example, the KPI of "improve on-time deliveries by 8 percent" might be tightly adhered to by one company, so that no or very little deviation under the 8 percent is tolerated. However, another company with a different risk tolerance level might find 5 or 6 percent improvement acceptable. An organization defines its risk tolerance with levels representing tolerance from low to catastrophic. See the exhibit "Risk Tolerance for KPIs."

Determining the risk tolerance for each KPI can also help in the event corrective measures are necessary when a KPI is not met. Linking the corrective measure with its identified tolerance level for the KPI promotes consistency

Risk Tolerance for KPIs

Strategic Objective	Critical Success Factor	Key Performance Indicator	Risk Tolerance
Customer Trust	Safe transport of customer valuables	Reduce transport breakage claims by 5%	Low—expectation met > 95 percent of time
			Medium—expectation met > 75 percent of time
			High—expectation met > 50 percent of time
			Severe—expectation met < 50 percent of time
			Worst Case—no improvement, claim number rises
Stable Workforce	High employee morale	Reduce employee turnover by 5%	Low—reduce turnover by 4 percent to 5 percent
			Medium—reduce turnover by 3 percent
			High—reduce turnover by 2 percent
			Severe—reduce turnover by 1 percent
			Worst Case—no improvement, turnover rate remains unchanged
Technological Excellence	Customer-focused website	Increase customer interactions with website	Low—completion on target
			Medium—completion within 10-12 months
			High—completion within 12-18 months
			Severe—completion within 24 months
			Catastrophic—completion after over 24 months

[DA10447]

throughout the entire process and further confirms the value of meeting the KPI.

Apply Your Knowledge

A small courier company collects and delivers packages by bicycle in the center of a large metropolitan area. The company's owner wants to attract new customers by guaranteeing on-time deliveries. Given this information, suggest a strategic objective, a CSF, a KPI, and the applicable risk tolerance for the owner to help build his business.

Feedback: A strategic objective would be to develop a reputation for excellent customer service. A CSF would be on-time deliveries. A KPI would be 100 percent on-time deliveries, and a suggested risk tolerance would be "low" (less than 5 percent late deliveries, all clients notified of delays).

KEY RISK INDICATORS

An organization can effectively manage its strategic risks by identifying issues before incidents occur that can lead to losses. Key risk indicators help organizations identify these issues.

Key risk indicator (KRI)

A tool used by an organization to measure the uncertainty of meeting a strategic business objective.

Organizations use **key risk indicators (KRIs)** to plan for and respond to risk. KRIs can reveal emerging risks, identify risk exposure levels, and detect changes or trends in existing risk exposures.

Purpose of KRIs

It is important to distinguish between KRIs and key performance indicators (KPIs). KPIs measure an organization's progress toward achieving its objectives; KRIs measure risk and volatility related to achieving those objectives. Although KPIs are lagging in nature—they measure the consequences of change that has occurred—KRIs are always leading (predictive) indicators. See the exhibit "Relationship Among Objectives, Risk, and Key Indicators."

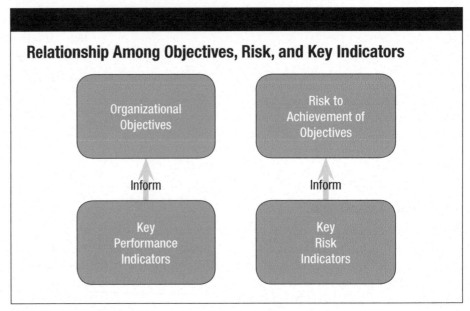

[DA10434]

Risk threshold

Predefined tolerance range that measures variances from expected outcomes.

Risk criteria

Information used as a basis for measuring the significance of a risk.

Effective KRIs provide objective, quantifiable information about emerging risks and trends in existing risks that can affect an organization's success. A KRI can reveal an upward trend in the level of a risk that, if it continues, will exceed the designated **risk threshold** for that risk. Alerted to the situation, management can take action to mitigate the impact to the organization.

Risk thresholds are developed from **risk criteria** determined for each risk. For example, a risk criterion for a bank might be the level of interest rates, with risk thresholds based on shifts in the level of interest rates. Risk criteria relating to an organization's strategic risks serve as the bases for KRIs.

KRIs help an organization maintain a level of risk within its defined risk tolerance level. Risk thresholds define the boundaries of risk tolerance; KRIs sound the warning when the boundaries are, or are about to be, breached.

For example, a financial organization may have a KRI relating to missed reporting deadlines, which can expose it to penalties and regulatory censure. Determining that a low number of missed deadlines in a designated period may be unavoidable, the organization sets that number as a threshold. If missed deadlines show a steady increase toward that threshold or repeatedly exceed it, the organization will take steps to determine why and implement corrective action. See the exhibit "KRI and Risk Threshold."

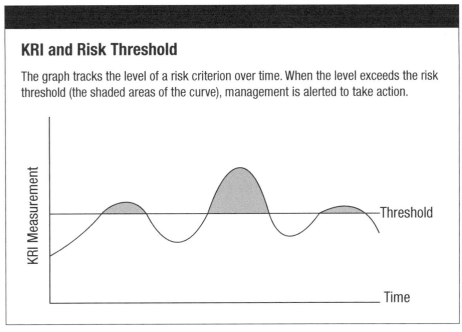

KRI and Risk Threshold

The graph tracks the level of a risk criterion over time. When the level exceeds the risk threshold (the shaded areas of the curve), management is alerted to take action.

[DA10436]

KRIs can be internal or external indicators. For example, internal changes such as budget variances, collection delays, and increases in employee turnover or the frequency of system outages can indicate emerging risks that, if not addressed, can become costly. External KRIs that a steel fabrication plant might monitor could relate to the cost of raw materials, the availability of labor, regulations that affect steel importation, and purchasing shifts by competitors. See the exhibit "KRI Measurement."

Sources of KRIs

Effective KRIs are founded on an organization's objectives. Management identifies areas of potential risk for each objective and then defines the

KRI Measurement

KRIs include the metrics that are used to identify abnormal patterns and exceptions to policy. KRIs and their calculation formula rules include these areas of measurement:

- Percentage change from prior period—current result divided by prior period (day/month/quarter/year)

- Budget variance percentage—current result divided by expected result

- Aged accounts receivable—unpaid customer invoice amounts greater than a given number of days that may affect bad debt reserves

- Aged accounts payable—unpaid vendor invoice amounts greater than a given number of days that may result in legal action

[DA10435]

information needed to measure and monitor the risks as they emerge or change (the risk criteria). KRI thresholds are developed for the risk criteria.

KRIs arise from various sources:

- Corporate strategies and objectives—Strategies and objectives often include performance metrics that can provide information to develop KRI measurements.

- Company policies, regulations, and legal requirements—Corporate policies and regulations governing the company set standards against which to measure compliance.

- Loss experience—An organization's historical loss data can identify processes or events that may lead to losses.

- Stakeholder requirements—The expectations of stakeholders, including shareholders, customers, suppliers, employees, and rating agencies, may be the basis for KRIs.

- Risk assessments—Assessments of risk throughout an organization may reveal areas of potential risk that would benefit from KRI measurement.[1]

- Internal and external subject-matter experts—Experts can identify specific areas of concern that can be addressed by KRIs. Experienced personnel within an organization may be aware of such areas. External experts can provide objective analysis.

- Trade publications and loss registries—These external sources can help an organization identify potential risks affecting its industry.

Key Characteristics of KRIs

In developing KRIs, an organization should strive for quality rather than quantity. Numerous, quickly developed KRIs can scatter focus. A more effective approach is to develop a limited number of KRIs linked to the risks that have the greatest potential impact on the organization. See the exhibit "Relating KRIs to Big Data."

Relating KRIs to Big Data

Big data, which is data that is too extensive to be gathered and analyzed by traditional methods, can provide an organization with information regarding emerging risks related to its KRIs. The purpose of big data is not to develop a large number of KRIs, but rather to provide the most relevant information regarding the KRIs that are most in line with the organization's business goals.

For example, competition would likely be a key risk for most organizations. Big data can provide information from social media, journals, patent applications, and other sources quickly. Data analysis techniques can be applied to this information to identify a potential new product that a competitor plans to introduce or a new company that is attracting customers.

[OV_12093]

Effective KRIs share several key characteristics:[2]

- They are based on quantifiable information.
- They are tied to risk categories.
- They are tied to the organization's objectives.
- They support management decisions.
- They can be benchmarked.

KRIs can be established for various levels within an organization. The degree of detail addressed by a KRI depends on the types of decisions required at each level. For example, business-unit KRIs are typically more specific than organization-wide KPIs. A specific department KRI would roll into a less specific KRI at the business-unit level and then be aggregated across all business units into a broad, general KRI for senior management.

ERM in Practice

Management at a large manufacturing company has determined that when employee turnover increases, workplace injuries also increase. Managers have decided to use employee turnover as a KRI for employee injury risk. This KRI is based on quantifiable information (the rate of employee turnover), tied to the category of hazard risk (safety), tied to the organization's objectives (productivity, profit, and social responsibility, for example), supportive of management decisions (to reduce turnover and improve safety), and capable of being benchmarked. To keep employee turnover levels below the established threshold, management has instituted employee retention programs, including enhanced employee benefits and incentives.

Uses of KRIs

As part of a risk management program, KRIs are used to assess, define, and measure potential changes in known risk conditions or identify and monitor emerging risk. They can provide early warnings of emerging risks, trends, or changes in risk exposures, giving the organization sufficient time to prevent or minimize any potential losses.

KRIs have other applications, including these:[3]

- Validation and monitoring—KRIs can help define performance targets, business strategies, and objectives as part of the organization's strategic planning efforts. In the process of linking KRIs to goals and objectives, managers can gain insight into the validity of those goals and the strategies that support them. Used in management reporting, KRIs can indicate progress toward organizational goals.

- Enhanced efficiency—KRIs can identify operational areas within the organization that have higher levels of risk. Management uses this information to balance risk and return when making resource allocation decisions.

- Clarification of risk-taking expectations—Thresholds and standards embodied in KRIs communicate and reinforce organizational values, **risk appetite**, risk tolerance, and accountability expectations to staff management. The clarification function of KRIs should supplement—not replace—formal communication efforts.

- Monitoring risk exposures—KRIs promote timely identification of risks using various risk identification and assessment tools.

- Measuring risk—Large financial institutions use KRIs to identify and maintain the appropriate level of **economic capital** to avoid unanticipated losses and calibrate capital models.

Risk appetite

The total exposed amount that an organization wishes to undertake on the basis of risk-return trade-offs for one or more desired and expected outcomes. (Used with permission of RIMS.)

Economic capital

The amount of capital required by an organization to ensure solvency at a given probability level, such as 99 percent, based on the fair value of its assets minus the fair value of its liabilities.

Apply Your Knowledge

In reviewing its sales data and customer base, an organization's management determines that 47 percent of its product is purchased by three major customers. These three customers pay for each order 90 to 120 days after receiving it. Failure of any of the three customers to pay for an order poses a significant risk to the organization. Management decides to develop KRIs to alert them to changes in the customers' behavior that would increase this risk exposure.

Which of the following proposed actions would qualify as a KRI for the risk described?

a.   Create a quarterly report of the number of products ordered by each of the three major customers.

b.   Have the sales force visit each customer every quarter and report on the customer's level of satisfaction with the product and the estimated size and frequency of future orders.

c.   Establish a method to monitor the financial results of each of the three major customers.

d.   Require the customers to pay for the product before delivery.

Feedback: c. Monitoring the customers' financial reports can alert management to potential changes that may directly affect the customers' ability to pay for the product. Option a. is not a KRI; it measures performance, not risk. Option b. does not directly address the customers' ability to pay. Although dissatisfaction with already-delivered products could cause loss of a customer, it is not causally related to the risk being measured. Option d. is not a measurement and is therefore not an indicator.

BUSINESS PROCESS MANAGEMENT

Utilizing business process management allows an organization to systematically manage and improve its products and services, meet the needs of customers, and gain a competitive advantage.

Business process management (BPM) focuses on coordinating all activities of an organization toward the preferences and needs of its customers. This management process includes five life-cycle steps—identifying processes, designing/redesigning processes, modeling scenarios, executing process changes, and monitoring results. Mapping risks to processes can expedite risk-treatment decisions and facilitate effective risk optimization.

Business process management (BPM)

A systematic, iterative plan to analyze and improve business processes through life-cycle phases to achieve long-term goals and client satisfaction.

The Nature of BPM

BPM is a structured approach that aligns an organization's operational components with its strategic goals and objectives, giving the organization the capability to be flexible, innovative, and attuned to emerging issues. BPM not only aims to improve processes, but to do so in an ongoing manner. Through BPM, the organization can quickly adjust to market- or risk-driven changes that can affect all aspects of that organization's products and services. BPM uses **risk indicators**, which provide feedback that helps the organization identify needed process improvements.

Risk indicator

A tool used by an organization to measure the level of uncertainty in an activity, project, or process.

Although incorporating information technology was the initial focus of BPM, human-driven processes are usually considered as well, because judgment or intuition is an important component of managing business processes. BPM is supported by technology to respond to clients, enable change quickly, and ensure the dynamic delivery of products and services, thereby helping the organization reach and maintain a competitive advantage. BPM uses technological and human applications in a systematic, structured approach that requires continual input, evaluation, and adjustments of operational activities.

These are some benefits of BPM:

- Providing senior management with regular feedback on process efficiency
- Enabling efficient use of resources
- Maximizing benefits from technology
- Responding quickly to client, regulatory, and market demands

The goal of BPM is achievement of organizational objectives through process improvements that incorporate technology, manage risks, improve efficiency, and increase profitability through life cycles of continual measurement and feedback.

BPM Life Cycle

The BPM life cycle incorporates five steps:

1. Identify processes—Critical processes that support achievement of the organization's goals are selected for analysis, design, redesign, or automation.
2. Design/redesign processes—The identified processes are designed or redesigned by considering workflows, affected personnel, reporting procedures, operating requirements, and referral mechanisms. Workflows include person-to-person, person-to-automated-system, or system-to-system interactions.
3. Model scenarios—Variables are applied to the process design to identify the response to various what-if scenarios.
4. Execute process changes—Software defines and executes the process, with human input as necessary. The entire process is driven by the collaboration of human and technological input.
5. Monitor results—Processes are tracked so that statistics on their performance can be gathered and compared with performance indicators. Performance indicators can measure areas such as productivity, defect rates, and cycle times, pointing to individual processes that need attention.

Based on data gained in the monitoring step, adjustments to the processes are identified and considered for improvement. Often, the identify processes step can be skipped at this point, with the life cycle starting over at the design/redesign processes step. See the exhibit "BPM Life Cycle."

BPM Life Cycle

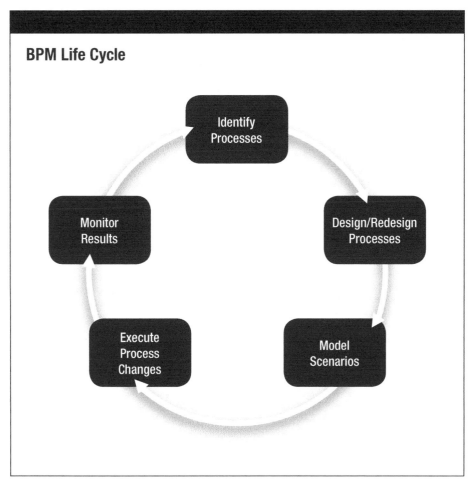

[DA10437]

As an example, New Tablet Inc. (NTI) is an organization employing the BPM life-cycle model to better design and manage the critical processes that support its supply chain. NTI manufactures medium-size tablets sold to schools and adult educational facilities throughout the United States. Although the company originally assembled the tablets from start to finish in its California factory, it later outsourced the initial production steps to a large assembly facility in Utah, and then again to a factory in China. The Utah facility still produces the partially assembled tablets for adult educational facilities, and the remaining partially assembled tablets are obtained from the contracted facility in China. All tablets are ordered and paid for by the purchasing schools prior to any assembly. After an order is received, NTI sends the order to the appropriate outsourcing facility, which partially assembles the tablets and ships them to California within one week for final assembly. The NTI factory in California does a quality check on the partially assembled tablets, adds specialized components, and ships the order to the school within two weeks. This schedule guarantees that customers receive their school tablets within thirty days of order placement. Each customer receives a follow-up questionnaire that solicits quality and service feedback.

Although operational year-round, NTI delivers the majority of its orders between June and September, as most schools make the subsequent school-year plans after the current school year ends but want their requested tablets received by the first day of school in the fall. The processing of orders for adult learning institutions is on a more consistent, year-round schedule.

NTI identified six critical processes in its supply chain that support achievement of its goals: (1) initial production, (2) personnel management, (3) inventory control, (4) information management, (5) distribution, and (6) customer service. For example, NTI uses BPM to improve efficiency in its inventory-control process by reviewing the technological and human interactions that track inventory and by clarifying the standards of, reporting form for, and frequency of quality control activities.

Business Process Risk

Uncertainty can have varying effects on an organization and may involve internal or external risks. Internal risks may include exposure to human factors such as talent availability or the organization's technological vision and capacity, or to physical factors such as equipment failures. External risks may be floods, tornadoes, changes in interest rates, or new government regulations.

When designing or redesigning its processes using the BPM life cycle, an organization should consider the risks to each process and the risk indicators for each. Risk indicators alert the organization to be proactive by intervening and mitigating an impending event before the harm occurs. Examples of risk indicators are unfavorable quality control reports or increased numbers of late shipments.

An organization should also consider the risks from all its processes taken together. A company might identify a fire risk to its property management process, an offsite-breakdown risk to its information management process, and a risk to its hiring process from a proposed minimum wage increase. If any of these risks is realized and occurs independently of the other two, the other two processes would likely remain intact and be available to support the organization. However, if two or three occurred at one time, the potential consequences to the company could be more serious and costly.

Continuing with the example, after NTI identified six critical processes that support the goals for its supply chain, it identified risks for each of the processes and developed risk indicators to assess the level of each risk. Mapping risks to processes and developing appropriate risk indicators can signal unacceptable risk levels and promote timely implementation of appropriate risk treatments. See the exhibit "NTI Supply Chain Processes, Risks, and Risk Indicators."

NTI identified initial production as one of the critical processes in its manufacturing supply chain. It recognized that a risk to this process, such as a natural disaster, would disrupt production at the China facility. NTI hopes the

NTI Supply Chain Processes, Risks, and Risk Indicators

Process	Risks to Process	Risk Indicators
Initial Production	Delay or disruption to China facility because of natural disaster or foreign government regulations affecting NTI	Political unrest in area
		Lapse of communication with foreign facility manager
		Any negative labor reports from foreign facility manager
	Delay or disruption to Utah or California facility because of natural disaster	Reports of predicted disasters, weather forecasts
Personnel Management	Inadequate staff coverage for California facility in summer months	High absenteeism in summer months
		Poor job performance reviews or remediation
		Negative employee feedback
	Delay or disruption to China facility because of worker conditions/human rights issues	Any lapse in communication without explanation—phone, Internet, fax, etc.
		Negative news reports of working conditions/ human rights focus in area
Inventory Control	Quality is compromised by poor assembly methods	Any change in quality control results on receivables from Utah or China facility
		Intermittant, unplanned, or late receivables from Utah or China facility
		Unfavorable reports from China's or Utah's QC report on assembled goods
Information Management	Delayed or compromised communications because of Internet, hardware, software failure, or obsolete equipment	Newly emerging software/hardware/ networking/cloud management options
		Any lapse of communication between California and each other facility
	Cyberattacks on any of the facilities	Any reported security breach to NTI technology or equipment
		Reported security breach to any NTI design, plans, facility, bank, or customer
Distribution	Late/higher-priced deliveries to customers from labor disputes, fuel prices	Predicted fuel shortages, reported looming labor disputes affecting any facility
Customer Service	Loss of customers/damage to reputation because of China's poor working conditions	Poor attitudes toward this from general public (news reports)
		Customer complaints toward this issue
	Loss of customers/goodwill from interrupted or late deliveries	Poor ratings on customer questionnaires
		Increased number of late shipments

[DA10438]

BPM life cycle will help it optimize its California and Utah facilities for initial production in the event of a disruption to the China facility. After redesigning the processes by updating workflows, refining communications between facilities, and refreshing scheduling criteria, NTI modeled various scenarios to determine the feasibility of using the Utah and California facilities as contingent assembly locations. It determined that each location could make up 50 percent of the lost production from China and meet the thirty-day delivery standard. NTI implemented the contingent production process.

After monitoring the process over the next year, NTI confirmed that its Utah facility would be able to assume 50 percent of the China facility's production, but that the California facility would only be able to assume 25 percent. NTI then went to the design/redesign processes step and changed some procedures to enable the California facility to undertake 50 percent of China's business. In a worst-case scenario, in which the China facility production would be completely halted, the improved contingency plan would be effective in redirecting all partial-assembly tablet production to both Utah and California.

Using BPM, NTI discovered many risks to its individual supply chain processes and identified numerous risk indicators to help it be aware of impending risk and intervene proactively. NTI also now views combined risks of the entire process. See the exhibit "Using Big Data for Business Process Management."

Using Big Data for Business Process Management

Big data, or data too extensive to be gathered and analyzed by traditional methods, and analytics can provide valuable insights into an organization's business process management. For example, an insurer wanted to improve its claims-assignment process. Seventy percent of its complex claims were not recognized as complex until six months or more after they were reported to the insurer. Because complex characteristics, such as surgery or litigation, developed gradually, resources such as an experienced claims adjuster or a nurse case manager were not initially assigned to the claims.

The insurer's data science team used the insurer's large database to develop a predictive model based on the attributes of claims that gradually became complex. By applying this predictive model to new claims, the insurer was able to identify fifty percent of its complex claims within a week of their report to the insurer and assign appropriate resources to those claims, an improvement of twenty percent over randomly assigning claims to experienced claims adjusters and nurse case managers.

[OV12094]

Apply Your Knowledge

Which statement is true in regard to BPM?

a. BPM is a technology-driven approach attempting to automate procedures to more quickly achieve long-term goals.

b. For the BPM life cycle to function as designed, the life cycle always starts again with the identify processes step.

c. BPM's iterative approach enables not only improvement, but continual improvement.

d. An emerging competitor would be an internal risk for an organization.

Feedback: c. BPM's iterative approach emphasizes a life cycle of continual identification, analysis, and monitoring of results, which enables not only improvement, but ongoing improvement. BPM is a technology-driven approach in conjunction with human input, a collaboration that drives change to achieve long-term goals—so a. is incorrect. The BPM life cycle does not always begin anew with the first step; often it starts over with second step—design/redesign processes—so b. is incorrect. Finally, d. is incorrect, as an emerging competitor would be an external, not an internal, risk for an organization.

SUMMARY

A CSF is an activity deemed crucial for an organization to move forward and attain its goals and objectives. A KPI measures the progress of a CSF, or how well a CSF has been put into effect. An organization will assign a certain level of tolerance in its adherence to each KPI, from a low tolerance of meeting the KPI most or all of the time to a worst case scenario, which could yield no improvement or even a worse situation than existed previously. The interrelationship among a strategic objective, CSF, KPI, and the acceptable risk tolerance contributes to an organization's efficiently and consistently achieving its long-term goals in a predictable and measurable manner.

KRIs are linked to an organization's objectives and strategy and are used as part of the risk management process to identify and analyze risk. By revealing emerging risks and changes or trends in existing risk exposures, KRIs help organizations plan for and respond to changing risk exposures. KRIs are often measured against thresholds or performance standards and may be internal or external. In addition to their role in risk identification, KRIs can be used to validate planning, enhance efficiency in prioritizing risks, clarify risk-taking expectations, monitor exposures, and measure risk.

BPM aims to improve an organization's performance in an ongoing manner by analyzing critical business processes through the five steps of the BPM life cycle: identify processes, design/redesign processes, model scenarios, execute process changes, and monitor results. Mapping risks to processes and tasks in the BPM life cycle can provide meaningful metrics and facilitate treatment decisions. BPM can help an organization align its business processes to achieve its goals while managing its risks.

ASSIGNMENT NOTES

1. James Lam & Associates, "Emerging Best Practices in Developing Key Risk Indicators and ERM Reporting," Cognos Business Intelligence (sponsor), 2005, p. 7.
2. "Emerging Best Practices in Developing Key Risk Indicators and ERM Reporting," p. 7.
3. Susan Hwang, "Identifying and Communicating Key Risk Indicators," in Enterprise Risk Management, eds. John Fraser and Betty Simkins (Hoboken, N.J.: John Wiley & Sons, Inc., 2010), pp. 129-134.

Index

Page numbers in boldface refer to pages where the word or phrase is defined.